"For my Mom and Dad,
who still worry"

Rocky
Mountain Books

SUMMITS & ICEFIELDS

Chic Scott

Skiing the Dezaiko Range of the northern Rockies. Photo George Evanoff

"In the end, to ski is to travel fast and free–free over the untouched snow covered country. To be bound to one slope, even to one mountain, by a lift may be convenient but it robs us of the greatest pleasure that skiing can give, that is, to travel through the wide, wintery country; to follow the lure of the peaks which tempt on the horizon and to be alone for a few days or even a few hours in clear, mysterious surroundings."

Hans Gmoser

Front cover: Skiing the Selkirk Mountains near Durrand Glacier Chalet. Photo Ruedi Beglinger (Selkirk Mountain Experience).

Inset: Northern lights dance above the Lawrence Grassi Hut, Clemenceau Icefield. Photo Clive Cordery

© Chic Scott, 1994,
2nd printing revised 1996
3rd printing revised 1999

We acknowledge the financial support of the Government of Canada through the Book Publishing Industry Development Program (BPIDP) for our publishing activities.

 **Published by
Rocky Mountain Books
#4 Spruce Centre SW**
RMB **Calgary, Alberta T3C 3B3**

Printed and bound in Canada by Kromar Printing Ltd., Winnipeg

ISBN 0-921102-34-8

Canadian Cataloguing in Publication Data
Scott, Chic, 1945-
  Summits and icefields

  Includes index.
  ISBN 0-921102-34-8

  1. Cross-country skiing--Rocky Mountains, Canadian (B.C. and Alta.)--Guidebooks. 2. Cross-country skiing--British Columbia--Columbia Mountains--Guidebooks. 3. Rocky Rocky Mountains, Canadian (B.C. and Alta.)--Guidebooks. * 4. Columbia Mountains (B.C.)--Guidebooks. I. Title.
GV854.8.C3S36 1994   796.93'2'09711   C94-910763-8

*The Columbia Icefield, showing the route up Mount Columbia.
Photo Ruedi Setz Collection*

Contents

South Canoe Glacier, Southern Cariboos Traverse. Photo Alf Skrastins

Acknowledgements

In a book of this scope it would be difficult indeed to have up-to-date personal experience of all the areas. I have therefore relied heavily on the experience of other ski mountaineers for information. In particular I would like to thank:

Bob Enagonio and Eric Trouillot (Great Divide Traverse), Bob Saunders (Clemenceau, Drummond and Bonnet Icefields, Southern Purcells Traverse), Terry Duncan (Bugaboos to Rogers Pass Traverse), Joe Nixhipi (McMurdo Hut), Larry Stanier (Olive Hut), Phil Janz (Mount Field, Fairy Meadow), Marc Ledwidge (Cirrus Mountain), Bob Ollinger (Silver Spray Cabin), Trevor Holsworth (Valhalla Traverse), Steve Smith (Northern Cariboos Ski Traverse), Al Schaffer (Southern Cariboos Ski Traverse), Chuck Young (Clemenceau Icefield, Fairy Meadow), Clive Cordery (Kokanee Glacier Park, Clemenceau Icefield), Murray Toft (Columbia Icefield, Rogers Pass), John Tweedy (Kootenay Pass), Peter Tucker (Great Divide Traverse), Frank Campbell (Mount Wilson), Alf Skrastins (The Commercial Lodges), Steve Chambers (The Commercial Lodges), Ruedi Beglinger (Monashee Traverse, Adamant/Goldstream Traverse), Tony Daffern (Mount Joffre, Skyline Trail, Southern Cariboos Ski Traverse).

I would specially like to thank Dave Smith, his wife Molly and their children Chris, Ian and Sarah for their wonderful hospitality while I did research in the Nelson area. As always my stay at the Smith household was delightful. Dave provided much of the information for Kootenay Pass, the Whitewater Ski Area, Mount Brennan, Commonwealth Peak and Kokanee Glacier Park.

For many years, the ACC Clubhouse in Canmore has been my refuge in the mountains. I would like to say thanks to Keith Haberl, Dan Verral and all the others who have made me feel so welcome.

My sincere thanks to Don Gardner for introducing me to backcountry skiing in the sixties and for being an inspiration all these years.

Disclaimer

There are inherent risks in glacier and high-mountain ski touring and many of the routes described in this book will, at times, be unsafe due to potential snow or ice avalanches or to weakly bridged crevasses. While the author has done his best to provide accurate information and to point out potential hazards, conditions may change due to weather and other factors. It is up to users of this guide to learn the necessary skills for safe ski touring and to exercise caution in potentially hazardous areas, particularly on glaciers and in avalanche prone terrain.

Skiers and others using this book do so entirely at their own risk and the author and publisher disclaim any liability for injury or other damage by anyone ski touring, snowboarding or Telemark skiing in any of the areas described.

On the South Cariboos Traverse. Photo Alf Skrastins

11

Skiing above the Durrand Glacier Chalet. Photo Ruedi Beglinger (Selkirk Mountain Experience)

Preface

There is something very special about ski mountaineering. To reach a peak or a high pass after a long and demanding ascent, and then to gaze out on an endless panorama of mountains is deeply rewarding. And so is the climb itself with its moments of meditation and silence, alternating with rich conversation.

Years ago when I was a teenager, just discovering the mountains, I attended a lecture given by a prominent guide and mountaineer. He told us that we must relearn the joy of hard physical work in the mountains. He said that we must shun the easy mechanized life and climb to the top of our mountains on our own two feet. I have never forgotten his words and have devoted much of my life to doing just as he suggested.

Here in this book is the result of a lifetime quest for adventure. There are fabulous ski descents over untracked snow, wilderness cabins in silent forests, snowfields surrounded by glistening peaks and even traverses of whole mountain ranges.

I hope this book helps to open the doors to your world of ski adventure and that you find the pleasure and satisfaction exploring these mountains, that I have.

Good skiing,

Chic Scott

Introduction

SKI MOUNTAINEERING IN THE ROCKIES AND THE COLUMBIA MOUNTAINS

The mountains of Western Canada offer a great opportunity for ski adventure of all kinds. You can spend a few hours making Telemark turns on a slope not far from your car, or you can head off on one of the grand traverses for a three week wilderness expedition. And there is everything in between—marvellous descents in powder snow, cosy mountain lodges under starlit skies, sun-drenched glaciers and shimmering icefalls.

For those of you unfamiliar with this part of the world, you should appreciate that the distinctive characteristic of the tours described in this book is 'wild'. This country is wilderness and there is little in the way of man-made amenities. In these mountains you are on your own, so self reliance is required. You must be prepared to deal with all eventualities yourself.

However the plus side to this is that you often have the ski descent or perhaps even the mountain range to yourself. In fact it seems to me that this area of Western Canada offers the finest combination of access to modern facilities (hospitals, communications, banking, hotels, restaurants, transportation), coupled with almost immediate access to wilderness which can be as little as 100 m from your doorway.

In this book I have collected information on some of the best and most popular ski tours in the Rockies and the Columbia Mountains. Yes, there are many ski tours and ski descents left out —I have chosen only the classics. This is the first guidebook to describe these mountain ski tours and I am sure that it

will grow and evolve with future editions. However this first edition should still be enough to keep most of you busy for many years.

Remember also that this book covers a huge area—almost the size of the European Alps—so this guide does not go into as much detail as guides for smaller areas. All the information needed to open the door is presented here but to walk through that door, you must be prepared to do some further investigation on your own.

To venture very far into these mountains requires a solid background of mountain skills and considerable depth of experience. If you are new at the game then don't be afraid to take some time to learn these skills and pay your dues on the less demanding tours before venturing onto the more serious ones. It is always advisable to invest some time and money in taking a few courses. Finally there are many good clubs here in Western Canada where you can meet people of like mind and get a chance to share a trip or two with some seasoned veterans.

Snow Conditions

The Rockies
The early season snowpack in the Rockies is shallow, uncompacted and unstable. As a result of long spells of cold weather combined with the shallow snowpack, large loose snow crystals called depth hoar often develop at the base of the snowpack. Trail breaking can be extremely frustrating, and it

is not uncommon to find yourself sinking almost a metre into unconsolidated snow overlying depth hoar.

Surface hoar, feathery crystals formed on the surface of the snow in cold clear conditions, is very common in the Rockies and can lie hidden to the unsuspecting ski tourer as a weak layer in the snow pack, for long periods of time. The principal hazard in the Rockies is from soft slab avalanches which may be triggered several days after a snowfall and which often release right down to the ground.

The general consensus is that snow stability evaluation in the Rockies is a very difficult business. Although the snowpack may not be much more than a metre or two deep, it can be made up of numerous layers including depth hoar, wind slab and surface hoar. The interpretation of all these layers can be quite a puzzle even for the experts so it is advised to be very cautious.

The Columbia Mountains

The snowpack in the Columbia Mountains is deeper, and as a general rule, more stable than in the Rockies. After all there are good reasons why all the heli-ski operations are located in these mountains.

The snow is generally moister and the temperatures are more moderate. There is also the insulating effect of a snowpack which can be many metres deep. However, there have been numerous avalanche incidents and deaths in this range most of them due to skiers trying to push the limits of what is skiable or from layers of surface hoar buried deep in the snow pack.

Avalanches

Snow stability is difficult to evaluate even for knowledgeable and experienced ski tourers. Avalanche accidents are a regular occurrence every year and usually occur during periods when professional forecasters are predicting high or extreme hazard.

Ski tourers should all wear an avalanche transceiver, carry a snow shovel, and use probe poles. Your transceiver should be switched on at the beginning of the tour and worn until you are safely back to your car. Batteries should be fresh and your group should do a check of transceiver operation at the start of the day. Everyone should know how to conduct a transceiver search in the event of an avalanche incident. Avalanche transceivers should not be an excuse to push the limits of safe judgement—remember that despite these electronic devices many avalanches still prove fatal.

You should ski with a high degree of awareness. Most of the tours in this book take you deep into the heart of avalanche country. Because the nature of the snowpack changes drastically from one slope to the next, it is necessary to have a good 'feel' for terrain, wind direction and snow conditions. It is not always possible to dig a pit on every slope and you must be able to extrapolate from one slope to another. You must be able to make quick and correct decisions, particularly on one of the long icefield traverses where you may cover 10-15 km in a day.

Keen observation, good routefinding and extreme caution are the keys to many years of safe backcountry skiing in Western Canada.

Before Setting Out

If you are going to ski tour in the areas covered by this book you should have taken an avalanche awareness course in order to learn how to travel safely in avalanche terrain and how to recognize signs of snowpack instability.

In addition you are advised to call the appropriate agency (see numbers at the back of the book) for the latest snow conditions and stability evaluation. Remember, there is a lot of information available on the snowpack in these ranges. Avalanche control agencies at Rogers Pass and Kootenay Pass and the heli-ski operators do literally thousands of studies and tests each season.

Glacier Travel

Glaciers in the Rockies and Columbia Mountains are most dangerous early in the season. The autumn and early winter snowfalls bridge the crevasses which have opened up over the summer but serve only to hide them, not to safely cover them. It is only later in the winter and in the spring that these crevasses are sufficiently well covered to offer reasonably safe travel.

Remoteness

Most of the tours in this book take you through wilderness areas. There are no man-made facilities and often there are no other skiers in the area. You are on your own and you must deal with any problems with your own resources. Self reliance is the byword in the Western Canadian Mountains. Remoteness is indeed one of the great attractions of these mountains.

Weather

The Rockies

Weather in the Canadian Rockies can be extreme. There can be long periods of intense cold, when the thermometer drops to -30°C or -40°C. On the other hand Chinook winds can change this in a matter of hours and raise the temperature well above freezing. Carrying the proper protection against the wind and cold is essential. A night out in the Rockies can be a serious matter so carry survival equipment at all times.

The mean temperature in the Rockies is reasonable however, and the area receives large amounts of sunshine. A typical Rockies day is perhaps -15°C and sunny. Spring time ski touring can of course be a real treat—often a sweater or a windbreaker is all that is needed.

The Columbia Mountains

The Columbia Mountains are snow country. This area receives some of the highest snowfalls in the world, consequently the sun can be absent from the sky for days while the white stuff piles up all around. Down in the valleys, in places like Nelson and Golden, the skies can be grey and overcast for long periods and rain is not unknown in the winter.

Temperatures are much more moderate in the interior of BC than in the Rockies. Normally the arctic cold front, when it descends from the north does not penetrate far into the western mountains—but it can. I have seen the Rogers Pass locked in a -30°C deep freeze just like the Rockies—but it is uncommon. Usually higher up the temperatures are in the -10°C range while down in the valleys the temperature would more commonly be around 0°C.

Hours of Daylight

The area covered in this guidebook is at approximately 52 degrees North Latitude. Consequently in winter the days can be very short and the nights long. In December it is dark by 5:00 pm and the sun is not up until 8:00 am the following day. If you are forced to bivouac that means the night is 15 hours long!

Environment

Many of these ski tours are within National or Provincial Parks where very high environmental standards are maintained. Whether your tour is within a park or not you should try to leave the area as beautiful and clean as you found it. There should be no cutting of trees or branches and all garbage must be packed out.

Emergency Procedures

Before venturing far into the back country you should obtain the knowledge and skills to carry out a few basic emergency procedures. You should know how to build an emergency shelter, how to start a fire, and how to stay warm and dry. You should also be familiar with avalanche rescue procedures because it is unlikely that by the time outside help arrives they will be able to do more than recover bodies. Before undertaking glacier travel you should be able to perform a crevasse rescue.

When embarking on any of the more serious ski tours you should consider registering out with the local wardens or rangers, for some added security.

In an emergency phone the appropriate number listed on the final page of this book.

Maps

It is expected that you will be using the 1:50,000 National Topographical Series maps in the field.

Grid References (e.g. Bow Hut GR 355203) are used throughout this book to help locate specific geographical features and man made objects on the map, such as passes, peaks, huts, lakes, etc. On the right hand border of each NTS map you will find instructions on how to use the Universal Transverse Mercator Grid System.

Take care when using some of the newer maps where the contour interval is 20 m below 2,000 m and 40 m above. These maps are truly hard to read.

Many of the trails marked on the topographical maps are incorrect. It is best to crosscheck with other references wherever possible.

Maps can be obtained from private sources such as the ACC office in Canmore, or from the Mountain Equipment Co-op and Map Town in Calgary. If you live far away you can obtain them from the federal government in Ottawa.

Canada Map Office
130 Bentley Avenue
Nepean, Ontario
Canada, K1A 0E9
US & Canada 1-800-465-6277
613-952-7000

Equipment and Clothing

Here are a few tips on the type of equipment and clothing commonly used by experienced tourers.

Skis Metal-edged Telemark skis are very popular for the type of tours described in this book, as are the wider 'randonee' or mountaineering skis. It is really a matter of personal choice which style of ski you use. The tours described in this book are high and rugged and the lighter Nordic skis are not suitable.

Ski Poles Poles which adapt to form an avalanche probe are very popular. However it is recommended that someone in the group carry a regular sectional avalanche probe.

Skins or Waxes Most of the tours in this book will require skins for the ascent. However, it is suggested you carry a small wax kit, particularly on the grand traverses where long horizontal sections will be encountered. Klister waxes are handy for wet or frozen conditions. You may also wish to carry a piece of plain paraffin wax (candle) for use on your skins! and skis when the snow is balling up on them.

Avalanche Transceivers Although single-frequency (457 kHz) transceivers are now the standard in North America, many people are still using dual frequency models.

Headgear A warm toque or insulated hat is essential. A balaclava which can be pulled down to cover the face and neck is highly recommended.

Glacier Goggles High quality eye protection, impervious to the high levels of ultra-violet light at these altitudes, must be worn even on cloudy days. There should be at least one spare pair in the party.

Handgear Warm mitts, rather than gloves, are the most effective.

Boots There are many good quality Telemark boots and ski mountaineering boots on the market. The boot should be warm particularly if you intend to ski in the Rockies. If you have poor circulation, consider using a double boot.

Insulating Material Down is still the insulating material of choice in the Rockies. The climate is dry and the cold is often extreme, necessitating a high quality four season bag. In the Columbia Mountains the temperature is much more moderate and at times it can even rain during the winter. Often the snowfall is wet and consequently many skiers prefer jackets with a synthetic fill.

Synthetic pile fabrics are popular for clothing and work very well. Synthetic underclothes are now used almost exclusively.

Shell Materials Breathable fabrics are popular in the dry climate of the Rockies for jackets, shells, overpants, down bags and down jackets. Gore-Tex tends to ice up on the inside in extremely cold weather. However in the Columbia Mountains where snowfalls can be extremely wet, Gore-Tex is by far superior.

Stoves Butane cartridge stoves are not recommended in the Rockies, because the fuel has difficulty vaporising in extreme cold. White gas stoves such as the MSR Whisperlite are the norm.

Shovel A solid two-piece metal shovel with extendable handle is recommended. It should have a wide, grain shovel type scoop to facilitate fast and easy digging.

Ropes Although ropes with a diameter of 10.5 mm give maximum security, many ski mountaineers use 8.5 mm ropes for glacier travel.

Trip Planning

You should always have at least an informal plan in the back of your mind, even for the most casual day of skiing. The more serious the trip the better planned it should be. If you do one of the multi-day grand traverses virtually nothing should be left to chance. The following are some items that you should consider when planning your tour:

- Let someone know where you are going and when you will be back.
- Study the map and any other information so as to be completely familiar with the route. Be aware of options, alternatives and escape routes along the way.
- Know the people you are skiing with and their skill and experience level. Do not get them in over their head.
- Establish a start time and a finish time. Leave plenty of room in your schedule to deal with the unforeseen. Check your time along the way to gauge your progress. You should decide on a turn back time and stick to it.
- Run through an equipment check before departing. Check your group for proper skis, boots and clothing and for compatible avalanche transceivers.
- Obtain the latest weather forecast before starting out.
- Check on avalanche hazard and snow stability with the local avalanche forecast centre before making a final decision on your route.

Food, Gear and Other Supplies

The mountain communities of Canmore, Banff, Lake Louise, Jasper, Golden, Revelstoke and Nelson have a wide selection of grocery stores and other shops to serve you. White gas for stoves is readily available as is gasoline for your vehicles.

Ski equipment and back country gear can be purchased at:

Calgary
Mountain Equipment Co-op
(403) 269-2420
The Hostel Shop (403) 283-8311

Canmore
Altitude Sports (403) 678-1636

Banff
Mountain Magic (403) 762-2591
Monod's (403) 762-4571

Lake Louise
Wilson's Sports (403) 522-3636

Jasper
Totem Men's Wear and Ski Shop
(780) 852-3078

Revelstoke
The Villager Ski Shop (250) 837-2006
Free Spirit Sports and Leisure Ltd.
(250) 837-9453

Golden
Selkirk Sports (250) 344-2966

Nelson
Kootenay Experience (250) 354-4441
Snowpack (250) 352-6411
Rivers and Oceans (250) 354-2056

Equipment Checklist to refresh your memory

Equipment
Skis
Poles
Boots
Skins
Wax kit
Avalanche transceiver
Shovel
Avalanche probe
Snow saw
Spare ski tip
Compass
Altimeter
Map
Repair kit
First aid kit
Emergency toboggan
Snow study kit
Headlamp
Emergency bivouac sac
Water bottle
Thermos
Sun glasses
Ski goggles
Pocket knife
Toilet paper
Camera and film
Lighter or matches
Lip balm
Sun cream
Notebook and pencil
Appropriate pack sack

Clothing
Synthetic Underwear
Wool or synthetic socks
Pants or knickers
Overpants
Jacket
Shirt
Pile jacket or sweater
Down jacket

Toque
Mitts
Polypro gloves
Gaiters
Spare mitts, socks
Spare underwear

If you are going overnight
Tent
Sleeping bag
Insulated sleeping pad
Insulated booties
Stove and fuel
Pots
Pot scrubber
Cup, bowl and spoon
Toilet kit

For glacier travel
Harness
Rope
Several prussik slings
Several locking carabiners
Several regular carabiners
Ice axe

Guides

Ski guides and instruction can be obtained by writing or phoning:

Company of Canadian Mountain Guides web site:
www.mountainguide.com

Yamnuska Inc.
#200, 50-103 Bow Valley Trail
Canmore, Alberta T1W 1N8
Phone (403) 678-4164
Fax (403) 678-4450
email: yamnuska@telusplanet.net
web site: www.yamnuska.com

Many of the tours lie within the boundaries of National Parks (Banff, Jasper, Yoho, Glacier) or are located within a BC Provincial Park (Kokanee, Bugaboo). With the exception of Glacier National Park, which has very strict rules on closed areas, these parks have similar back country regulations of which a summary is provided here.

Back Country Use Permits

In the national parks it is necessary to get a backcountry use permit if you spend at least one night in the back country. Permits can be obtained at park information centres. The cost is $6/person/night. Season pass $42.

Registration

A voluntary registration system is provided by the National Parks Service for hazardous activities within the national parks. You are strongly advised to use the service if you are skiing in some of the more remote areas.

It is necessary to register in person during regular office hours at either park information centres or at a warden office because registering out is a contractual agreement that requires a signature. All overdue registrations are checked out. There are three important considerations to bear in mind when you register:

• Because all overdues are checked out you must provide a reasonable estimate of your trip time. This is to avoid unnecessary use of costly helicopter flights by rescue personnel.

• You must notify the Parks Service upon completion of your trip by either dropping the registration slip off at one of the warden offices or information centres, or by telephoning . If you are late, phone at your earliest convenience. Failure to notify the Parks Service of your return or of cancellation of a trip is grounds for prosecution.

• Rescue personnel exercise some discretion about when to commence a search. This depends upon many factors like weather conditions, amount of time overdue, estimate of the individuals ability, number in party, etc. For this reason you must be prepared to spend at least one night out before expecting help to arrive.

Glacier National Park (Rogers Pass)

In recent years regulations in this park have been relaxed and it is no longer necessary to register out for back country ski tours. There is, however, a day-use fee for ski touring of $6/person/day or you can purchase a yearly pass for $42. See page 151 for further regulations.

Kootenay Pass
(The Salmo/Creston Highway)

This pass also has an intensive avalanche control program and avalanche control operations can be started at any time. When avalanche control is in progress all areas north of Highway #3 are closed to ski touring and the highway will be closed.

Vehicle Permits

All vehicles stopping in a national park are required to have a Park Motor Vehicle Permit. These can be obtained at park information centres, or at the east entrance to Banff Park, the west entrance to Kootenay Park and the east and west gates of Jasper Park. You can buy either a one day, four day, or annual permit. If you intend to stay for longer than a few days the best buy is to pay the $70 (1999 price) for the annual permit.

Travel Information

The Rockies and the Columbia Mountains are best reached by air or bus. Rail travel is very limited. Consult your travel agent for schedules and fares.

By Air

There are international airports in Edmonton, Calgary and Vancouver. It is possible to fly directly to these cities from within North America, and from Europe and Asia. The areas described in this book are 2-10 hours drive along excellent highways from the airports. There is an airport at Castlegar, near Nelson, which receives connector flights from Calgary and Vancouver; however, schedules are sometimes unreliable due to poor visibility in winter.

By Bus

There are regular scheduled buses which run east and west along the Trans-Canada Highway. They stop at Revelstoke, the Rogers Pass, Golden, Lake Louise, Banff and Canmore. There are also regularly scheduled buses which serve the other centres referred to in this book—Nelson and Jasper. Phone Greyhound Bus Lines for further information. Check with Brewster Transport (403) 762-6767 for Icefield Parkway buses.

By Car

Public transportation in the western Canadian mountains is poor, particularly in the winter. It is almost imperative to have a vehicle if you want to reach most of the trailheads.

Cars can be rented from the major international chains (Hertz, Avis, Tilden, etc.) in all the centres referred to in this book—Calgary, Edmonton, Vancouver, Banff, Jasper, Golden, Nelson, Revelstoke. The highways described in this book are all normally well main-tained in winter (with the exception of the Icefields Parkway, which often goes several days before being plowed). However, severe cold and sudden snow storms can make extreme demands on both the car and driver.

Be sure your vehicle has antifreeze adequate for -40°C, and that it is equipped with snow tires, a block heater and a strong battery. You should carry jumper cables in the event of a dead battery, and a snow shovel in the event you become stuck. It is also a good idea to always have a sleeping bag and some survival equipment in the car in the event of a breakdown. If the thermometer plunges it is advisable to plug your car in if at all possible. Diesel and propane powered vehicles can be hard to start on cold winter mornings. It is best not to park on the roadside as high speed snowplows regularly maintain the highways.

Time Change

The areas covered in this book are in two different time zones. The areas lying to the west (Revelstoke, Rogers Pass and Nelson) are on Pacific time and are one hour earlier than those areas to the east, (Canmore, Banff, Lake Louise, Golden and Jasper) which are on Mountain time. When travelling the Trans-Canada Highway the time changes just east of the Rogers Pass. When travelling Highway #3 the time changes at the Kootenay Pass between Creston and Salmo.

Telephone Exchanges

The areas covered in this book are within four different telephone exchanges. Numbers in southern Alberta (Banff/Lake Louise area) carry the prefix 403 and numbers in northern Alberta (Jasper region) carry the prefix 780. Numbers in the Vancouver area of British Columbia carry the prefix 604 while elsewhere in British Columbia the prefix is 250.

Where to Stay

When you get off the plane in Calgary, Edmonton or Vancouver you are in a major city, each with a population in excess of 800,000. There is an endless variety of accommodation from five star hotels to hostels. The major mountain communities referred to in this book— Banff, Canmore, Lake Louise, Jasper, Golden, Revelstoke and Nelson—all have a variety of hotels, bed and breakfast establishments and hostels. For more information, write:

> Travel Alberta
> 300, 10155-102 Street N.W.
> Edmonton, Alberta
> T5J 4G8
> Phone 1-800-661-8888
> local (780) 427-4321
> Fax (780) 427-0867

> Tourism British Columbia
> Box 9830
> Station Provincial Government
> Victoria, B.C.
> V8W 9W5
> Phone 1-800-663-6000
> web site: www.travel.bc.ca

Alpine Club of Canada

The ACC operates a luxurious clubhouse and many backcountry huts. They are all reasonably priced (particularly if you choose to become a club member) and bookings can be made through the main ACC office in Canmore, Box 8040, Indian Flats Road, Canmore, Alberta, T1W 2T8, (phone 403-678-3200). The ACC facilities are as follows:

The Club House Located on the outskirts of Canmore, this lovely facility has beds for 60. There is an attractive library and lounge, complete kitchen facilities, sauna and a bar.

Huts

The ACC operates many backcountry huts which tend to be rustic and lean towards a philosophy of self reliance. Normally no custodian is present. A number of the huts referred to in this book (the Class A Huts) are locked with a combination lock. Booking can be a simple matter of exchanging your Visa or Mastercard number for the combination lock number! The huts described in this book are:

Class A Huts equipped with foamies, cooking and eating utensils, Coleman stoves and lanterns, and a wood heating stove.
Stanley Mitchell Hut (Little Yoho)
Bow Hut (Wapta Icefields)
Wheeler Hut (Rogers Pass)
Fairy Meadow Hut (Northern Selkirks)

Class B Huts equipped as above but there is normally no heating stove. They are much less luxurious.
Balfour Hut (Wapta Icefield)
Peyto Hut (Whyte Hut)
    (Wapta Icefield)
Scott Duncan Hut (Wapta Icefield)
Lawrence Grassi Hut
    (Clemenceau Icefield)
Great Cairn Hut (Mount Sir Sandford)

Hostels

The Southern Alberta Hostelling Association operates two luxurious hostels as well as a number of more rustic hostels throughout the Rockies. They are moderately priced and are extensively used by backcountry skiers. For reservations and/or further information write or phone:

SAHA
#203, 1414 Kensington Road N.W.
Calgary, Alberta, T2N 3P9 Canada
Phone (403) 283-5551

The Banff Hostel is a large modern structure with beds for 154. There is a restaurant, lounge and self serve kitchen. Phone (403) 762-4122 for information and reservations.

The Lake Louise Alpine Centre is owned and operated in conjunction with the Alpine Club of Canada, the centre offers over 100 beds and a fully modern facility. There is a restaurant, sauna, library, lounge and a self serve kitchen. Phone (403) 522-2200 for reservations and information.

Castle Junction Hostel Located on the 1A Highway (Bow Valley Parkway) near the Radium turn-off.

The Icefields Parkway Hostels There are several hostels which are more rustic and are almost like backcountry cabins. These are located along the Icefields Parkway at Mosquito Creek, Ramparts Creek and Hilda Creek. They are inexpensive, but comfortable. Phone the Banff Hostel for bookings.

The Alberta Hostelling Association operates a number of hostels near Jasper. Information on these can be obtained through:

AHA
10926 - 88 Ave.
Edmonton, Alberta, T6G 0Z1
Phone (780) 432-7798
Phone 1-877-852-0781 for reservations at Jasper hostels.

Jasper Hostel (7 km from Jasper)

Maligne Canyon Hostel
(11 km from Jasper)

Athabasca Falls Hostel
(30 km south of Jasper)

Edith Cavell Hostel (ski access only, 13 km from the trailhead)

Beauty Creek Hostel
(82 km south of Jasper)

There are two hostels in British Columbia in the area covered in this book.

Nelson
Dancing Bear Inn
171 Baker Street
Nelson, BC
V1L 4H1
Phone (250) 352-7573
e-mail: dbear@netidea.com
web site: www.dancingbearinn.com

Fernie
Raging Elk Hostel
892-6 Ave.
Fernie, BC
V0B 1M0
Phone (250) 423-6811

Commercial Lodges
In this book 16 backcountry commercial ski lodges are described in some detail. See page 279 for the start of more information.

Miscellaneous Huts
There are several other huts described in this book. They are:

McMurdo Hut (BC Forest Service)

Olive Hut (BC Forest Service)

Slocan Chief Cabin
(Kokanee Provincial Park)

Glacier Circle Cabin
(Glacier National Park)

Sapphire Col Hut
(Glacier National Park)

Malloy Igloo

Conrad Kain Hut
(Bugaboo Provincial Park)

Campgrounds
The Canadian Parks Service plows several campgrounds and keeps them open all winter for folks with RV vehicles. Contact the park information service for more up-to-date information.

Hot Springs

There are several excellent hot springs in the Rockies and Columbia Mountains. After a long day skiing it is a delight to soak in one of these pools. Here are five of the best.

Nakusp Hot Springs

This is a developed pool/resort and there is an entrance fee of $4.50. However it is well worth the money. The pool is hot with a water temperature of 53°C - 54.5°C. The pool is located in Nakusp Hot Springs Provincial Park just north of the town of Nakusp on the East Shore of Upper Arrow Lake. From Nakusp drive north on Highway #23 for 2.0 km then turn right and drive up an access road for 12 km. The pool is open in winter 11:00 am to 9:30 pm.

Halcyon Hot Springs

This is a rustic hot spring and has not been commercialized. The springs have been diverted into two large wooden tubs or pools. The smallest tub which is the hot pool will hold about 4 comfortably and the larger tub will hold about 6. The water temperature is 46.5° C - 50.5°C. The hot springs are located on the east side of the road (Highway #23), 33 km north of Nakusp. In the winter you must hike in the snow about 300 m up a steep road, then turn right for another 100 m to reach the pools.

Ainsworth Hot Springs

This is a fully developed resort but is highly recommended. It is usually not crowded in the winter time. Located 46 km north of Nelson on Highway #31 towards Kaslo, the hot spring centres around a cave that was a former mine shaft. When the miners hit hot water the shaft was abandoned. Over the years the walls of the shaft have been coated with calcite and are now unique. The hottest part of the pool is deep in the cave where the water pours out of the rock. The temperature of the water here is about 45°C. At the mouth of the cave is another pool of more moderate temperature and there is a large swimming pool at about 37.5°C. For those who like a refreshing dip during their hot soak there is a plunge pool of water straight from the creek at a temperature just marginally above freezing—it takes your breath away and leaves your skin tingling. The admission fee for this experience is $5.

Radium Hot Springs

This hot spring is located 1.5 km east of the town of Radium just inside the gates of Kootenay National Park. This large commercial operation is very popular and makes a pleasant way to finish a ski holiday. The average temperature of the pool is 40°C. The hours of operation are 9:00 am to 10:30 pm and the entrance fee for adults is $3.50

Upper Hot Springs - Banff

This hot spring is situated on the slopes of Sulphur Mountain, 3.5 km from the centre of Banff. It is a very popular hot pool and is delightful in the snow on a winter day. The temperature of the pool averages 40°C. The admission fee is $4 for adults. Winter hours are 12:00 noon to 9:00 pm weekdays and 10:00 am to 11:00 pm weekends.

USEFUL PHONE NUMBERS

Park Administrative Offices

Parks Canada Regional Office, Calgary — (403) 292-4401
BC Provincial Parks, East Kootenay District Office — (250) 422-4200
BC Provincial Parks, West Kootenay District Office — (250) 825-3500

BC Forest Service District Offices

Invermere — (250) 342-4200
Golden — (250) 344-7500
Revelstoke — (250) 837-7611
Nelson — (250) 354-6200
McBride — (250) 569-3700

National Park Information Centres

Banff (English or French) — (403) 762-1550
Lake Louise (English or French) — (403) 522-3833
Yoho — (250) 343-6324
Jasper (English or French) — (780) 852-6176
Glacier — (250) 837-7500

Travel Alberta

Field — (250) 343-6312
Canmore — (403) 678-5277

Weather Reports

Banff — (403) 762-2088
Jasper — (780) 852-3185
Castlegar — (250) 365-3131

Reservations

Alpine Club of Canada Huts — (403) 678-3200
Banff National Park Huts — (403) 762-1550
Canadian Alpine Centre (Lake Louise) — (403) 522-2200
Southern Alberta Hostelling Association — (403) 283-5551
Alberta Hostelling Association — (780) 432-7798
Banff Hostel — (403) 762-4122
BC Forest Service Huts — (250) 342-4200
Jasper Park Hostels — 1-877-852-0781

Helicopter Companies

Alpine Helicopters (Golden) — (250) 344-7444
e-mail — dsmctighe@redshift.bc.ca
Canadian Helicopters (Golden) — (250) 344-5311
Canadian Helicopters (Nelson) — (250) 352-5411
Frontier Helicopters (Invermere) — (250) 342-6535
High Terrain Helicopters (Nelson) — (250) 354-8445
Yellowhead Helicopters (Valemount) — (250) 566-4401
Selkirk Mountain Helicopters (Revelstoke) — (250) 837-2455

HOW TO USE THIS BOOK

Summits and Icefields is written for those who know something about backcountry skiing. It is presumed that you are familiar with map reading and route finding, whiteout navigation, snow stability evaluation and avalanche avoidance. If you are not, you should be skiing with someone who is.

This book covers a huge area and includes many ski runs and backcountry tours. They are not described in minute detail. Enough information is given in the form of written text, maps and photographs for an experienced ski mountaineer to form a good picture of what is involved. You must be able to fill in many of the details for yourself.

Grades No grades are given for the tours. You should be able appreciate the relative seriousness of a day Telemarking at Bow Summit or a month skiing the Great Divide Traverse. However I have made comments on all tours to help you to come to the right conclusions. All the tours described in this book are serious—they all offer real avalanche potential and what is a pleasant and safe ski tour one day can be extremely dangerous the next. You must have the ability to make this judgement.

Hazards As well as avalanche potential many of these tours offer other dangers such as crevasses, icefalls, river and creek crossings, cliffs. Often I have drawn the readers attention to some particular danger, but just because I have not mentioned a hazard does not mean that it is not there—this book covers such a large area that it is impossible to be thoroughly intimate with all the details and hazards of every tour.

Times No specific times are given for any of these tours. It may be indicated that the tour is one day or two days or that it is a month long tour but beyond that it is very difficult to be specific. Depending on the depth of snow, the strength of your party and the weight of your packs, the same tour can vary anywhere from four hours to two days. You must assess how long your party will take depending on conditions.

Maps The maps in this book are meant to be only a rough guide to the route. Intricate details such as which side of the stream the route follows, where it crosses the stream or how the route works its way through the crevasses on a glacier are not illustrated on the maps. You must work these out for yourself. The maps in this book are not meant to be used in the field for navigation or compass work. For all tours you must obtain and use the topographical maps referred to in the tour description.

Distances All distances are given in metres or kilometres and refers to horizontal distance.

Elevations Elevation gains and losses are referred to as "vertical metres".

Directions All directions such as turn left or turn right are given relative to the direction of travel. "Ski along the left bank of the stream" means ski on the left bank in the direction of travel. This is not necessarily what is known as the "true left bank" which is relative to the direction of flow of the stream.

Page 31 Wapta Icefields. Steep slopes below Mount Saint Nicholas not far from the Bow Hut. Photo Alf Skrastins

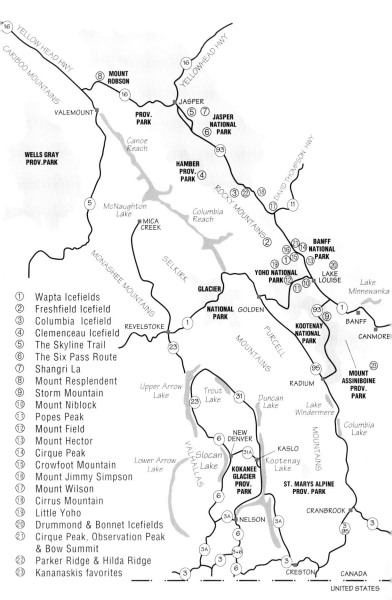

YELLOW HEAD HWY

CARIBOO MOUNTAINS

⑯

⑯ YELLOWHEAD HWY

⑧ MOUNT ROBSON

⑯

JASPER

VALEMOUNT

PROV. PARK

Canoe Reach

⑤ ⑦

⑥

JASPER NATIONAL PARK

93

WELLS GRAY PROV. PARK

HAMBER PROV. PARK ④

ROCKY MOUNTAINS

⑳ ⑱

DAVID THOMPSON HWY

⑰ ⑪

McNaughton Lake

⑤

Columbia Reach

MICA CREEK

②

㉑ ⑭

⑯

BANFF NATIONAL PARK

⑮

⑲ ①

⑬

⑳

LAKE LOUISE

Lake Minnewanka

MONASHEE MOUNTAINS

SELKIRK

YOHO NATIONAL PARK

⑫

⑪ ⑩

GLACIER

93

①

NATIONAL PARK

GOLDEN

⑨

BANFF

REVELSTOKE

①

PURCELL

KOOTENAY NATIONAL PARK

CANMORE

23

MOUNTAINS

㉓

MOUNT ASSINIBOINE PROV. PARK

95

RADIUM

Upper Arrow Lake

Trout Lake

㉛

Duncan Lake

Lake Windermere

MOUNTAINS

Columbia Lake

⑥ NEW DENVER

Slocan Lake

KASLO

㉛ᴬ

Lower Arrow Lake

VALHALLA

⑥

Kootenay Lake

KOKANEE GLACIER PROV. PARK

ST. MARYS ALPINE PROV. PARK

③ᴬ NELSON

③ᴬ

CRANBROOK

③ᴬ

⑥

③+⑥

③ ⑨⑤

③

⑥

③

CRESTON

CANADA

UNITED STATES

① Wapta Icefields
② Freshfield Icefield
③ Columbia Icefield
④ Clemenceau Icefield
⑤ The Skyline Trail
⑥ The Six Pass Route
⑦ Shangri La
⑧ Mount Resplendent
⑨ Storm Mountain
⑩ Mount Niblock
⑪ Popes Peak
⑫ Mount Field
⑬ Mount Hector
⑭ Cirque Peak
⑮ Crowfoot Mountain
⑯ Mount Jimmy Simpson
⑰ Mount Wilson
⑱ Cirrus Mountain
⑲ Little Yoho
⑳ Drummond & Bonnet Icefields
㉑ Cirque Peak, Observation Peak & Bow Summit
㉒ Parker Ridge & Hilda Ridge
㉓ Kananaskis favorites

the Rockies

ICEFIELD TOURS

The Wapta Icefields

The Wapta Icefields have become, for good reason, the most popular area for ski mountaineering in Canada. The mountains are spectacular, the glaciers are extensive and relatively safe, access from the highway is easy and there is an excellent system of huts operated by the Alpine Club of Canada.

The Wapta Icefields cover an area of 5-600 km² and are really composed of two distinct icefields—the Wapta and the Waputik.

On a sunny day it is a joy to explore the icefield. There are enough different variations of the 'Wapta Traverse' to keep the ardent ski mountaineer busy for a number of years. There are also many fine slopes to satisfy Telemark skiers and a wide choice of peaks to climb.

Although the Wapta Icefields have come to be regarded as pretty tame adventure, one should not take lightly the dangers that are waiting for the unsuspecting. In the winter time, with extremely cold temperatures or violent storms, sheer survival can become an issue even for the most experienced ski mountaineer. With reduced visibility, navigation becomes a challenge for all of us and getting lost, with limited survival gear, is very serious indeed. Avalanche terrain and numerous crevasses require good route finding skills and experience in roped glacier travel. In the event of an avalanche or crevasse fall you should be prepared to locate and dig up the victim or extricate them from the crevasse. It is recommended that before venturing out onto this icefield you become trained in all the necessary skills,

and for your first few trips travel in the company of an experienced ski mountaineer or even a guide.

There are four huts on the Wapta Icefields and a fifth hut in the Little Yoho Valley nearby (Stanley Mitchell Hut). It is worth remembering that in poor visibility it may be very difficult to locate some of these huts. You should be prepared to construct an emergency shelter and bivouac.

The Wapta Icefields are covered by 4 topographical maps (82 N/7 Golden, 82 N/8 Lake Louise, 82 N/9 Hector Lake and 82 N/10 Blaeberry River), and this has been a nuisance in the past. However it is now possible to purchase one map which covers the entire region. It is printed on waterproof, tearproof and erasable paper, and on the back has aerial photographs showing the major ski routes. It is recommended that you purchase the map and use it as a companion to this guide book. Referred to as "Touring the Wapta Icefields", it was prepared by Murray Toft, and sells for about $15.

Early Ski Exploration

The first ski exploration onto the Wapta Icefields was in May of 1932. A. A. McCoubrey, Roger Neave, Ferris Neave and Campbell Secord skied up the Yoho Valley and set up a base at Twin Falls Chalet. On May 6 they ascended Mount Des Poilus. On May 9 they skied up the Yoho Glacier, climbed to the summit of Mount Gordon, descended to near Vulture Col and ascended Mount Olive. Finally on May 11 Roger and Ferris Neave traversed Yoho Peak.

In June 1934, Guide Victor Kutschera led D.E. Batchelor and B.G. Moodie from the Calgary Ski Club and Lloyd Harmon from Banff, up the trail to Sherbrooke Lake where they set up camp. The weather was not good but on June 10 it dawned clear and they skied through Niles Pass and carried on across the Waputik Icefield to make an ascent of Mount Balfour.

In May 1936, Georg Lillienfeld with unnamed companions (likely Victor Kutschera), established headquarters at Jim Simpson's camp, north of Bow Lake near the present day site of Num-ti-jah Lodge. They found an excellent route up onto the Wapta Icefields which is in fact the route followed today. They made ascents of a peak they called 'Snow Dome', Mount Gordon and the south peak of Mount Rhondda. In a mammoth one day effort they skied from Bow Lake, up the canyon, then crossed a pass and a small icefield to the south between Mount Saint Nicholas and Crowfoot Mountain, then descended into Balfour Creek. From here they ascended the Balfour Glacier, rounded Lilliput Mountain and climbed Mount Balfour! They returned via the Balfour Glacier, then skied out to Hector Lake where they spent the night at a nearby cabin. Quite an effort! Lillienfeld captures the spirit of ski adventure of those days in this quote (things have not changed a lot in sixty years).

"The characteristic difference that strikes the European visitor almost on his first day in the Canadian Rockies and impresses itself more and more profoundly upon his mind during a long stay, may be seen correctly in the tremendous vastness and still unspoiled wilderness of these rugged ranges and trailless valleys and the complete solitude of the 'high country' and the big icefields. Although detailed maps with ski routes, major crevasses and avalanche gullies marked on them, an elaborately set up hut system, human settlements in every little valley have done a great deal to lessen the dangers of skiing and ski mountaineering in the Alps, they have also taken away a good part of the fun that lies for the experienced mountaineer in being dependent only on his own ability and in pioneering excursions off the beaten path." [1]

After this early burst of activity the Wapta Icefield saw limited ski activity for a number of years. In April 1944 soldiers training in winter warfare made the traverse of the Wapta Icefields by ascending the Peyto Glacier, then descending the Yoho Glacier.

In 1960 ski exploration on the Wapta and, indeed, all other icefields along the divide underwent a major boost when a group led by Hans Gmoser attempted to ski the Continental Divide from Kickinghorse Pass to Jasper. They ascended to Sherbrooke Lake and gained the Waputik Icefield via Niles Pass. They then traversed the Waputik and Wapta over several days, crossed Baker Col and descended into the Blaeberry Valley to the west. From here they continued via the Freshfield, Mons and Lyell Icefields as far as the Alexandra River. The article Gmoser wrote in the Canadian Alpine Journal in 1961 about this partially successful trip opened the eyes of many to the opportunity for ski adventure along the icefields of the Continental Divide. Within a few years many parties began to venture onto the icefields on skis and by 1965 the first hut was erected.

[1] A Spring Ski Excursion into the Bow Lake District" by Georg Von Lillienfeld, CAJ, Vol. 24, 1936, page 75.

The History of the Huts

Much of the credit for the huts on the Wapta Icefields belongs to a small number of individuals. In the early days it was Peter Fuhrmann who conceived of the idea and championed it to completion, Philippe Delesalle who designed and oversaw the construction of the huts and Art Patterson, who with the help of the Calgary Ski Club did much of the work in erecting the huts. In more recent years a new generation of huts has been constructed on the Wapta Icefields under the direction of Mike Mortimer, Chairman of the ACC Huts Committee, using the tremendous volunteer energy of the Alpine Club of Canada.

The beginnings of this fine hut system date back to the early 1960's when Peter Fuhrmann, who was guiding groups on the icefields, saw the need for some simple shelters to facilitate these ski adventures. Two of his clients from Chicago, Vicki and Lucio Mondolfo offered to pay for a hut. He enlisted the help of architect Philippe Delesalle who designed a simple fibreglass igloo style of structure. After obtaining permission from the Federal Government, the hut was erected in October of 1965, near Balfour Pass, by Fuhrmann, Patterson and a group from the Calgary Ski Club. Ownership of the hut was given to the crown and it was open to the public at no charge.

It was not long before the shortcomings of this hut were apparent—chief among these being the fact that wandering wolverines could break into the hut and make a tremendous mess. In 1967 a new Panabode structure was built by Banff National Park and the old structure was scrapped.

Over the years this building also suffered from the elements and from abuse. In 1989 ownership of the hut was transferred to the Alpine Club of Canada in a complex arrangement whereby the government transferred most of its remaining backcountry huts in the park to the club. Then in exchange for the removal of the Lloyd MacKay Hut on the Freshfield Icefield, Banff National Park tore down the old Balfour Hut and replaced it with a fine new building in 1990. A new site for this building was chosen several kilometres east of the old location.

The second hut on the Wapta Icefield was the Peyto Hut (Whyte Hut), a small fibreglass igloo similar to the first Balfour Hut, again designed by Philippe Delesalle. It was paid for by prominent Banff citizen and ski pioneer Catharine Whyte. On February 26, 1967 the hut was erected on a rock outcrop below Mount Thompson by Art Patterson and a group from the Calgary Ski Club.

This hut encountered the same problems with wolverines that had plagued the Balfour Hut and in 1970 was replaced with two oblong fibreglass 'bubbles' which were acquired from the National Parks. These were erected by the Banff Section of the Alpine Club of Canada, but were soon found to have their own shortcomings, the ceilings dripped heavily from condensation.

In 1983 the present hut was built. It was designed and constructed by Bernie Schiesser and Eric Lomas with manpower supplied by the Alpine Club of Canada. Major funding for the hut once again came from the Whyte family and Art Patterson was again involved. In 1989 Banff National Park transferred ownership of this hut to the Alpine Club of Canada as well.

Although the Bow Hut is now the most luxurious and most popular hut on the Wapta, it was the third hut to be erected. The same players were involved in this hut. It was designed by

Philippe Delesalle, funded by Catharine Whyte and the cause was championed and organized by Peter Fuhrmann and Art Patterson. The hut was constructed in February, 1968 by a crew made up of members of the Alpine Club of Canada, the Calgary Mountain Rescue Group, the Calgary Mountain Club, the Calgary Ski Club, and the Association of Canadian Mountain Guides. The crew was supervised by Bob Hind of the Alpine Club of Canada.

This hut was abused and heavily overused right from the beginning. For 20 years it suffered from pollution and poor management. It was finally handed over by Parks to the Alpine Club of Canada in 1989. Part of the agreement was that the ACC would be allowed to build a new environmentally sound hut near the old location.

That same year the new hut was built. It was a mammoth project costing $98,000 for materials and helicopter alone. Hundreds of volunteers donated all the labour involved. Chief amongst those responsible for this hut were Mike Mortimer, Carl Hannigan, Malcolm Talbot, John Lajeunesse and Wayne Shackleton.

In 1988 the Scott Duncan Hut, named after a young ski mountaineer who died in November of 1985, was built on the shoulder of Mount Daly at the southern extremity of the icefield. This fine hut was also designed and constructed by Bernie Schiesser and Eric Lomas with manpower provided by volunteers from the Alpine Club of Canada.

Since its beginnings in the early 1960's an excellent hut system has evolved on the Wapta Icefields. In the early years the huts were donated to the Canadian Government and were open to the public at no cost. Banff National Park found it a tremendous expense to try to manage these huts and eventually realized that the solution was to give them to the Alpine Club of Canada. Although we now pay to use the huts we are certain that they are clean when we arrive and through the club's booking system we are guaranteed there will be room for us. The huts are now environmentally responsible and are always well outfitted and maintained. The fees are a small price to pay for such a comfortable way to enjoy the Wapta.

Victor Kutschera

Vic Kutschera was one of the first ski guides in the Rockies. Although he guided during the summer his first love was the mountains in winter. He was one of the first European-trained ski instructors around Banff and was a product of Hannes Schneider's ski school in Austria. Victor put a lot of time and energy into helping the local young skiers perfect their skills—skiers like Norman Knight, Rupe and Chess Edwards and the Paris Boys, Ted, Cyril and Herb. Kutschera worked around the Mount Norquay, Skoki and Mount Assiniboine ski lodges and is known for his early ski explorations on the Wapta Icefields.

Vic Kutschera during early ski ascent of Mount Balfour, 1934. Photo Lloyd Harmon

Approaches

The Wapta Icefields are not far from the Trans-Canada Highway and, consequently, make a very popular weekend destination. There are two main access routes—via the Peyto Glacier and from Bow Lake. Both routes are reasonably safe and can be managed by almost any group. A third route onto the Wapta to the Scott Duncan Hut from Sherbrooke Lake is used only occasionally.

Peyto Glacier Approach

Distance 10 km one way to Peyto Hut
Height gain 550 m
Max elevation 2480 m

This is a very pleasant way to access the Wapta Icefields. Depending on conditions, the weight of your pack and your fitness and skill level, it can be either an easy day trip or a marathon march. The route is generally easy to follow.

Hazards There are slopes on this tour that could slide in certain conditions. In addition, caution should be exercised when circling around the crevasses on the upper end of the Peyto Glacier. The rope should be worn when near these crevasses.

Access A plowed parking lot on the west side of the Icefields Parkway, 2.5 km down the hill, north of Bow Pass.

From the parking lot find an old road which is just a short distance away. It is easiest to head north along the highway for about 100 m, then descend west down the bank for another few metres to hit the road. Descend the road for several hundred metres, keeping your eyes open for a trail which takes off through the woods to your left—usually there is a piece of flagging to mark the spot. Follow the trail as it rolls up and down through the woods for about 1 km to Peyto Lake. This section can be tricky and often it is best to do it with your skins on!

Ski across the lake heading for the Peyto Creek drainage on the other side. Be certain that the lake is adequately frozen and snow covered.

Once you reach the gravel flats on the far side of the lake, head towards the narrowing. At the first narrows, only a short distance from the lake, it is usually necessary to cross the creek then climb up onto the left bank for a short distance. Cross the creek again, then continue beyond this point along the gravel flats for about 0.5 km. When the stream begins to curve gradually to the left towards a narrowing canyon, climb up the slopes above on the right towards a large and prominent moraine that can be seen higher up.

Climb up into a protected little basin behind the moraine, then continue to the point where the crest of the moraine butts up against the hillside. Take off your skis and climb the hillside (caution—avalanche potential), continuing on foot for another 75 vertical metres until the angle lays back. Here you can usually put your skis back on and traverse to the Peyto Glacier (passing the Glaciology Research building).

Ascend the glacier in a southwest direction, aiming for the groove in the slope at the end. Ski up the groove staying well to the right of the crevasses. Above the crevasses circle back to the east. The Peyto Hut is directly to the east on a knoll, below the slopes of Mt. Thompson. The precise grid reference for the hut is 314237.

Peyto Hut
(Peter and Catharine Whyte Hut)

Map 82 N/9 Hector Lake,
82 N/10 Blaeberry River
Location On the moraine below the NW ridge of Mt. Thompson GR 314237
Reservations Alpine Club of Canada
Capacity 18
Facilities Foamies, Coleman stoves & lanterns, dishes
Water Snowmelt

Ascending the Peyto Glacier towards the two peaks of Rhondda. The Peyto Hut is located above the icefall to the left.
Photo Gillean Daffern

Photo Chic Scott

Bow Hut Approach

The most popular and easiest access onto the Wapta Icefields takes you to the Bow Hut which is the largest and most luxurious of the Wapta Huts. The trail is usually broken and easy to follow. However, if there has been a heavy snowfall and you are unfamiliar with the route, it can be more challenging.

Distance 8 km one way to the Bow Hut
Height gain 390 m
Max elevation 2330 m

Facilities Num-ti-jah Lodge on the edge of Bow Lake makes an excellent base of operations for ski touring the area offering comfortable accommodation and fine dining.

Hazards There is potential avalanche hazard on this route, particularly along the canyon, on the hillside above the canyon and then on the steep hillside below the Bow Hut. Be particularly aware that the large cirque below Mount Saint Nicholas is threatened by avalanches from the ice cliffs high above. Move quickly through this exposed area.

Access There is a large parking lot on the west side of the Icefields Parkway, about 6 km south of Bow Pass (north end of Bow Lake) at the turn off to Num-Ti-Jah Lodge.

Ascending the second canyon.
Photo Tony Daffern

From the parking lot ski gently down to the lake. Head out across the lake (be certain that it is well frozen!) and cross to the gravel flats on the far side. Continue up the stream for about 0.5 km until you can see that the way ahead is blocked by a narrow canyon. At this point angle left and ski up through the trees on a trail which climbs gradually up a small side drainage until it bumps up against a steep mountainside, complete with avalanche paths. Climb a short hill to the right, traverse around the corner (west) then descend into the main drainage again. You have now circumvented the first canyon.

Follow the creek, heading almost due south, up the second canyon. The walls above you are steep and overhung with snow—you should not linger here. In the late spring the creek may be open in places and present difficulties. After about 1 km the way ahead becomes difficult and the route ascends to the left, onto the east bank. Continue through broken forest, climbing gradually, until the trees end and the route breaks out into a large open cirque below the threatening ice cliffs of Mount Saint Nicholas.

Cross the cirque in a southerly direction, climbing gradually, and contour around to the base of the steep hillside on your right. It is critical that you pick the right point to climb this hillside as there is avalanche potential here. The route normally climbs a shallow groove up the left end of the hillside, with a series of traverses and kick turns, until it can break out over the right edge of the groove onto the slopes above. Continue up these slopes to the hut which is about 100 vertical metres higher up. The precise grid reference for the Bow Hut is 355203. Please note that this is a new hut, built in 1989, and any information of an earlier date will give an incorrect hut location.

Bow Hut

Map 82 N/9 Hector Lake
Location NE of St. Nicholas Peak, on a rocky ridge overlooking the main drainage leading down to Bow Lake GR 355203
Reservations Alpine Club of Canada
Capacity 30
Facilities Two buildings separated by a vestibule. Foamies, wood stove, Coleman stoves & lanterns and utensils in common room
Water Snowmelt or drainage to south
Notes Common room locked when custodian not present. Combination required.

Bow Hut. Photo Gillean Daffern

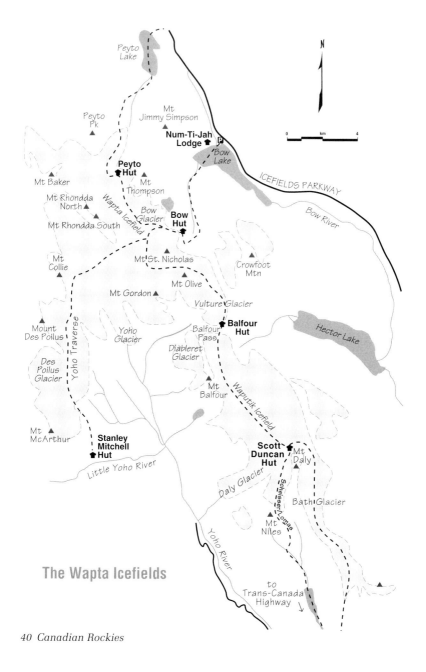

The Wapta Icefields

Traverses

The Wapta Icefields are normally traversed in one of four ways, with some minor variations. These are:

- The Complete Traverse from Peyto Lake to Sherbrooke Lake (there are three possible exits)
- The Partial Traverse from Bow Lake to Sherbrooke Lake (three exits)
- The Mini Traverse from Bow Lake to Peyto Lake
- The East to West Traverse from Bow Lake to The Little Yoho Valley

In this section the components of these traverses are described and should be combined with the approaches from the previous section and with the exits in the following section.

At the end of the day. The terrific descent beneath Mount Saint Nicholas to Bow Hut. Photo Roger Laurilla

Peyto Hut to Bow Hut

Distance 6 km
Height gain 150 m to Rhondda/Thompson Col
Height loss 300 m to Bow Hut
Max elevation 2670 m

This connection is straightforward in good visibility, but can be a challenging routefinding problem in a whiteout.

From the Peyto Hut ski southeast to the broad pass between Mount Thompson and Rhondda South. Continue southeast, traversing so as to maintain your height. The most common mistake here is to lose elevation too quickly, and be drawn down into the Bow Glacier drainage. Stay high above the Bow Glacier and traverse through a little notch just above a small unnamed peak (GR 343209). From here descend southeast to the Bow Hut. Watch out for crevasses.

Bow Hut to Balfour Hut

Distance 7 km
Height gain 580 m to Olive/Saint Nicholas col
Height loss 430 m to Balfour Hut
Max elevation 2930 m

This connection is also very straightforward in good visibility but can be challenging in a whiteout.

From Bow Hut climb up the hill in a northwest direction. Once you reach the glacier, the direction of travel becomes westerly. Climb up beneath the impressive north face of Mount Saint Nicholas and work your way around the west side of the peak until you can ski up into the pass between Mount Olive and Mount Saint Nicholas.

From the pass, head east out onto the Vulture Glacier, then curve around to the right. Continue descending in a southeast direction to the hut. There are numerous crevasses at the toe of the glacier, directly in your path, so it is best to avoid the crevasses by picking a line which takes you along the east side of the glacier, then curves around to the south at the very end.

In poor visibility the best tactic is to ski east (with the aid of a compass) from the Olive/Saint Nicholas Col until the escarpment which runs all along the east side of the Vulture Glacier can be seen. Then descend the glacier using this escarpment as a handrail (it usually shows up through the mist as assorted cliffs and scree slopes). As you near the end of the glacier, the escarpment can actually be followed to the right (south) to the hut (GR 375157) at Balfour Pass. (Note that the location of the Balfour Hut has changed since 1990).

Peyto Hut to Balfour Hut

Distance 7 km
Height gain 430 m to Olive/Saint Nicholas Col
Height loss 430 m to Balfour Hut
Max elevation 2930 m

This tour offers the essence of icefields touring. It stays high and traverses across 'endless' expanses of snow. In some conditions, the descent to the Balfour Hut can be fast and fun.

Many people ski directly from the Peyto Hut to the Balfour Hut. The trip is straightforward when there is good visibility. Refer to page 41 and page 42 for the route. These two tours can be connected easily—instead of descending to the Bow Hut, when traversing from the Peyto Hut, simply continue high across the icefield to the Olive/Saint Nicholas Col and follow the usual route to the Balfour Hut.

Balfour Hut

Map 82 N/9 Hector Lake
Location On low, rocky hills at the toe of the Vulture Glacier GR 375157 as of 1990
Reservations Alpine Club of Canada
Capacity 18
Facilities Foamies, Coleman stoves & lanterns, dishes
Water Snowmelt
Note May be difficult to find in whiteout conditions

Opposite top: From Balfour Pass looking back up the Vulture Glacier to Vulture Col and Mount Olive. Photo Clive Cordery

Opposite bottom: Balfour Hut at Balfour Pass. Balfour High Col and Mount Balfour in the background. Photo Murray Toft

Balfour Hut to Scott Duncan Hut

Distance 10 km
Height gain 520 m to Balfour High Col
Height loss 320 m to Scott Duncan Hut
Max elevation 3020 m

This is one of the most challenging sections of ski mountaineering on the Wapta Icefields. It should only be undertaken in good visibility, as it is very hard to navigate by map and compass in the complicated terrain below Mount Balfour.

From the Balfour Hut, descend a short distance then ski across the flats in a southerly direction to reach the lower slopes of Mount Balfour. Ascend the slope and ski out onto the glacier, heading towards a rock cliff which sticks up prominently in the middle of the glacier. High above you on the right is another bench which is sometimes used as a route up the glacier. As you approach the rock cliff, the route turns to the right and climbs steeply up a narrow ramp. The angle then eases, the route turns left and continues across to Balfour High Col for another 1 km. This route is subject to icefall from the northeast face of Mount Balfour and you should travel as quickly as possible without rest stops!

From High Col the route descends in a southeast direction across the Waputik Icefield, heading almost directly for Mount Daly. There are a few crevasses across here, and you should still ski with caution. The hut is located at the base of the spur which descends in a northwest direction from Mount Daly (GR 417084).

Opposite top: Balfour High Col and Mount Balfour. Photo Alan Kane
Opposite bottom: Crossing the Waputik Icefield towards the Scott Duncan Hut, located at the base of the ridge on Mount Daly. Photo Alan Kane

The route to Balfour High Col. The safest route ascends from lower left to below the small black cliff. Balfour High Col is located directly above the cliff. Mount Balfour to right. Photo Don Gardner

Scott Duncan Hut

Map 82 N/9 Hector Lake
Location On a bench at the bottom end of the NW ridge of Mt. Daly GR 417084
Reservations Alpine Club of Canada
Capacity 12
Facilities Foamies, Coleman stoves & lanterns, dishes
Water Snowmelt
Note May be difficult to find in whiteout conditions.

View from the Scott Duncan Hut of the Waputik Icefield and Mount Balfour (left). It shows the route from Balfour High Col. Photo Murray Toft

Scott Duncan was a very promising alpinist and ski mountaineer from Calgary who died in 1987. During his brief life he became a veteran of the Grand Traverses, skiing the Northern Rockies Traverse in 1978, The Southern Rockies Traverse in 1980, the Northern Selkirks in 1981 and the Northern Cariboos in 1982. Scott travelled widely and made journeys to South America, Nepal and New Zealand. At the time of his death he was establishing himself as an adventure photographer. In 1987 he made his last major mountain expedition. Over a period of 26 days he and his companions made a 380 km traverse of the St. Elias Range, climbing 4725 m-high Mount Wood along the way.

Exits

From the Scott Duncan Hut there are three exits to the Trans-Canada Highway at West Louise Lodge. Today, most parties follow the exit discovered by Bernie Schiesser and Eric Lomas in the 1980's.

The Schiesser/Lomas Route

Distance 12 km from the Scott Duncan Hut to the West Louise Lodge
Height loss 1,060 m
Max elevation 2710 m

This is the most pleasant and safest way to descend from the Scott Duncan Hut to the Trans-Canada Highway. In reasonable visibility it is easy to follow. However, if you are unfamiliar with the terrain it can, in a whiteout, require advanced navigational skills in the upper section.

From the Scott Duncan Hut descend to the glacier below. Traverse south towards the pass between Mount Niles and Mount Daly. Ski around the right side of the small peak which is located in the centre of the pass, then descend a slope which takes you out onto a broad bench high above the Niles Creek Valley.

Descend the bench for almost 2 km. Very near the end of the bench the route swings to the right and begins to curve back around the shoulder towards the west. Be sure to swing right around to the west so that you are clearly above the upper Sherbrooke Creek. Descend open slopes, then ski through the trees into upper Sherbrooke Creek. Continue directly down the creek bed to the flat, open meadow where it joins Niles Creek. There are a few short steep sections in this creek bed which can be difficult in poor conditions.

After you reach the junction of Niles Creek with Sherbrooke Creek, continue to just short of the brow of a steep hill not far above Sherbrooke Lake. From here it is best to traverse out to the right, through the trees, to the brow of the hill. Then descend steeply for a short distance until you reach an open slope which descends to more gentle terrain. Ski down to the lake and cross it (be sure the lake is well frozen).

Once across the lake, continue above the left bank of Sherbrooke Creek for a short distance, then search up to the left to find the summer trail. From here the trail turns east and heads down and around the shoulder of Paget Peak to West Louise Lodge. This section of the trail is steep and challenging—it can be the most difficult part of the descent, particularly if you have a large pack and the trail is icy or rutted.

The Bath Glacier Exit

The exit via the Bath Glacier offers an interesting variation and in good conditions can be a viable alternative to the Schiesser/Lomas Route. There is one very steep slope of about 300 vertical m which you should feel very certain of before descending!

From the Scott Duncan Hut head back to the north and curve around to the right (east). Ski through a gentle pass on the northeast side of Mount Daly and out onto the Bath Glacier. From here the route continues south across the Bath Glacier, high above the valley. The route is generally safe along here, but there are a few sections where the slope is steep enough to be dangerous in certain conditions.

After about 8 km the route climbs to a pass between Paget Peak and Mount Bosworth. The descent of the south side of this pass is extremely steep and should be undertaken only if you are absolutely certain of the safety of the slope (often it is windblown and bare). From the bottom of the hill continue south down the valley. After about 1 km swing right above the upper edge of the trees and work your way over to a large avalanche path which descends from Paget Peak. Ski down this path, then continue through the trees to West Louise Lodge almost directly below.

Below the Scott Duncan Hut skiing towards Mount Niles. Photo Rod Plasman

The Traditional Sherbrooke Lake Exit

The Scott Duncan Hut was built to enable parties exiting the Wapta to get an early start and descend this route while conditions were well frozen. Previously, parties had been forced to descend dangerous slopes late in the day. The traditional exit down Niles Creek can still be dangerous and is not recommended unless the snowpack is very stable. The route goes through the pass between Mount Niles and Mount Daly, staying on the left side of the little peak in the pass, then descends the Niles Creek Drainage.

The Yoho Traverse

Distance 20 km from the Bow Hut to
the Stanley Mitchell Hut
Height gain 820 m
Height loss 1,100 m
Max elevation 2,900 m

From the Bow Hut you can traverse to the
Stanley Mitchell Hut in the Little Yoho
Valley. Most parties will find this a very
long day—so be prepared to bivouac if
necessary. There are several slopes
which provide serious avalanche potential in certain conditions, so it is best to
wait for a period of high stability before
attempting this trip. Routefinding in whiteout conditions would be extremely difficult on this tour.

From Bow Hut climb northwest up the
hill and head west out onto the icefield.
Ski west to the broad open pass between Rhondda South and Mount Gordon. From the pass descend gently for
several kilometres and ski across to the
broken section of glacier descending
southeast from Mount Collie. This is

the first challenge of the trip—to find a
way through these crevasses.

Once above them head southwest to
the top of a very steep slope above the
Des Poilus Glacier. This is the second
challenge of the tour—to descend this
slope safely. In certain conditions it
may not be possible.

Cross the Des Poilus Glacier heading
south. People often camp in this area
rather than stay at the Bow Hut. The third
challenge is to ascend the steep ramp
which works its way from right to left
under Isolated Peak up to Isolated Col
(GR 298101). Caution is required here as
the slope is steeper than it appears.

The descent of the south-facing slope
of Isolated Col is also steep and requires
caution. Continue down the valley,
then descend steeply through the trees
to the Stanley Mitchell Hut which is
located on the edge of a meadow, along
the banks of the Little Yoho River (GR
303081). To ski out to the highway refer
to the Approach to the Little Yoho Valley on page 125.

*The pass, with Mount Collie in the
background. Photo Alan Kane*

Ascents

The Wapta offers many fine ski mountaineering ascents. On some of them, like Mt. Gordon and Rhondda South you can ski right to the top. Most of them, however, like Mt. Collie, Mt. Balfour, Mt. Olive and Rhondda North require some climbing to reach the summit. However, the climbing is not difficult and usually all that is required is a rope and an ice axe.

Mount Saint Nicholas

Distance 6 km return from the Bow Hut
Height gain 610 m
Max elevation 2970 m

This spectacular peak is one of the most popular ascents on the Wapta Icefields. It is not a ski ascent but is included here because ski mountaineers often attempt the climb.

From the Bow Hut ascend northwest to reach the toe of the glacier. Continue climbing to the west onto the icefield under the imposing north face of Mount Saint Nicholas, then circle around the west flank of the mountain to reach the Olive—Saint Nicholas Col on the south side of the peak. Leave your skis here and continue on foot along the ridge, heading north. The ridge is moderately technical and involves some rock scrambling and steep snow. Most parties will want to put a rope on. On the left is a very steep cliff while on the right a steep slope falls away. At the top a short scramble up a gully takes you to the summit.

Top: The ridge of Mount Saint Nicholas. Photo Keith Morton

Mt. Gordon

Distance 12 km return from Bow Hut
Height gain 850 m
Max elevation 3203 m

This is one of the most scenic ski ascents on the Wapta. It is possible to see almost the whole icefield stretched out before you. The ascent is straightforward in good weather, but can be tricky if visibility is poor.

From the Bow Hut climb up the hill in a northwest direction. Climb the toe of the glacier in long switchbacks, ascending west beneath the impressive north face of Mount Saint Nicholas. Continue angling southwest towards Mount Gordon. The route climbs easily to the right hand shoulder of the mountain, passing a deep wind scoop below some outcropping rocks, then works up and left to the ridge. Once on the ridge the angle eases and the summit is only a short distance away.

Olive   Balfour   Gordon

                    Vulture Col

        Saint
        Nicholas

*Top and following four pages: Panorama of
the Wapta Icefields from Mount Thompson.
Photo Clive Cordery*

*Previous page: The final easy slopes of
Mount Gordon. Photo Roger Laurilla*

Mt. Olive

Distance 6 km return from the Bow Hut
Height gain 770 m
Max elevation 3130 m

This is another easy scramble which is a
very popular ascent with ski mountaineers.

From Bow Hut ascend northwest to
reach the toe of the glacier. Continue
climbing to the west onto the icefield
under the imposing north face of
Mount Saint Nicholas, then circle
round the west flank of the mountain
to reach the Olive—Saint Nicholas Col
on the south side of the peak. Leave
your skis here and climb the ridge
above the col in a southeasterly direction. Although the climbing is easy
scrambling, novices may appreciate
the comfort of the rope. About half
way to the summit the route breaks out
onto a scree-covered slope and essen-
tially follows a trail to the summit.

Rhondda South Peak

Distance 10 km return from Peyto Hut
Height gain 530 m
Max elevation 3015 m

The peak labelled Mount Rhondda on
the topo map is one of a pair of peaks. It
is often referred to as Rhondda South
while its slightly taller neighbour is known
as Rhondda North. The ski ascent of
Rhondda South is very popular. It is not
a difficult peak and skis can be taken to
the summit.

From Peyto Hut cross the névé of the
Wapta Icefield heading south to reach
the southeast ridge of Rhondda South
(GR 323208). The slope steepens here
and is often windblown and hard packed.
Work your way back and forth with several kick turns, gaining about 100 vertical metres to reach lower-angled terrain
above. From here simply follow the ridge
crest for about 2 km to the summit. Along
the way there are several steep steps
where one may have to remove skis and
kick steps for a short distance. Most parties return via the same route although
the northeast face of the peak offers an
interesting alternate descent (be wary of
large crevasses).

The summit ridge of Rhondda North Peak. In the background is Mount Collie.
Photo Gillean Daffern

Rhondda North Peak

Distance 6 km return from Peyto Hut
Height gain 570 m
Max elevation 3055 m

The large peak which dominates the ice-field across from the Peyto Hut is referred to as Mount Rhondda. It, too, is a very popular ski ascent and gives a good ski run on the way back down.

From the Peyto Hut ski across the glacier in a southwest direction to enter the cirque between Rhondda North and Rhondda South. As you ascend into the cirque, work your way around and climb up north to reach the east ridge of Rhondda North. The snow becomes wind packed along the ridge and after ascending on skis as far as possible, continue on foot. The final summit tower offers some technical climbing where a rope is required.

The descent of the southeast facing slopes into the basin offers some excellent skiing.

Mt. Collie

Distance 18 km return from the Bow Hut
Height gain 750 m
Max elevation 3116 m

The ascent of Mount Collie is a major undertaking. It is a long day with some climbing near the summit. Take a rope and crampons.

From the Bow Hut ascend northwest to gain the Wapta Icefields. Gradually turn west and ascend the slope up onto the névé of the icefields. Continue west for about 3 km to reach the broad pass between Mount Gordon and Rhondda South (GR 324204), then descend gently out onto the upper reaches of the Yoho Glacier. Continue southwest for several kilometres, then climb up towards Mount Collie, working your way through the crevasses which are prevalent here. Once above the crevasses go either of two ways.

Either follow the route as marked on Murray Toft's map which ascends to the south ridge. Some rock scrambling is encountered en route to the summit. Or ascend to the low point of the northeast ridge (GR 286185), then climb the ridge to the summit. Usually a cornice impedes progress and it is necessary to traverse around it on the steep slope to the right.

Mount Thompson

Distance 8 km return from the Peyto Hut
Height gain 580 m
Max elevation 3065 m

This peak is occasionally climbed by ski mountaineers. The boulder slope leading to the summit is often windblown and presents tedious travelling conditions.

From the Peyto Hut ski south up to the bottom of the broad southwest ridge which descends from the summit of Mount Thompson. From here the route simply ascends the wind blown slopes above. Sometimes it is necessary to proceed on foot. Sinking into deep snow and slipping on the boulders can prove frustrating and possibly dangerous.

Opposite: Ascending the northeast ridge of Mount Collie. Photo Alan Kane
Opposite inset: The cornice traverse. Photo Alan Kane

Baker

Baker Col

Trapper

Baker Col

Trapper Col

Mt. Des Poilus

Distance 5 km return from camp on glacier below peak
Height gain 800 m
Max elevation 3161 m

This mountain offers a ski descent of about 700 m to the Des Poilus Glacier below. If conditions are right and you know what you are doing you can reach the summit. However, the upper slopes are very steep and avalanche prone and it is best to leave your skis and scramble the last 100 vertical metres along the ridge to the top. There are a number of crevasses on this tour (very apparent in summer) and you should ski with caution and take all safety precautions.

From the Des Poilus Glacier the route of ascent follows straight up the glacier towards the summit. Higher on the climb, just below the summit pyramid, several large crevasses must be avoided. The final pyramid itself is very steep. However ,it may be possible to traverse to the left hand ridge, then scramble to the summit on foot.

Mount Baker

Distance 8 km return from the Peyto Hut
Height gain 680 m
Max elevation 3172 m

This is a frequently climbed peak. It is not a ski ascent but is often climbed by ski mountaineers.

From the Peyto Hut ski west across the head of the Peyto Glacier then ascend northwest to the col on the north side of Mount Baker, between that peak and a small unnamed peak (Baker Col). Leave your skis a short distance above the col and proceed on foot to the summit. The climb involves steep step kicking in wind-blown snow. Although the ascent is not difficult, novices may appreciate the protection of a rope and an ice axe.

Opposite: Approaching the northeast ridge of Mount Baker. Photo Alan Kane

Mount Balfour

Distance 12 km return from the Scott Duncan Hut
Height gain 570 m
Max elevation 3272 m

Mount Balfour is the highest peak on the Wapta Icefield and a real prize. The ascent is more serious than most of the other climbs on the Wapta due to the combination of elevation, remoteness and difficulty of access.

From the Scott Duncan Hut descend to the glacier below and make your way in a northwest direction to Balfour High Col (GR 384119). The glacier is straightforward to cross and there is little problem with crevasses.

The route ascends the shoulder of Mount Balfour above High Col in a westerly direction and gains about 50 vertical metres over a distance of about 0.5 km. Be careful of hidden crevasses. This takes you to the edge of a steep drop-off which must be descended. Remove your skis and scramble down scree and snow slopes for about 50 vertical metres to the glacier below.

Ski northwest across the glacier on the southwest flank of Mount Balfour. The glacier becomes steep as it nears the summit. If you wish, leave your skis

behind and kick steps. (This slope could present serious avalanche risk in certain conditions.) The glacier turns to steep snow with bits of rock sticking through just as it reaches the ridge. The last 50 vertical metres along the summit ridge is not difficult but one should be careful of cornices overhanging the northeast face. An ice axe is handy on the last part of this ascent.

The Columbia Icefield is one of the premier ski mountaineering locations in Canada. It is a huge and complex icefield surrounded by numerous mountain giants between which glaciers wind their way to the valley bottom. The icefield covers about 225 km^2 with ice up to 365 m thick.

The icefield is the hydrographic apex of North America—the summit of Snow Dome is the point from which snow melt flows to the Arctic, Atlantic and Pacific Oceans. Water from the Athabasca Glacier flows north via the Athabasca River and Mackenzie River into the Arctic Ocean. Water from the Castleguard and Saskatchewan Glaciers flows via the North Saskatchewan River east to Hudson Bay and the Atlantic Ocean. Water from the western reaches of the icefield flows via the Bush and Sullivan Rivers into the Columbia River and on to the Pacific Ocean.

There are other icefields nearby: to the north the Chaba and Clemenceau Icefields and to the south the Lyell and Mons Icefields. All of these icefields have been linked together in a ski traverse which stretches from Jasper to Lake Louise (see page 211).

Spring is the most popular time for skiers, the winter being generally too cold. Folks from Calgary and Edmonton can be found camped on the névé, particularly at the Easter break and on the Victoria Day long weekend. But even at the busiest of times it is a wild and wind swept place and most folks will appreciate a little company.

Opposite: Ascending the final slopes of Mount Balfour. In the background is Mount Daly (left), Mount Niles (right) and the Niles/Daly Col in between. Photo Alan Kane

The normal approach is via the Athabasca Glacier, although groups occasionally ascend the Saskatchewan Glacier. It takes a full day to work your way up onto the névé and to establish a camp. Prepare your campsite with an eye to changing weather. It may be a beautiful sunny afternoon when you set up your tent but the next morning when a howling gale is blowing you will wish that you secured your tent well and built that wind wall. You will also wish that you had taken some compass bearings the night before and placed a few wands so that you can find your way back to your car.

History

The first white men to reach the fringes of the Columbia Icefield were Walter Wilcox and R. L. Barrett. Led by packers Fred Stephens and Tom Lusk, they reached the toe of the Athabasca and Saskatchewan Glaciers in 1896 but were unaware of the extent of the icefield from which these glaciers flowed.

Two years later, in 1898, J. N. Collie, H. Woolley and Hugh Stutfield, led by Bill Peyto, made their way to the icefield. On August 18, Collie and Woolley climbed Mount Athabasca and discovered what lay behind.

"The view that lay before us in the evening light was one that does not often fall to the lot of modern mountaineers. A new world was spread at our feet. To the westward stretched a vast icefield probably never before seen by human eye, and surrounded by entirely unknown, unnamed and unclimbed peaks."

A few days later Collie and Woolley, joined by Stutfield, made an attempt on the giant, Mount Columbia. They made their way up the Athabasca Glacier to:

"...the edge of an immense icefield, which stretched mile upon mile before us like a rolling snow covered prairie. The peaks we noticed, were all a long way off,..."

They were unsuccessful in climbing Mount Columbia,

"...for several hours we tramped steadily on over the almost level icefield, but Mount Columbia proved to be much farther off than it looked."[1]

...but they did manage to reach the summit of Snow Dome on their return.

Collie had a great desire to make the first ascent of Mount Columbia but was beaten to the summit by James Outram. Led by his guide Christian Kaufmann, Outram reached the summit during July of 1902. On that same trip they also made a remarkable first ascent of Mount Bryce—an ascent which involved difficult rock climbing in the dark and a bivouac on the mountain without food, water or protection from the elements.

For twenty years the area was largely forgotten by alpinists and was visited only three times; by Mary Schäffer in 1907, by the Provincial Boundary Survey in 1919, and by Caroline Hinman in 1919 leading her 'Off the Beaten Track' tours (14 young women from the eastern United States and their cowboy guides!).

During the twenties there was a rebirth of interest and soon the major peaks were all climbed—North Twin (1923), South Twin (1924), Mount King Edward (1924), Mount Kitchener (1927), Mount Stutfield (1927) and Mount Andromeda (1930).

Skiing in the area got its start in 1929 when Joe Weiss made a solo trip from

Jasper to the Columbia Icefield. In 1930 Joe and several companions made another ski trip to the Columbia Icefield and this time the group explored the icefield itself. In poor weather they made an attempt on Mount Castleguard and got to within a few metres of the summit. Later that same year, Joe and four companions skied from Jasper, past the Columbia Icefield, on their epic traverse from Jasper to Banff. In 1931 Joe repeated the Jasper to Banff traverse, but this time he and his group stopped and made a ski ascent of Snow Dome. In 1933 Joe was back one more time and he and his team very nearly made a ski ascent of Mount Columbia. Along with C.V. Jeffery, A.D. Jeffery and A.L. Withers he reached a point only 100 vertical metres below the summit after spending a frigid night bivouacked in a trench dug in the snow.

With the opening of the Banff-Jasper Highway (now called the Icefields Parkway) in 1940, the nature of mountaineering changed completely. It was now possible to reach the Athabasca Glacier in several hours from Lake Louise or Jasper.

In January 1944 the newly constructed Columbia Icefield Chalet was home to the Lovat Scouts, Scottish soldiers who were being trained in mountain warfare by Canadian guides and instructors. During their stay in the icefield area they made first winter ascents of Mount Columbia, Mount Kitchener, Mount Andromeda and Nigel Peak. Their Canadian guides and instructors included Joe Weiss, Ken Jones, Bruno Engler and Stan Peyto.

In April 1947 the Alpine Club of Canada held their annual ski camp at the Columbia Icefield, using the garage building of the Icefield Chalet for their base camp. In 1957, the Alpine Club was back again for their spring ski camp.

[1] Climbs and Exploration in the Canadian Rockies, H.E.M. Stutfield and J.N. Collie, Longmans, Green and Co., London, 1903.

The Icefields Parkway was reconstructed and resurfaced between 1955 and 1962 and access to the Columbia Icefield became even easier. Over the years the attraction of this area has grown. Some of the greatest climbing routes in the world are on peaks that ring the icefield - the North Ridge of Mount Columbia, the North Face of Mount Kitchener, the North Face of North Twin, the North Face of Mount Alberta and Slipstream on Snow Dome. In the springtime many parties venture up onto the icefield in hope of making a ski ascent of one of the giants—perhaps Mount Columbia or North Twin.

Past Huts There have been several huts used by mountaineers in the vicinity of the Columbia Icefields. None proved satisfactory and they no longer exist today.

The Saskatchewan Glacier Hut was originally built by the United States Army in 1942 and was used as a base for testing vehicles over snow and ice in mountainous terrain. The original build-

Cliff White on Snow Dome in 1931.
Photo Joe Weiss

ing collapsed under the heavy snow load during the winter of 1942-43. It was rebuilt by the Canadian Army Engineers as a smaller hut and used to train the Lovat Scouts during the winter of 1943-44. After this it was turned over to the Alpine Club of Canada. The hut was located on the south bank of the stream issuing from the Saskatchewan Glacier, only a very short distance from the glacier itself. Originally you could drive right to the door of the hut, but in the 1960's the road washed out, and after this the hut was rarely used. The lease of occupation expired in 1972 and the hut reverted back to the Crown. It was torn down a short time later by Parks Canada.

The Athabasca Glacier Hut was located on bed rock above the south lateral moraine of the Athabasca Glacier, below the Andromeda Icefall. Its origin is shrouded in mystery but it was likely built during WW II by the Lovat Scouts or for them by Jack Brewster. It was a simple frame building and by the 1960's had fallen into complete disrepair. It was burned down by Parks Canada in 1974.

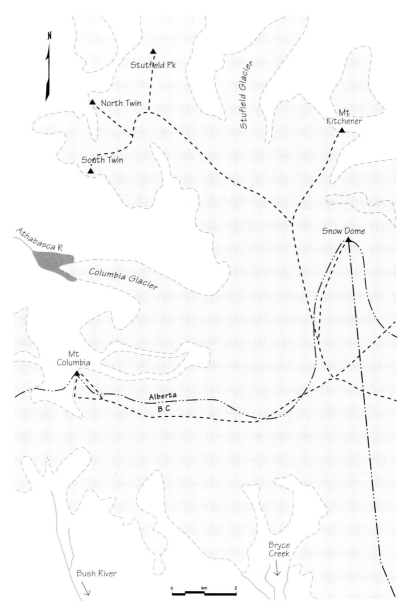

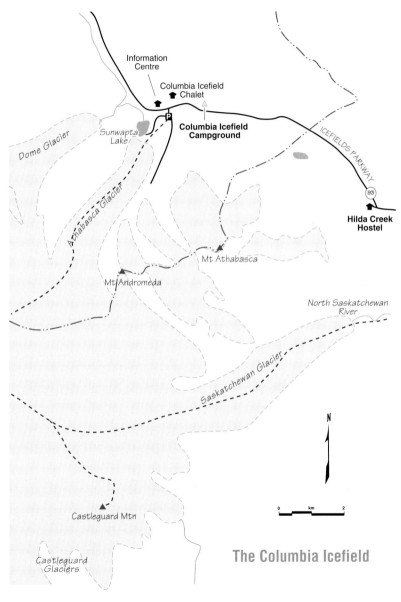

Information Centre

Columbia Icefield Chalet

Columbia Icefield Campground

Sunwapta Lake

Dome Glacier

Athabasca Glacier

ICEFIELDS PARKWAY

93

Hilda Creek Hostel

Mt Athabasca

Mt Andromeda

North Saskatchewan River

Saskatchewan Glacier

N

0   km   2

Castleguard Mtn

The Columbia Icefield

Castleguard Glaciers

Approaches

Most peaks on the Columbia Icefield are climbed from a high camp. It is normal to ski up the Athabasca Glacier the first day and establish a camp high on the névé (at about GR 780780), just before reaching 'the big dip'. From this high camp you can fan out and make ascents of many peaks.

It is big country on the icefield and you should be very careful about heading out on a day trip and being unable to locate your camp after the clouds roll in. Put some wands around your camp in a large X so that you have a bigger target to shoot for on your way home. Keep your map and compass handy and know how to use them.

Maps

The Columbia Icefield is one of the few locations which is confined quite conveniently to one map. All the approach routes and peaks described in this guidebook are on one topo sheet, 83 C/3 Columbia Icefield. Also available is 'Exploring the Columbia Icefield', prepared by Murray Toft, which shows the ski touring routes on a waterproof, tearproof and erasable map.

The Athabasca Glacier

Distance 10 km one way
(to high camp)
Height gain 950 m (to high camp)
Max elevation 2900 m (at high camp)

Most people approach the Columbia Icefield via the Athabasca Glacier. It usually takes a full day to ski up the glacier, ascend the headwall, then get established well out on the névé. There are lots of crevasses on this approach and it is

recommended that you ski roped up. There is also icefall danger from high on the side of Snow Dome so keep your eyes open and be very careful where you stop for lunch breaks.

In the winter and spring the small side roads which lead from the Icefields Parkway to the toe of the Athabasca Glacier, or up to the Snowcoach Tours, are not plowed so you park just a short distance after turning off the highway. From here make your way down the snow covered road or across country to the toe of the Athabasca Glacier.

After putting the rope on head up the centre of the glacier. For several kilometres travel is very straightforward. As you approach the heavily crevassed upper reaches of the glacier work your way to the right flank to bypass some crevasses. There are three steps in the glacier—the first two being relatively minor and the last step (or the headwall) being a long climb of about 300 vertical metres. All three steps are threatened to some degree by icefall from the seracs high above you on the right. The first two steps are usually negotiated towards the right side of the glacier. The final headwall is ascended pretty well up the centre, between large icefalls on the left and the right. While climbing the headwall and just above there is a great risk of crevasse falls so pay attention to the variations in snow texture. Above the headwall the angle gradually eases and the expanse of the Columbia Icefield spreads out before you.

Opposite top: Ascending the Athabasca Glacier headwall. Note the seracs on the side of Snow Dome. Photo Murray Toft

Opposite bottom: Typical camp on the Columbia Icefield, with Mount Bryce in the background. Photo Ruedi Setz Collection

Saskatchewan Glacier

Distance 15 km one way
(to névé of icefield)
Height gain 900 m (to névé of icefield)
Max elevation 2575 m (on névé)

The approach via the Saskatchewan Glacier is not often used. It is long and tedious and most of the major ascents on the icefield are along the north flank. Mount Castleguard is however the one exception and is often approached via the Saskatchewan Glacier.

Park your car at a large, plowed parking lot at the 'Big Bend' on the Icefields Parkway, located at the bottom of the big hill, 12 km south of Sunwapta Pass.

From the parking lot, angle south a short distance, crossing the creek then continue across open flats to the trees. (If there is not enough snow to cross the creek, you can head back east along the highway for about a kilometre where you will find an old abandoned bridge.) Find an old road heading up the hill through forest (marked on the map). Do not attempt to follow the creek through the canyon—it is impassable. Climb up the road gaining about 75 vertical metres of elevation, then pass through a bit of a notch and follow the road down the other side. The descent is exposed to avalanches from the slopes above on the left, and you should proceed as quickly as possible to the safety of the valley flats below.

Cross the open gravel flats for several kilometres, then climb easily onto the toe of the glacier. The angle of ascent is gentle. Even though there are not a lot of obvious crevasses, you should travel roped up. Ten kilometres of skiing up the glacier will take you out onto the névé of the Columbia Icefield.

The upper reaches of the Saskatchewan Glacier with Mount Castleguard on the left.
Photo Murray Toft

On the summit of North Twin. Photo Alan Kane

ASCENTS

Don't expect to simply ski up the névé and bag a few peaks—the weather is often poor here and it can take several attempts before you're successful. Before heading out from camp take compass bearings and place your tent position accurately on the map, then keep checking your position throughout the day. It can be very serious if the clouds roll in midway through your climb and you are unable to locate your camp.

Mount Columbia

Distance 8 km one way (from high camp)
Height gain 1000 m (from big dip)
Max elevation 3747 m

Mount Columbia is of course the big prize on the Columbia Icefield. It is the second highest summit in the Canadian Rockies and is a magnificent peak. Normally it takes a few tries to get the right weather to make a successful ascent so don't get discouraged. The climb is not particularly difficult but it is a serious ascent.

From your high camp ski west, descend into the big dip then begin the long ascent to the base of the summit pyramid. From here there are two popular variations to reach the top.

- It is possible to climb the centre of the southeast face. It is necessary to take your skis off as the angle steepens and kick steps to the top.
- If you have doubts about the snow stability it is also possible to ascend the left ridge (the south ridge). There are several rock steps on the ridge which must be avoided by kicking steps up steep snow, to the right of the crest.

Opposite top: Mount Columbia, showing ascent route up the southeast face.
Photo Andy Riggs
Bottom: The Columbia Icefield from Mount Castleguard. Photo Tony Daffern

Mt. Columbia

South Twin North Twin Snowdome

Kitchener

Snow Dome

Distance 5 km one way (from high camp)
Height gain 600 m (from high camp)
Max elevation 3451 m

Snow Dome is perhaps the most popular and the easiest ascent on the Columbia Icefield. It is a gentle ski ascent right to the top. It is best to stay towards the southwest flank of the mountain where there are fewer crevasse.

Mount Kitchener

Distance 8 km one way (from high camp)
Height gain 600 m (from high camp)
Max elevation 3480 m

Mount Kitchener is another straightforward ski ascent. Ski north from the high camp, rounding the west flank of Snow Dome. From the broad pass between the peaks continue to the summit.

Top and next 4 pages: Panorama of the Columbia Icefield from North Twin. Photo Clive Cordery

Stutfield Peak

Distance 12 km one way
(from high camp)
Height gain 550 m (from high camp)
Max elevation 3450 m

A straightforward ascent from the saddle between Stutfield Peak and North Twin. Stutfield has two summits—the south summit (GR 722874) is slightly higher. To begin the ascent there is a small rock band just above the saddle which is rounded on the left.

It is possible to make several ascents in one day. Snow Dome, Kitchener, Stutfield, North Twin and South Twin are all along the margin of the icefield and any number of combinations is possible.

Snowdome

North Twin

Distance 12 km one way
(from high camp)
Height gain 750 m (from high camp)
Max elevation 3730 m

After Mount Columbia, North Twin is perhaps the second most popular prize. The reason is, of course, that it is the third highest peak in the Canadian Rockies (and one of the four 'twelve thousanders'). You need good weather for this ascent as well because you must travel a long distance to reach the peak.

From your high camp ski north across the long arm of the icefield to the saddle between North Twin and Stutfield Peak (GR 716855). From here traverse out left (south) on a bench to avoid the icefall on the east face of North Twin above you. The route then swings right and ascends the southeast face of the peak.

Be careful on this ascent as there are a number of big crevasses to negotiate (you might even want to mark them with wands for your descent afterwards). You can ski to within a few metres of the summit, but it is advised that you walk the last bit. Approach the summit warily (cornices!).

You can get a good view of North Twin from the bump in the icefield just to the southeast (GR 727847). It is advised that you stop here for a moment and check out the ascent route.

From the top is one of the greatest panoramas in the Rockies. To the south and west across the névé is the great north face of Mount Bryce and the north ridge of Mount Columbia, while to the north is the tower of Mount Alberta, one of the most difficult summits in the Rockies. Below you, the north face of The Twins drops off into what is called "The Black Hole". On this wall are two of the most difficult climbing routes in North America.

Lyells

Bryce

Columbia

South Twin

South Twin

Distance 14 km one way
(from high camp)
Height gain 700 m (from high camp)
Max elevation 3580 m

Ski north from your high camp across
the long northern arm of the icefield to
reach the saddle between North Twin
and Stutfield Peak (GR 716855).
Traverse left (south) on a bench to reach
the col between North Twin and South
Twin (GR 703843). From here you can
continue to the top of South Twin. Before long it is necessary to remove your
skis and proceed on foot along a very
narrow ridge to the summit.

*Opposite bottom: North Twin, showing the
route of ascent. Photo Murray Toft*

Mount Castleguard

Distance 6 km one way (from high
camp), (15 km via the Saskatchewan
Glacier)
Height gain 500 m (from the icefield
névé), (1350 m via the Saskatchewan
Glacier)
Max elevation 3090 m

The summit of Mount Castleguard can
be reached quite easily. The route up
the final summit pyramid is up the
centre of the northeast face. Skis can be
taken to within 50 metres of the summit, then you have to kick steps to the
top. Although the mountain can be
climbed from the icefield névé, it is
often approached via the Saskatchewan
Glacier and Castleguard Meadows.

The summit gives a tremendous
panorama of the Columbia Icefield as
shown on pages 68/69.

The Clemenceau Icefield

The Lawrence Grassi Hut.
Mount Clemenceau in the background.
Photo Chuck Young

The Clemenceau is one of the more remote icefields in the Rockies. Coupled with the Chaba Icefield it forms an immense area with great peaks rising from an endless expanse of snow. It is difficult to access and rarely visited. Those searching for solitude and adventure will find this an appealing destination.

Although the Lawrence Grassi Hut, located towards the northwest edge of the icefield, is a good base for an ascent of Mount Clemenceau, there are few other ski ascents in the immediate area. It is suggested that, if you fly in, you take a tent with you and explore farther afield.

From the hut a one day ascent of Mount Clemenceau is possible up the Tiger Glacier on the southwest flank of the mountain. It is not an ascent to be taken lightly as the climb offers cre-

Lawrence Grassi Hut

The Lawrence Grassi Hut is a well insulated, metal sided, Gothic arch structure, with a single room.

Map 83 C/4 Clemenceau Icefield
Location The hut is located on the southeast end of Cummins Ridge, southwest of Mount Clemenceau at 2100 m (GR 320813).
Reservations ACC in Canmore
Capacity 18
Facilities Foam mattresses, kitchen area outfitted with utensils and pots. Coleman stoves, lanterns and an oil heater.
Water from snow melt.

vasse and icefall danger as well as some non-technical climbing. It is a very big peak and in the winter or spring conditions can be very cold.

Other objectives in the vicinity of the hut are Mount Sharp and Mount Morrison which are located along the ridge which separates the Cummins Glacier from the Tusk Glacier.

There is good, sheltered skiing to the north and west of Cummins Ridge. The descent to the Cummins Glacier to the northeast is about 100-150 vertical metres. Skiing can also be found in the glacial bowl southwest of Tusk Peak, between Tusk and Mount Shipton.

Access by air

Access by air to the Clemenceau Icefield is an expensive proposition as you must fly by helicopter all the way from Golden. For further information contact Alpine Helicopters in Golden (250) 344-7444.

Num-ti-jah Lodge

Located on the shore of Bow Lake, along the Icefields Parkway, Num-ti-jah Lodge provides a delightful mix of old fashioned ambiance and modern convenience. Although you can drive to the door of this 1940s structure, it has the feel of a back country lodge. Offering fine dining, hot showers and a roaring log fire in the evening, Num-ti-jah also provides easy access to some of the best ski mountaineering in the Rockies. Open year round, rooms for two range from $65 to $125 per night. Meals are $45 per day. For further information phone: (403) 522-2167 or e-mail: reserve@num-ti-jah.com

---

Access on foot

Access on foot to the Clemenceau Icefield is a serious undertaking. There are no easy routes and you must have a sense of adventure and a bit of the pioneer spirit to get yourself there without the help of a machine. There are several routes to consider:

• There are logging roads which ascend high up the Sullivan River and are said to reach a point not far from the icefield (GR 505717). From this point, ski in a northwesterly direction, crossing a pass (GR 454808) after about 10 km which takes you onto the head of the Clemenceau Glacier just south of Apex Mountain. The roads may be clear of snow or you may need to use a snowmobile. For further information contact Evans Forest Products in Golden at (250) 344-8800.

• Traditionally, parties have skied up the Athabasca River and the Chaba River to Fortress Lake, crossed the lake, descended the Wood River, then turned south and ascended Clemenceau Creek to reach the icefield. It may be difficult to cross the Wood River to reach Clemenceau Creek and it will take several days to reach the edge of the icefield.

• It is possible to reach the Chaba Icefield by ascending the Athabasca River, and following the Chaba River to the toe of the East Chaba Glacier. This glacier is extremely broken up and it is best to ascend to the south beneath the north flank of Chaba Peak to a pass (GR 551834) just east of Chaba Peak, then continue south onto the Chaba Icefield.

• For the really adventurous an exciting alternative to consider is skiing out via the Columbia Icefield. It is possible to ski from the Lawrence Grassi Hut across the Clemenceau Icefield and the Chaba Icefield to reach the main body of the Columbia Icefield which can be

Powder skiing below Mount Clemenceau. Photo Clive Cordery

crossed to the Athabasca Glacier and thence to the Icefields Parkway. However, there is a major routefinding challenge in rounding the southwest flank of Mount Columbia (see page 217).

Maps

83 C/4 Clemenceau Icefield
83 C/5 Fortress Lake
83 D/1 Wood Arm
83 D/8 Athabasca Pass

Lawrence Grassi and Hut History

Lawrence Grassi was born in Italy in 1890 and emigrated to Canada in 1912. He very quickly found his way west to the Rocky Mountains where he spent most of his life working as a coal miner in Canmore.

Lawrence Grassi also built a reputation as a mountain guide. He guided the first ascents of The Tower on Castle Mountain and the difficult First Sister near Canmore. He worked for many years at the Alpine Club of Canada General Mountaineering Camps, and one year guided Mount Sir Donald five times in five days. He climbed Mount Louis sixteen times, often as a guide, and in the 1930's he even made an attempt on Mount Waddington. He loved the mountains so much and enjoyed guiding people so much, legend has it that he never took any money for his services.

Lawrence was also a pioneer trail builder. He built trails for the Hostel Association linking their hostels between Calgary and Banff and also built trails in the Skoki area. However, he is best known for creating the wonderful network of trails at Lake O'Hara for which the area is so famous.

The Lawrence Grassi Hut was built by the Alpine Club of Canada in 1981. It was paid for with funds donated from the Lawrence Grassi estate and also with funds donated by Edmund Hayes Sr. Mr. Hayes was past owner of Canmore Collieries Ltd. and was Lawrence's employer for many years. Together they had shared many mountain adventures.

The Freshfield Icefield

The Freshfield Icefield offers a marvellous array of peaks and slopes for ski exploration. Although there is lots of good skiing, the area is especially suited for those who want to do a little ski mountaineering in a wild setting and reach a few summits. The scenery is truly impressive with many crevasses and wild icefalls. Some of the peaks that are regularly attempted are:
• The north side of Mount Barlow makes a fine ski ascent right to the summit and offers an excellent run back down.
• Mount Gilgit is skiable right to the top via the Nanga Parbat/Gilgit col.
• Nanga Parbat can be ascended via the north face. There is a bergschrund to cross then some steep step kicking to gain the rounded summit ridge.
• Mount Barnard makes an excellent ascent. Ski to the Barnard/Bulyea col then climb steep snow and ice slopes to the corniced summit.
• Mount Bulyea offers a straightforward snow climb from the Bulyea/Walker col.
• Mounts Trutch and Waitabit can be tricky right at the top with narrow ridges and cornices.

Access to the Freshfield Icefield is by helicopter. The most reliable landing site is in the Helmer/Barlow col. From here you can just ski north out onto the icefield. Exit from the Freshfields is usually on foot, either to the Icefields Parkway at Saskatchewan River Crossing or back down the Mummery Glacier (descend the true left bank of the glacier from the Gilgit/Helmer col) to the Blaeberry River.

For further information contact Alpine Helicopters in Golden, phone (250) 344-7444.

Looking southwest towards Gilgit, Nanga Parbat and Trutch. Photo Chic Scott

The Forgotten Drummond & Bonnet Icefields

East of the Trans-Canada Highway, near Skoki, lie two small icefields which offer a great opportunity for ski adventure. Once upon a time, during the heyday of Skoki Lodge in the 1930's and 1940's, these two icefields were popular. However, in recent years they seem to have been forgotten.

The Drummond Icefield

Distance 26 km (one way)
Height gain 1540 m
Max elevation 3120 m
Maps Lake Louise 82 N/8
82 K/9 Hector Lake
82 O/12 Barrier Mountain

The Drummond Icefield is highly recommended for those skiers who want an adventure without the crowds often found on the Wapta Icefields. A mini-

mum of 3-4 days is required if you are to allow some time for a ski ascent or two. This is an excellent venue for those who are looking for something new with a wilderness touch.

The Drummond Icefield normally is approached from Temple Lodge at the Lake Louise Ski Area and then via Baker Lake. Park at Fish Creek parking lot near the Lake Louise Ski Area and take the bus to Temple Lodge. The bus is operated by the ski area. For information regarding fares and schedules phone (403) 522-3555.

From Temple Lodge follow the trail towards Skoki Lodge up Corral Creek to Boulder Pass. Continue across Ptarmigan Lake and across Baker Lake, then ski around the corner into Cottongrass Pass (GR 677065). Continue north for about 4 km to Red Deer Lakes. Turn east for another 4 km, following the Red

Deer River until you can turn northwest up the stream that drains the Drummond Icefield (GR 697119). Follow this stream for about 2 km, then begin the climb onto the Drummond Icefield along the right flank, following the edge of the creek.

Once you are on the icefield it is possible to ascend a number of peaks. At the north end of the icefield are several easy peaks up to 3120 m in elevation. At the south end it is possible to get up Cyclone Mountain and Pipestone Mountain with some scrambling. Note that Pipestone Mountain is marked incorrectly on the map and is really the peak just to the west at GR 658128.

Right: Looking south across the Bonnet Glacier towards the Bonnet Peaks. Photo Reg Bonney

Bottom and previous page: Panorama looking north from Pipestone Mountain across the Drummond Icefield. Photo Bob Saunders

The Bonnet Icefield

Distance 26 km (one way)
Height gain 1390 m
Max elevation 3215 m
Maps 82 N/8 Lake Louise
82 O/5 Castle Mountain

Another good location for a wilderness adventure is the Bonnet Icefield. You will most likely have it all to yourself. Allow 3-4 days to give yourself some time to make a few ascents.

The access to the Bonnet Icefield is also from Temple Lodge at the Lake Louise Ski Area. To reach the lodge, park at the Fish Creek parking lot and take the bus to Temple Lodge. Phone the Lake Louise Ski Area (403) 522-3555 for information regarding fares and schedules.

From Temple Lodge follow the Skoki trail up Corral Creek to Boulder Pass. Continue across Ptarmigan Lake and Baker Lake. Descend into the headwaters of Baker Creek, then climb to a small lake northwest of Tilted Mountain (GR 693045). From here ascend an open valley to the east to reach a col on the northwest ridge of Lychnis Mountain (GR 711048). Ski out onto the flats in a northeast direction until it is possible to angle around to the right and climb back up open slopes to a col on the northeast ridge of Lychnis Mountain (GR 717048). From here you can travel southeast along the Bonnet Icefield for almost 10 km, crossing one small pass at GR 730023.

Several ascents are possible on the Bonnet Icefield. South Bonnet Peak (GR 779979) is a scree walk to the summit, while North Bonnet Peak (GR 776985), which is slightly higher, is more problematic and the ascent exposes you to

avalanche hazard. Mount Hickson (GR 753971) involves some rock scrambling and a rope is advised. Several other unnamed summits can also be reached.

A Little Aviation History

Al Gaetz was perhaps the first mountain pilot in the Rockies. He was a military pilot, trained during the Second World War, who afterwards tried to get a business going in the Banff area. However, he was always running into difficulties with the park officials. Ken Jones says of Al that *"He just put in enough gas he figured would do him so he could carry more load!"* That caught up to him occasionally and Jones says that at one time Gaetz had to make a forced landing on a frozen and snowy Lake Louise. Gaetz had a company called Inter-Mountain Airlines. In 1952 his little red and yellow aeroplane flew the participants of the ACC ski camp into Mount Assiniboine. He was unfortunately killed in a car accident along what is now the 1A Highway at Baker Creek in 1953.

After the death of Gaetz two other adventurous pilots tried their hand at Gaetz's business for a while. However, Stu Ames and Wally Lutz had some trouble of their own. Ames crashed a plane on snow-covered Lake Magog and the plane still is at the bottom of the lake. Around 1954 or 1955 Ames crashed a plane on the Bonnet Icefield and the body of the plane is still there (approximate grid reference 761986). Ski mountaineers can often spot this relic in the winter and spring even with the deep snow.

Ascending above Fossil Creek to the Drummond Icefield. The route ascends the bench below the big cliff.
Photo Don Gardner

The Traverse of the Drummond and Bonnet Icefields

For those skiers looking for a good wilderness adventure but perhaps lacking the time or experience for one of the major ski traverses described in this book, a great alternative is to traverse from Mosquito Creek to Johnston Canyon, crossing the Drummond and Bonnet Icefields along the way. It is a perfect one week backcountry trip and would allow time on each of the icefields to climb a few peaks. The terrain is not as intimidating as on a major icefield traverse and the trip not as committing. It is highly recommended for skiers who have done several trips onto the Wapta and are looking for something a little more challenging.

The traverse begins along the Icefields Parkway at Mosquito Creek. Follow the creek for about 7 km, then climb to North Molar Pass (GR 536228). From here descend to Fish Lakes, then down to the Pipestone River. Descend the Pipestone for a short distance before turn-

ing east up Fossil Creek (GR 603185). Ascend Fossil Creek (unnamed on the map) until it breaks out of the trees (GR 624189). From here an unlikely looking route ascends the slope to the south to gain a ramp (GR 627182) which is then followed in a southeast direction, eventually emerging on the Drummond Icefield. Several days can be spent camped on the icefield, making ascents of surrounding peaks.

Descend the Drummond Glacier to the southeast and continue into the valley, following the creek along the left flank (GR 676147). Ski down the creek to the Red Deer River. Work your way over to the valley which runs south, just to the east of Oyster Peak. Ascend this valley, then climb the slopes under Mount Douglas and Mount St. Bride to a high pass on the northeast ridge of Lychnis Mountain (GR 717047). From here you can ski south onto the Bonnet Icefield. Continue south through a small pass (GR 730023) and out onto the main névé of the icefield. Several days can be spent bagging peaks and doing some exploration.

From the Bonnet Icefield descend to the south through a pass along the south rim of the icefield (GR 767974). The descent below this pass can be hazardous and caution is advised. After about 1.5 km, the route turns to the right through Badger Pass (GR 771958) which may present problems with cornices. Descend the creek to the southwest to Johnston Creek. The trail is followed along Johnston Creek for over 20 km to the Bow Valley Parkway. Note that the trail does not descend along Johnston Canyon at the end as it approaches the highway. The trail in the winter branches to the right (about GR 811791) and reaches the highway at what is called Moose Meadows (GR 798787).

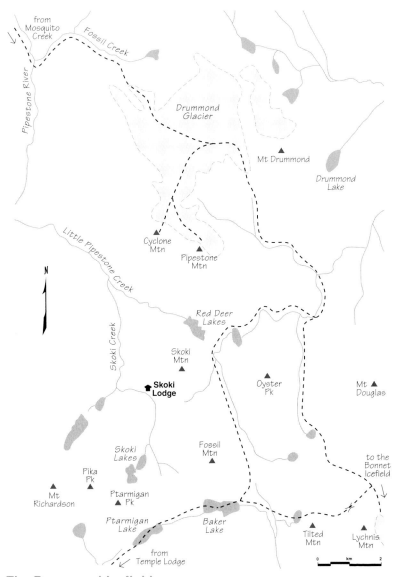

from
Mosquito
Creek

Fossil Creek

Pipestone River

Drummond
Glacier

Mt Drummond

Drummond
Lake

Little Pipestone Creek

N

Cyclone
Mtn

Pipestone
Mtn

Skoki Creek

Red Deer
Lakes

Skoki
Mtn

Skoki
Lodge

Oyster
Pk

Mt ▲
Douglas

to the
Bonnet
Icefield

Skoki
Lakes

Fossil
Mtn

Pika
Pk

Mt
Richardson

Ptarmigan
Pk

Ptarmigan
Lake

Baker
Lake

Tilted
Mtn

Lychnis
Mtn

from
Temple Lodge

0   km   2

The Drummond Icefield

82 Canadian Rockies

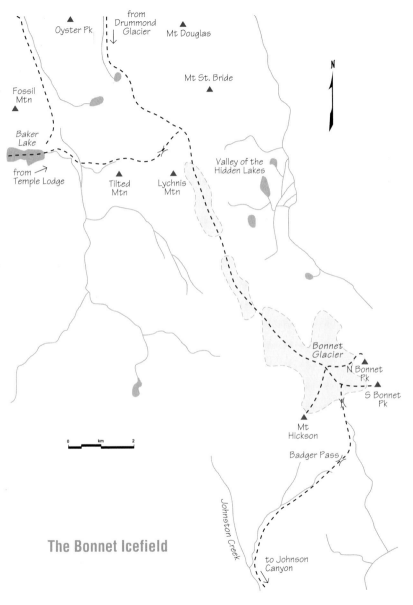

Oyster Pk

from Drummond Glacier

Mt Douglas

N

Fossil Mtn

Mt St. Bride

Baker Lake

from Temple Lodge

Valley of the Hidden Lakes

Tilted Mtn

Lychnis Mtn

Bonnet Glacier

N Bonnet Pk

S Bonnet Pk

Mt Hickson

0 km 2

Badger Pass

Johnston Creek

The Bonnet Icefield

to Johnson Canyon

SOME JASPER CLASSICS

The Jasper area has long been a ski centre and has its own history, heroes and classic tours. In the 1930's Joe Weiss, Rex Gibson, Ron Burstrom, Pete Withers and the Jeffreys Brothers were pioneering ski trails, building cabins and promoting the sport. Jasper has never quite caught on the way that the Banff/Lake Louise area has, but it still offers some fine ski touring. Here are four classic ski tours that you will enjoy.

The Six Pass Route

Distance 50 km
Elevation gain 2170 m
Max elevation 2475 m
Maps 83 C/12 Athabasca Falls
83 C/11 Southesk Lake
83 C/6 Sunwapta Peak

The once named Eight Pass Route has become a classic ski traverse in the Jasper region. At one time the tour began up Hardisty Creek, crossed a pass into the Evelyn Creek drainage, then continued over seven more passes to finish at Poboktan Creek, hence the name. Now, however, the trip starts from Maligne Lake, ascends to Bald Hills Lookout, then continues south, just brushing by a pass and then crossing another six passes. Consequently this trip is now often referred to as The Six Pass Route. No matter what you want to call it, the traverse it is well worth doing.

The route is made up of a number of short climbs up the north slopes, ascending generally moderate terrain, followed by enjoyable ski descents down the southern exposures into new valleys. The tour takes three or four days.

The climbs are respectively:
- to Bald Hills summit 700 m
- to first pass 360 m
- to second pass 150 m
- to third pass 360 m
- to fourth pass 150 m
- to fifth pass ('Elusive') 450 m
- to sixth pass ('Maligne') 0 m

Before embarking on the route it is necessary to leave a car at the parking lot, just across Poboktan Creek from the Sunwapta Warden Station, for the completion of the tour. Be sure to let the wardens know that you have left this vehicle as they will begin to worry when it sits there for several days. It is a good idea to register out either at the Sunwapta Warden Station or in Jasper at the Information Building.

To begin the tour drive from Jasper up the Maligne Lake Road and park in the plowed parking lot at the start of the lake, just across the bridge. This is a long drive (44 km) so make certain that you have sufficient gas in your car for the return trip. As well, the road is not plowed as often as it might be so it is imperative that you have good snow tires on your car.

Begin by ascending the fire road to the Bald Hills Lookout. This fire road starts immediately across the road from the south end of the parking lot. A climb of about 5 km and 480 vertical metres takes you to the 'Lookout' at the edge of treeline. From here you strike out across open meadows in a southerly direction, aiming for a small peak in the distance. It is best to ski to the summit of this peak (GR 539384) and scramble directly over the summit rather than to

Ascending to a pass. This photo is typical of the terrain on the Six Pass Route.
Photo Alf Skrastins

try to cut around the peak along the east flank. Descend easily down the south side of this peak to the flats below.

Put your skis back on and ascend a short distance to a broad rounded bump (GR 539377). Cross the bump and descend the far side in a southerly direction, passing very near a broad pass (GR 541370). Continue descending in a southerly direction to the edge of treeline in a small valley (GR 541356).

From here, descend the drainage a short distance, then cut right around the corner just at the edge of the thick trees (GR 547356). To try to cut around the corner any earlier than this would expose you to avalanche risk and offers no saving in time or distance. Once around the corner descend gradually, angling down through thick bush to the valley bottom. This section of the tour is a bit of a thrash for about 1.5 km.

Once in the valley bottom follow the creek in a southwest direction for about 2 km. As you approach the steep mountain wall ahead turn up to the left and climb over open windswept slopes for another 2 km to the first of the passes (GR 555307). From the summit of this pass it is best to descend in a southeast direction into the next valley, enjoying the skiing, rather than trying to contour and maintain your elevation.

Another gentle climb will take you to the second pass (GR 566294). From this pass another descent can offer good skiing. Stay to the right on open slopes rather than follow the drainage. Lower down on the right you can find glades through the trees.

From this valley climb straight up the other side, staying in a wedge of trees to avoid steep slopes on either side. The wedge of trees leads right up to a bench from which a gentle slope continues to the third pass (GR 592263). To get the best ski descent, climb a short distance south up the ridge above the pass then descend south-southeast down an open shoulder into the valley below.

Climb open slopes in a southeasterly direction to the fourth pass (GR 613238). The descent down the southeast slopes on the far side, following the fall line into the valley, can offer some excellent skiing.

Continue travelling southeast, ascending gradually for about 7 km, up to the fifth pass which is known as 'Elusive' Pass (GR 672186). This climb once again is very straight forward. However, the southeast side of the pass is usually overhung by a large cornice and a direct descent is not possible. To solve this problem scramble up the ridge crest on the northeast side of the pass, gaining

about 75 vertical metres. This takes you to the crest of a small shoulder from where you descend a few feet, then traverse out right onto windblown shale slopes which can be descended to easier-angled snow slopes below.

The route continues southeast out into Maligne Pass which is a broad and gentle pass. The descent down Poligne Creek to Poboktan Creek is tricky and requires a fine touch at route finding (note that the trail is incorrectly positioned on the map). To begin with the descent is gradual and follows generally open terrain for about 4 km. At this point the route reaches a giant avalanche path which descends from the west flank of the valley. It is necessary to cross this avalanche path, descend the creek bed for a short distance until it becomes very narrow then climb up and along the right flank of the creek for a short distance. Drop down to the creek again and cross it to the east bank.

N

FIRE ROAD

P

Bald
Hills

Evelyne Creek

Maligne
Lake

Pass
#1

Pass
#2

Pass
#3

0   km   2

*Opposite: The long ascent to the fifth pass
known as Elusive Pass. Photo Alf Skrastins*

The Six Pass Route 1

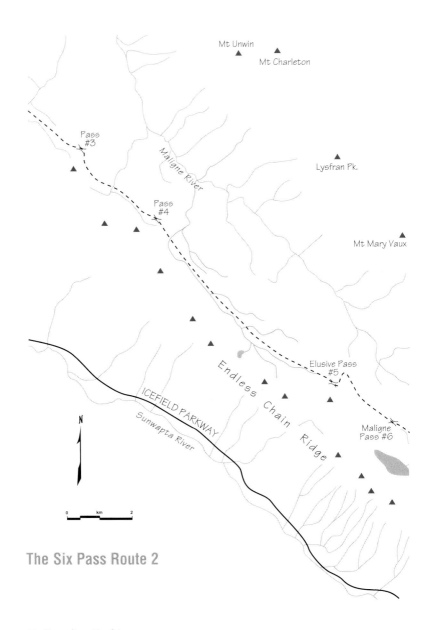

Mt Unwin

Mt Charleton

Pass #3

Maligne River

Lysfran Pk.

Pass #4

Mt Mary Vaux

Elusive Pass #5

Endless Chain Ridge

ICEFIELD PARKWAY

Sunwapta River

N

Maligne Pass #6

0   km   2

The Six Pass Route 2

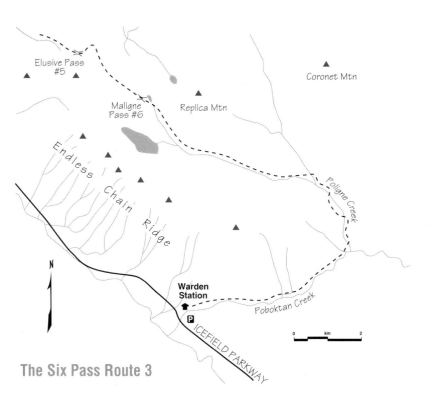

Coronet Mtn

Maligne
Pass #6

Replica Mtn

Endless

Chain

Ridge

Poligne Creek

N

Warden
Station

P

Poboktan Creek

ICEFIELD PARKWAY

0   km   2

The Six Pass Route 3

You are now in the V formed by two creeks. In the open trees there is a trail and you should be able to spot some blazes. Continue skiing through these open trees for about 0.5 km, then cross a shoulder in the trees to the left into another drainage. At this point there is a bridge which crosses this second creek (GR 741149). The trail continues up into the trees. You are now following the east bank of Poligne Creek, gradually descending. After about 1 km the trail reaches the creek again. Cross a bridge to the west side of the creek then traverse through the trees for another kilometre until the trail once again crosses a bridge to the east side of the creek. From here the trail climbs for a short distance to the brow of a hill overlooking Poboktan Creek. Several steep switchbacks take you to the bottom of the hill where a bridge is crossed to the west bank of Poligne Creek. A short gentle descent takes you to the junction with the Poboktan Creek trail.

Turn right and follow Poboktan Creek trail for about 7 km to the Icefields Parkway and your waiting car. Usually this last part of the trail will be well broken and packed.

Shangri-La

Distance 8 km
Height gain 400 m
Max elevation 2000 m
Maps 83 C/13 Medicine Lake
83 C/12 Athabasca Falls

Shangri-La is a beautiful log cabin located high in the mountains near Jasper in a place very aptly named Snow Bowl. It was built in 1936 by the legendary Curly Phillips and has the aura of history from a bygone day.

The bowl above the hut offers excellent skiing of both the Nordic touring and the powder skiing varieties. Snow Bowl is an alpine basin about 7 km across rimmed by many small peaks. Days can be filled touring the meadows, admiring the scenery, carving turns on the many delightful slopes, or scrambling to the summits. The descents are not long, generally 2-300 vertical metres but are more than adequate for a good day of skiing.

From Jasper drive east of town along Highway #16 for about 3 km to the Maligne Lake turn-off. Drive up this road towards Maligne Lake for almost 40 km. There are two ways to begin the tour:

1. If the river is completely frozen you can cross it at Rosemary's Rocks and ascend directly towards the valley of Jeffery's Creek. Park your car on the right at the point where the road leaves the Maligne River (GR 534477) and cuts inland (the large rocks are obvious in the river). Cross the river (Caution!), ascend the far bank and head off northwest through the trees following a trail with many blazes. The route seems to be going in the wrong direction but after several kilometres turns west and heads up the hillside, climbing steadily.

2. If the river is open, drive another 1 km along the road and park on the left just before the bridge. Cross the bridge then ski along the left bank of the river. Soon the trail begins to climb and work its way up the hillside (many blazes on the trees).

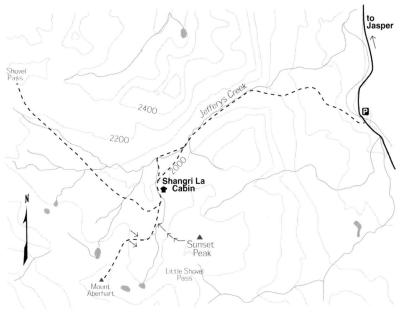

Shangri-La Cabin

Maps 83 C/13 Medicine Lake,
Location Near head of Jefferys Creek (GR 479448) just below treeline at an elevation of 2000 m
Reservations The cabin belongs to the Maligne Lake Ski Club and can be rented for $150 per night. To rent the cabin phone Bette Weir in Jasper at (780) 852-3665.
Capacity 6
Facilities Bunks and blankets. As well there is propane heating, a propane cooking stove, and all the pots, pans and utensils required.
Water The stream in the valley down the hill in front of the cabin

Opposite: Shangri-La. Photo Chic Scott

Eventually the two approaches join, ascend steeply then cross a wooded shoulder then descend to Jeffery's Creek (GR 509476).

Follow the creek bed for about 2 km until it opens up into a large meadow. Keep following the creek for several more kilometres. Then turn left up a subsidiary stream which enters from the left (GR 478457) and follow it for 1 km to the cabin. The cabin itself is tucked away above the left bank of the stream and would be easy to miss. Usually you spot the water hole dug in the stream and the steep footsteps leading up the bank. Many people take a short cut for the last kilometre to reach the cabin. Rather than following the small stream up to the cabin they turn up to the left (at about GR 483459) and ascend directly over a wooded shoulder.

Skiing across Snow Bowl towards Shovel Pass which is crossed by the Skyline Trail.
Photo Tony Daffern

Tours

There is a variety of tours that can be done in Snow Bowl above Shangri-La Cabin. All of them begin by skiing up the draw to the southwest which you see looking out the front door of the cabin. Very quickly this draw breaks out of the trees into the open meadow. Do not attempt to follow the stream bed itself which continues past the cabin in a southerly direction. The walls of this stream bed are very steep and narrow and pose a real avalanche threat.

Once out in the meadow you can tour for hours and find many excellent Telemarking slopes.

Here are some other suggestions:

• There is an excellent hill for making turns on the east flank of what is called Aberhart's Nose. This is the hill directly in front of you as you enter the meadow beyond the draw. Good ski descents can be had from this ridge (GR 470437).

• If you feel adventurous, ski and scramble along the ridge above Aberhart's Nose to reach the summit of Mount Aberhart (GR 464427) which gives a panoramic view of the area .

• If you want a pleasant Nordic tour you can ski in a northwest direction to Shovel Pass (GR 440478).

• At the end of the day, pleasant skiing can be had in the last rays of the sun on the west slopes of Sunset Peak (GR 485435).

The Skyline Trail

Distance 40 km
Height Gain 1500 m
Max Elevation 2450 m
Maps 83 D/16 Jasper
83 C/12 Athabasca Falls
83 C/13 Medicine Lake

This tour is not often done but could become a true classic. It is perhaps more serious than the Six Pass Route. Because it is above treeline for most of the way, routefinding would be very difficult in poor visibility. Leave a car at the parking lot at Maligne Lake if you plan to end your trip there. If you plan to carry on over the Six Pass Route, leave a car at the Poboktan Creek parking lot. Allow 3 days.

The Skyline Trail begins by climbing the Signal Mountain fire road not far from Jasper. A small parking lot is located at the trailhead about 5 km along the Maligne Lake Road from its junction with Highway #16. The climb is a steady uphill grind for 880 vertical metres.

Just short of timberline, head off left along a trail through the trees (GR 342584). The trail climbs up and to the left and works its way out into the open.

Contour across open slopes, maintaining the same elevation and crossing a small drainage, then follow the line of

Approaching Shovel Pass which is out of the picture to the right. Most parties traverse below the ridge to the right and so miss this view.
Photo Don Gardner

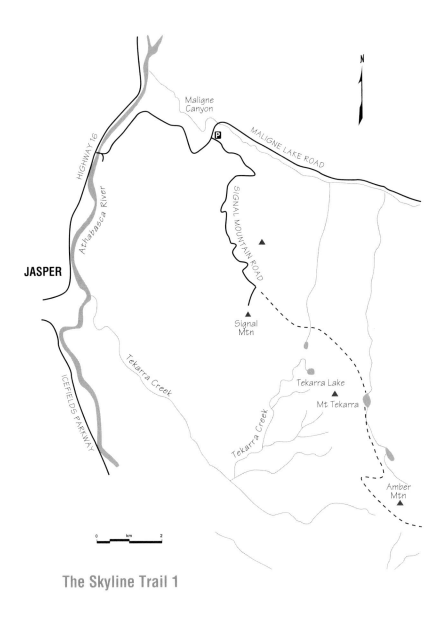

The Skyline Trail 1

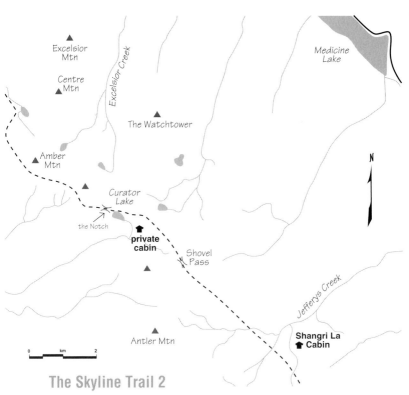

The Skyline Trail 2

the summer trail marked on the map around the corner and into a valley. Continue contouring at treeline over to an unnamed lake (GR 368547). Carry on up the valley to the south along the left flank of the creek to another small lake (GR 386529) from where it's an easy climb up the hillside to the southwest to reach the ridge (GR 380525). Continue southeast along the ridge over Amber Mountain, then cross southwest facing slopes beneath twin summits to reach the crux—the notch (GR 408499).

From the notch the route drops steeply to Curator Lake (GR 418494). It is easiest to descend at the left hand edge of the notch where the cornice is smallest. You may have to descend the initial slope on foot. At the bottom, cross the lake, ascend slightly, then contour across to the southeast to Shovel Pass (GR 440479). The cabin marked on the map just south of Curator Lake is not open in the winter.

From Shovel Pass descend to the southeast across broad open meadows. If you have made prior arrangements you might spend the night at the Shangri-La Cabin at the head of Jefferys Creek (GR 479447).

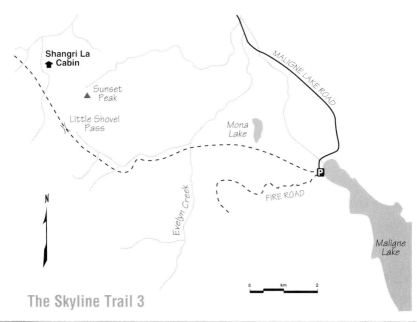

The Skyline Trail 3

From upper Jefferys Creek there are two ways to continue:

The usual route crosses Snow Bowl meadows at the head of Jefferys Creek, rounds the northeast ridge of Mount Aberhart (GR 475446), then climbs to Little Shovel Pass (GR 485430). Descend the drainage southeast from the pass into Evelyn Creek, travelling downstream to rejoin the trail at GR 527430. Cross the creek. On the east bank the trail becomes a well-used Nordic ski trail which is likely well-packed and fast. It descends through forest to the parking area on the shores of Maligne Lake.

Bottom: Panorama from Mount Aberhart north across Snow Bowl to Shovel Pass. Shangri-La Cabin is out of the photo to the right.
Photo Colin Jones

Combining the Skyline and Six Pass Routes
If you are really adventurous you can continue along the Six Pass Route. From Shovel Pass cross the Snow Bowl meadows, round the northeast ridge of Mount Aberhart (GR 475446), then head south up into an open valley. Climb steeply to the lefthand pass at the head of the valley (GR 471420). Extreme caution is advised here as the climb to the pass is very steep and subject to avalanches. Descend the wind-swept southwest side of the pass on foot for a short distance, then ski easily down and across to the southeast to Hardisty Pass (GR 490390). Descend into the valley to the southeast (Evelyn Creek) then ascend to the end of the valley (GR 511355). From here an easy climb takes you to another pass (GR 529347). Descend to the south, passing by several lakes to join the Six Pass Route (GR 538322). (See page 84).

Curator Mtn   Shovel Pass

Snow Bowl

Mount Resplendent

Distance 29 km one way
Height gain 2560 m
Max elevation 3410 m
Map 83 E/3 Mount Robson

This is an often overlooked classic ski ascent in the Rockies. Although it is rarely done due to its long and committing character, it was in fact on this mountain that ski mountaineering got its start back in 1930. On February 28 of that year a young adventurer by the name of P. L. Parsons made a solo ski ascent of the mountain. Two years later when Joe Weiss and Rex Gibson arrived to make another ski ascent of Mount Resplendent they found a note of this achievement carved on the wall of the cabin at Berg Lake.

Drive west of Jasper along Highway #16 for 88 km to Mount Robson and follow the short access road to the trailhead.

The trail to Berg Lake (17 km) is initially wide and easy, following alongside the Robson River and gaining elevation gradually. Just before Kinney Lake cross to the east shore. Continue across the lake (make sure it is well frozen) or follow the trail along the right shore (camp shelter), then head easily across the gravel flats at the end of the lake.

The valley narrows and you must climb the left flank to gain the higher Valley of a Thousand Falls. Routefinding can be a tricky. After the trail levels off, cross the Robson River to the east bank (suspension bridge). Near here you will see the Whitehorn Shelter.

Carry on up the east bank of the river for a little more than a kilometre then cross to the northwest side of the river (suspension bridge). The trail then climbs steeply, switchbacking up the hillside. Caution is advised.

Beyond Emperor Falls the angle lays back and the skiing becomes more reasonable. Follow the trail until it breaks out onto open gravel flats and ski across to the lake. Either ski down the lake or along the north shore almost to the other end where you will find the Berg Lake Shelter.

From the Berg Lake Shelter ski northeast across the lake and cross the gravel flats at the end. After about 1.5 km turn right and ski up to the toe of the Robson Glacier which is followed for several kilometres. Near Extinguisher Tower the angle steepens and it is necessary to move to the left flank to find a way into a higher basin. Ski south up the basin heading for the col (GR 582846) between the southeast ridge of Mount Robson and Mount Resplendent. Around here there are some very big crevasses—use caution. Turn left before the col and ascend the shoulder of Mount Resplendent. You can ski almost to the top. The last part of the ascent near the summit usually requires that skis be left behind and that you climb on foot. Be wary of cornices on your left and be very careful of the steep drop that rolls over the south face on your right. It is advisable to wear the rope.

Berg Lake Shelter

Map 83 E/3 Mount Robson
Location Along the northwest shore of Berg Lake not far from the northeast end of the lake
Reservations not necessary
Facilities Heating stove. No bunks, mattresses, pots or pans. Wood pile nearby. For more information contact the Mount Robson Provincial Park rangers at (250) 566-4325
Fee No charge

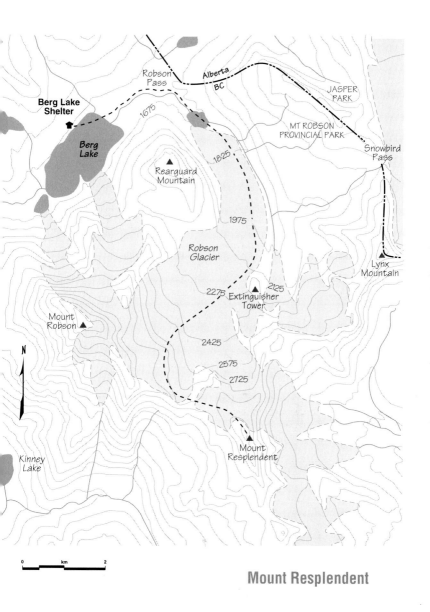

Robson Pass

Alberta

BC

JASPER PARK

Berg Lake Shelter

MT ROBSON PROVINCIAL PARK

1675

Berg Lake

1825

Snowbird Pass

Rearguard Mountain

1975

Robson Glacier

Lynx Mountain

2275

2125

Extinguisher Tower

Mount Robson

2425

2575

N

2725

Kinney Lake

Mount Resplendent

0   km   2

Mount Resplendent

SKI ASCENTS IN THE BANFF AREA

There are many excellent ski ascents in the vicinity of Banff and Lake Louise. Some of the more popular tours are included here. Tours like Mount Hector are great classics and have been done regularly for many years. Others like Cirrus Mountain and Mount Wilson are not often done, but are destined to become classics.

Many of these tours are best done later in the season when there is a deeper snowpack. So wait until March when the underbrush is well covered and the days are becoming longer.

Opposite: Ascending from the valley to the upper slopes of Storm Mountain.
Photo Doug McConnery

Storm Mountain

Storm Mountain

Distance 10 km return
Height gain 1500 m
Max elevation 3161 m
Map 82 N/1 Mount Goodsir

The ascent of Storm Mountain is a good day tour through a scenic upper valley with many hanging waterfalls. This tour is not recommended until late in the season when the deadfall is well covered with snow. Early in the season it is advised you ski or walk about 1.5 km west down the highway to a point directly below the hanging valley on the west side of Storm Mountain.

From the Divide parking lot at Vermilion Pass on Highway # 93, climb diagonally up the hill through burnt forest, and enter the narrow valley at GR 662731. It is necessary to do some bushwhacking for about 2 km until you break out of the trees into an open valley above timberline. Follow the valley to the cirque at the end then ascend to the left, around the east end of a cliff band. Continue to the summit over windblown scree slopes. There is some avalanche risk at the head of the valley and caution is advised.

On the way back, descend directly down the drainage to the highway. The slope through the burned forest is open and offers good skiing.

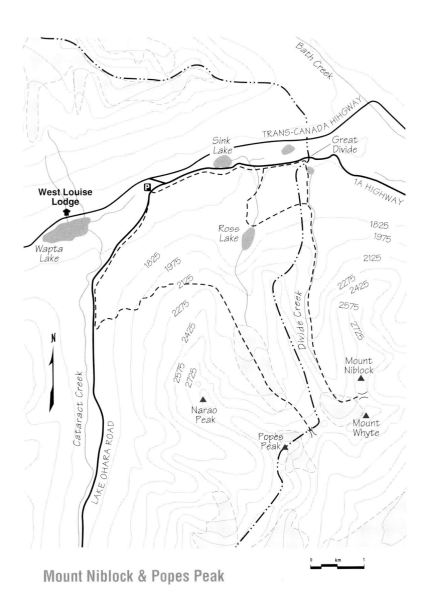

Mount Niblock & Popes Peak

Mount Niblock

Distance 14 km return
Height gain 1200 m
Max elevation 2800 m
Map 82 N/8 Lake Louise

This is an excellent tour for late in the year when the creek is well covered with snow. You can get a good ski descent from the col and the views are excellent. The more adventurous can scramble to the summit of Mount Niblock; the less experienced members of the party will appreciate the comfort of a rope. If you just want to ski you can simply yo-yo up and down in the upper bowl.

The tour skirts the edge of a glacier and it is suggested that you carry a rope.

The tour begins at the Lake O'Hara parking lot just south of the Trans-Canada Highway at Kicking Horse Pass. From here, there are two ways to start:

You may ski east along the snow covered 1A Highway for about 2 km. Turn right (signs) and follow the trail to Ross Lake. Just as you arrive at the lake a trail heads east on its way to Lake Louise. Follow this trail for about 1 km until it drops into the well defined drainage of Divide Creek. Climb steeply up the drainage.

The same point can be reached by skiing along the 1A Highway for about 3 km to 'The Great Divide'. Right beside the large monument which spans the road you turn right up the drainage of Divide Creek. The drainage is well defined to begin with, but after several hundred metres it fades. For the next 0.5 km you need a good eye to follow the creek bed. Eventually the drainage becomes better defined and you can follow it to join the route described above.

The creek bed now becomes a little steeper but is always reasonable to follow. About 2 km above 1A Highway the angle lays back and the creek meanders through the forest.

After another 0.5 km the terrain steepens again and you climb short, wooded hills. High above you on both sides are steep and impressive mountain walls.

When the trail breaks out of the forest, steep snow covered moraines block the way. They can be ascended on both the left and the right but the left flank offers a more moderate angle. Above these moraines the angle eases off and eventually a flat section leads towards the final climb.

The cliff band is negotiated on the left and brings you to large open slopes of a moderate angle. Traverse back and forth, gaining elevation until you are high enough to work your way out left towards the Mount Niblock/Mount Whyte Col. The last 100 m of elevation to the col is often quite windblown.

Most people make the col their destination but if you are adventurous you can carry on and scramble up Mount Niblock.

Popes Peak

Distance 18 km return
Height gain 1200 m
Max elevation 2780 m
Map 82 N/8 Lake Louise

This tour is popular with local ski tourers and offers some very good skiing. The trip gets you up high and offers good views.

Park your car at the Lake O'Hara parking lot, just south of the Trans-Canada Highway at Kicking Horse Pass.

Begin by skiing along the Lake O'Hara road. After about 2.5 km along the road, start climbing up to the left through the trees. The trees are open and the route finding is reasonable. After about 2-300 vertical metres elevation gain, work your way over to the left (northeast) to reach the crest of the shoulder of Narao Peak. Cross the shoulder along a bench, just above timberline.

Descend a short distance on the other side of the shoulder to reach the hanging valley below the north face of Mount Narao and Popes Peak. Ascend this valley for about 2.5 km, gradually curving to the left away from the north face of Popes Peak. Climb up and left, negotiate a small easy rock cliff, then reach the slopes above which descend from the east shoulder of Popes Peak. Ascend these slopes, which are steep, to reach a col between Popes Peak and a minor unnamed summit. From this col is a spectacular view down the other side to the Plain of Six Glaciers.

The ski run back down is rewarding but is marred by having to climb back up to the shoulder of Narao Peak.

Mount Field

Distance 8 km one way
Height gain 1300 m
Max elevation 2635 m
Map 82 N/8 Lake Louise

The ski ascent of Mount Field is becoming one of the classics in the Rockies. However, because the tour takes you onto huge slopes you should only undertake this ascent when the avalanche hazard is very low. If conditions are safe you can ski right to the summit. The run back down can be excellent.

There is a large parking area at the trailhead, which is reached by taking the turn-off for Yoho Valley, 4 km east of Field on the Trans-Canada Highway. If you are coming from Lake Louise, the turn is on your right, just after you descend the big hill from Kicking Horse Pass, and after crossing the bridge over the Kicking Horse River.

From the parking lot, ski across the bridge, past the campground entrance and head up the road towards Takakkaw Falls. Follow the road for about 4.5 km to the switchbacks where the road climbs steeply. Several hundred metres beyond the top of the switchbacks you come upon a giant slide path to the left. This is where you leave the road (GR 387003). Begin the ascent, following along the left edge of the slide path. It feels intimidating to climb up the centre of the path, so you will feel better staying along the edge of the trees. As the slope steepens you may feel more secure ascending in the forest along the edge of the avalanche swath. Keep climbing for about 600 vertical metres until you reach the uppermost tip of the trees (GR 383984).

From here the route angles out right along a bench for about 1 km into the huge bowl. The terrain is generally not too steep but this position is very exposed and intimidating. When you are well out in the bowl you turn back left and begin ascending towards Mount Field. Continue climbing for about 300 vertical metres. The route ascends below some rock cliffs just beneath the summit and gains the summit ridge at GR 376977. This final climb is very steep and you must be absolutely certain of snow stability before ascending this slope. It is possible to ski the last 50 vertical metres up the easy ridge to the actual top.

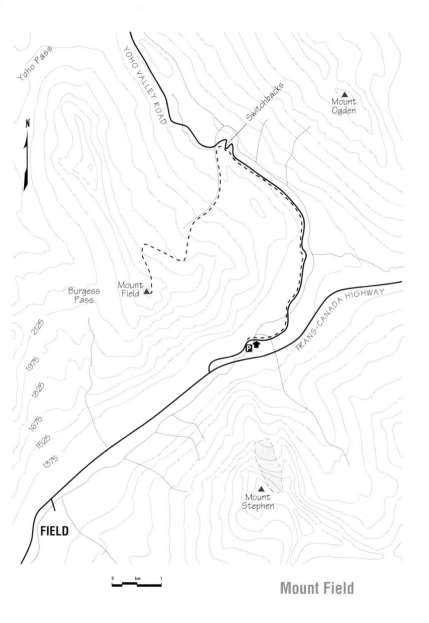

Mount Field

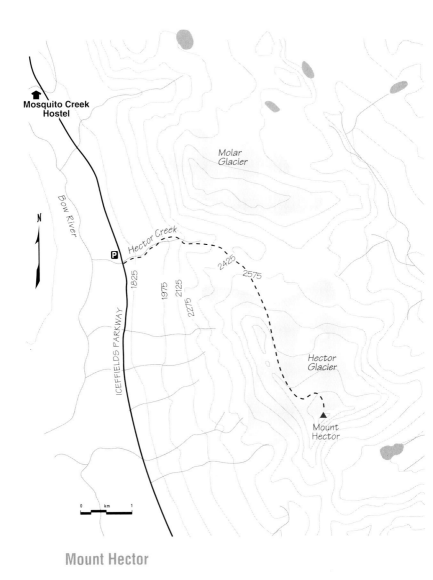

Mosquito Creek Hostel

Bow River

N

Hector Creek

P

Molar Glacier

1825

1975

2125

2275

2425

2575

ICEFIELDS PARKWAY

Hector Glacier

Mount Hector

0   km   1

Mount Hector

Mount Hector from the Hector Glacier.
Photo Andy Riggs

Mount Hector

Distance 5.5 km one way
Height gain 1600 m
Max elevation 3394 m
Map 82 N/9 Hector Lake

Mount Hector is one of the great ski tours in the Rockies. You get up high, enjoy a wonderful view over all the surrounding peaks, and then have a fabulous descent. This ascent should be saved for a sunny spring day when the snow conditions are good and the avalanche hazard is low. This is a long and serious climb and you should leave early and give yourself plenty of time. Take along a rope, crampons, ice axe and crevasses rescue equipment.

The tour to Mount Hector begins at Hector Creek, 19 km north on the Icefields Parkway (Highway #93) from the junction with the Trans-Canada Highway. There is a plowed parking area on the west side of the highway just across the creek.

Most people ski up the creek bed or just along the right flank through open trees. After about 0.5 km the forest ends and you emerge into an open area below a large slope. The route ascends this slope to the left of a band of cliffs. The slope is big (about 100 vertical metres) and is dangerous. The safe negotiation of this hillside is perhaps the crux of the tour. Do not continue if you are unsure of stability. This area is also threatened by large snowfields on the mountain high above. There are some trees on the left side of the slope which may give some extra security but, unfortunately, this ascent route is unavoidable.

From the top of the slope traverse right, at the base of some rock cliffs, above a lower cliff band, to reach a gully. The route then ascends this gully for about 50 vertical metres. In places it is steep and you must take off your skis and kick steps. There often is a small waterfall that must be circumvented.

Above the gully the angle lays back and you can continue easily up into the basin. Ascend gradually into a draw, keeping right of a black crest of rock. (The obvious route up the drainage to the left of the crest of rock is not as straightforward because it is blocked twice by cliffbands). Continue climbing into the draw for about 0.5 km, being cautious of the large snow slopes on the right, then angle up left onto the crest. Turn right and ascend more steeply up the windblown crest. After about 100 vertical metres the angle lays back again and the route continues southeast over windswept terrain for another 0.5 km to the edge of the Hector Glacier.

Ascend the glacier staying generally to the right, then as you approach the peak, swing to the left below the summit tower. Often the area just beneath the summit can be wind packed and may even be blown bare with ice showing. Crampons may be needed. The final scramble to the summit is about 50 vertical metres. Crampons may be needed if it is icy, and some folks will appreciate the protection of the rope.

Cirque Peak

Distance 6 km one way
Height gain 1100 m
Max elevation 2993 m
Map 82 N/9 Hector Lake

This peak has long been a favourite tour with local skiers. Save it for a sunny spring day and enjoy the view.

Park your car at the Helen Creek trailhead just north of Helen Creek bridge, 29 km north of the junction with the Trans-Canada Highway on the Icefields Parkway.

Initially, the trail climbs steeply for about 100 vertical metres until it reaches the crest of a ridge. It may be a bit difficult to locate the trail at first as it appears to have been abandoned by the park authorities. Look for it above and slightly left of the parking lot. Once on the ridge the angle eases and the trail continues northwest along the crest for a short distance. It then descends to the right to the creek bed. Cross the creek and continue along the opposite bank where the trail crosses large avalanche paths and cuts through the forest in between. After about 1.5 km the trail begins to climb, then crosses the creek again and works its way steeply up through the trees until they begin to thin out near timberline (GR 415253). Here the trail traverses left across lower angled slopes into a draw. Ascend this draw, continue through a gap, cross open meadows and ski through another gap. Below you on the left you will see Helen Lake. From here there are two choices. If you want to bag the summit of Cirque Peak follow route 1. If you want to have the best ski descent follow route 2.

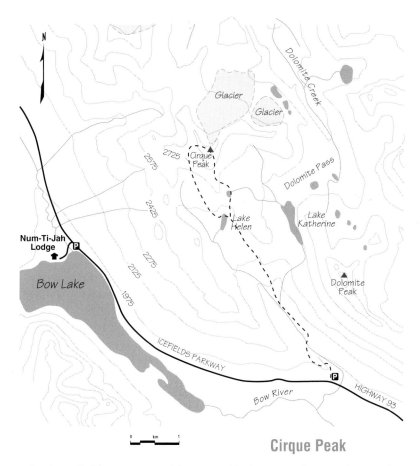

Cirque Peak

1. Continue climbing up to your right to reach the pass (GR 408266) immediately south of Cirque Peak. Stay to the left as you ascend and be careful near the top as the slopes are steep. From the pass work your way around onto the east flank of the south ridge of Cirque Peak. Ascend these east-facing slopes onto the ridge. There may be a cornice to negotiate just below the crest of the ridge. Scramble

and kick steps up the scree slope on the windblown crest. The slope is steep and should be treated cautiously. The last 25 vertical metres offers some rock scrambling to reach the summit.

2. Descend to Helen Lake, cross the lake, then climb up over a small shoulder to the west to reach wide open rolling terrain. Continue north, gradually ascending under the west flank of

Cirque Peak. Towards the end of the valley the slope steepens considerably and avalanche hazard is a real concern. However, if it is springtime and the slopes above you are frozen and stable you can climb to the col above (GR 398277) on the west ridge of Cirque Peak. At this point you can leave your skis and scramble through the rocks above to a summit. Although it is not the highest summit of Cirque Peak it is a wonderful viewpoint. To reach the highest point you must climb and scramble along the narrow summit ridge for several hundred metres to the east. It is tricky in the winter time and you will probably want a rope if you choose this option.

Note It appears as though there is another viable route to Cirque Peak from the Icefields Parkway. It follows a valley which curves south and reaches the col described in route 2 (GR 398277) from the north. Although this appears to offer a good ski descent, the author has not personally checked this route.

Descent On your way back down it is possible to descend the valley directly below Helen Lake, but you must be very careful not to become trapped in a very narrow canyon. At the point where Helen Creek drops over a steep headwall just at timberline (GR 409251) do not attempt to follow the creek itself. Stay up on the right along a bench and traverse south until it is possible to descend glades in the trees down to the creek bed again. About 0.5 km further down Helen Creek (GR 416245) there are very steep slopes along the west flank of the creek which offer real serious avalanche potential. Use caution.

Mount Jimmy Simpson

Distance 14 km return
Height gain 1000 m
Max elevation 2940 m

This is a ski tour which is rapidly becoming very popular. Because there are some steep slopes on this tour it should be done on a spring day when snow stability is very good. Get an early start so you can ski the south-facing slopes before the sun has been on them very long. In the right conditions this tour can offer an excellent ski descent.

Park at the large plowed parking lot at the turn-off to Num-Ti-Jah Lodge, on the west side of the Icefields Parkway (Highway #93), about 35 km north of the intersection with the Trans-Canada Highway).

Ski down a gentle hill to Bow Lake then head out across the lake (be sure it is well frozen). Cross to the far side of the lake, and continue southwest across the gravel flats. Continue up the stream for about 0.5 km until you can see that the direct route ahead is blocked by a narrow canyon. From here you have two choices.

The most direct route is to climb steeply through the trees on the hillside several hundred metres to the right of the canyon (GR 354234). The way is steep and the forest is thick but the climb is only about 75 vertical metres. When you reach the top of the hill continue southwest for a short distance until you break out of the trees into a huge amphitheatre with the frozen waterfall (Bow Falls) at the back.

Another alternative is to follow the traditional approach to Bow hut for a short distance to reach the large amphitheatre. To do this angle left and cross the

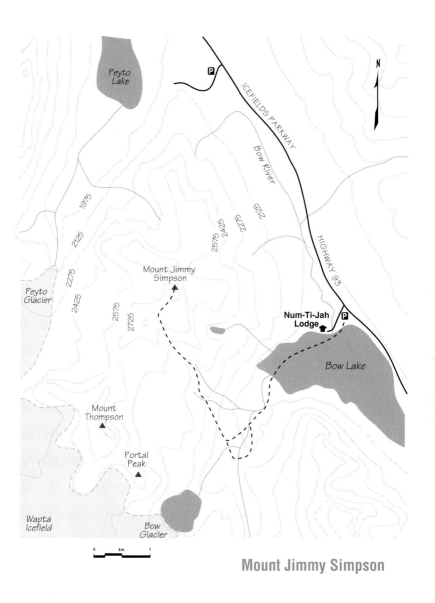

Mount Jimmy Simpson

creek as you approach the canyon. Ascend through the trees following a trail up a minor drainage until you bump up against a steep mountainside complete with avalanche paths. Climb a short hill up to the right, traverse around the corner (west), then descend into the main drainage again. You have now circumvented the canyon. Ski out to the right across the open gravel flats of the amphitheatre below the falls where the two routes join.

From here the climb begins in earnest. The route works its way up a ramp beginning at GR 352233, and reaches a col at GR 338254. This ramp is steep in places, and in the lower part there are large cliffs on your right over which you could be carried if you were to trigger an avalanche. So if you de-

Top: the final slope to the pass.
Photo Denis Roy

cide to continue up the ramp you must be certain that it is safe to do so.

To begin the ascent up the ramp, ascend through open trees, gaining perhaps 100 vertical metres. Soon, the trees thin out and the slope steepens. This is really the crux of the tour. For the next 150 vertical metres the route ascends the ramp in a very exposed position on steep slopes above cliffs. As you climb up and left into a draw the angle eases and the risk decreases. It is best to climb up into the first obvious draw rather than traverse across into the main drainage. Climb this draw until it crosses a minor crest and drops down into the main drainage.

From here the route ascends the drainage to the pass. To begin it climbs a steep slope (use caution), then continues up a bowl to the final slope before the pass (see top photo opposite). This slope is steep indeed and you need very stable conditions to climb it. It is perhaps up to 35 degrees and 150 vertical metres high so use caution.

From the col it is a straightforward scree walk up the windswept shoulder to your right to the summit. Usually skis are left at the col.

If you have doubts about descending the way you just came, it is possible to descend to the west then curve around to the southwest to reach the Peyto Glacier. This is an option that should be considered if you are late in the day and the south-facing slopes have become dangerous. Although this route will take you back to the highway via Peyto Lake and you will end up a few kilometres from your vehicle, it is far better than getting swept away by an avalanche.

Opposite bottom: Looking back towards Crowfoot Mountain (left) from Mount Jimmy Simpson. Photo Denis Roy

Crowfoot Mountain

Distance 14 km return
Height gain 870 m to summit of small peak, 1100 m to summit of Crowfoot Mountain
Max elevation 2800 m at summit of small peak, 3030 m at summit of Crowfoot Mountain
Map 82 N/9 Hector Lake

This is a moderate day trip that gets you up high, offers great views and the opportunity for some good turns. There is a glacier on this tour so carry a rope.

Leave your car at the parking area at the turn off for Num-Ti-Jah Lodge, located on the west side of the Icefields Parkway at the north end of Bow Lake, about 6 km south of Bow Pass.

Following the route to Bow Hut, ski from the parking lot down to Bow Lake, then cross the lake in a southwest direction. Cross gravel flats at the end of the lake, and continue up the drainage for about 0.5 km until a canyon completely bars the way. Ski up to the left through the trees (there is a trail) until the hill steepens and an avalanche path looms above. Climb up and right and over a shoulder, then drop down into the drainage on the other side. You have now bypassed the first canyon.

Ahead of you is the second canyon. Ski up the canyon for 1 km then climb up onto the left (east) flank when the canyon pinches off. Ski through the trees above the canyon until the route breaks out of the trees and a large alpine bowl is seen ahead.

Just before you reach a creek drainage, turn up to the left. The route line drawn on Murray Toft's map is perhaps

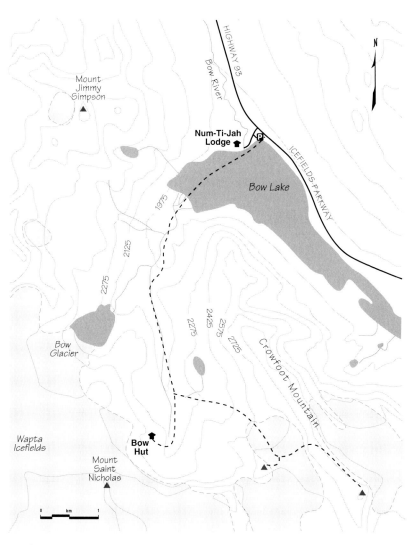

Crowfoot Mountain

Opposite: Crowfoot Mountain. Excellent skiing below the col. Photo Colin Jones

the best path to follow. Climb steeply above, staying in the trees on the left side of the small drainage. Do not attempt to ascend the creek bed itself as it narrows and is impassable. Gain about 100 vertical metres climbing through the trees until the terrain flattens out and you ski out into a broad open area. From this point the route to the pass generally follows the shallow drainage or just along its flanks.

Another route often followed to the pass is to ski across the small drainage just as you come out of the trees, then climb the wooded hillside on the right flank of the creek bed. The angle soon lays back and the route works its way up and over many small moraines and hills until it reaches the pass.

The pass itself is filled with a small glacier and precautions should be taken. Crevasses could be in the area and your group should be prepared.

Once you reach the pass a nice conclusion to the trip is to climb to the small unnamed summit just to the west, above the pass (GR 375197). The view from the top is excellent, with much of the Wapta Icefield spread out in front of you. On a nice spring day this is a glorious spot to sit and enjoy the mountains.

For those with more ambition and energy the summit of Crowfoot Mountain can be reached. Ski up above the pass as high as you can, then scramble up the scree on the southwest flank of the mountain to reach the broad ridge which is followed to the summit (GR 393194).

The descent below the col can offer excellent skiing (the slopes above the col are usually crusted and wind blasted). From the col it is best to follow the shallow drainage or to ski just along the flank. When the drainage narrows at the bottom move up on the right flank and descend about 100 vertical metres through the trees to regain the Bow Hut trail above the canyon.

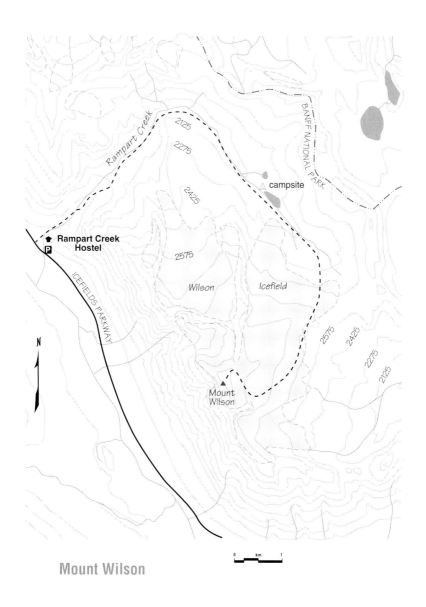

Rampart Creek

2125

2275

2425

Banff National Park

△ campsite

♠ **Rampart Creek**
Hostel
P

2575

Wilson　　*Icefield*

N

ICEFIELDS PARKWAY

2575

2425

2275

2125

▲ Mount
Wilson

0　　km　　1

Mount Wilson

Mount Wilson

Distance 26 km return
Height gain 1800 m
Max elevation 3240 m
Map 82 N/9 Cline River 83 C/2

This is a long tour that is usually done in two days. It gets you high to the summit of a major mountain. The route is protected from the wind and often has good snow conditions.

The tour begins at the Rampart Creek Hostel which is located on the east side of the Icefields Parkway (Highway #93) about 11 km north of the junction with the David Thompson Highway (#11). Direct access to the valley of Rampart Creek is not possible due to a narrow canyon so it is necessary to outflank this obstacle. Walk 300 m north along the highway then ascend tightly wooded slopes between two large cliff bands. After gaining about 100 vertical metres head back into the valley of Rampart Creek. Follow blazes along a rough trail along a bench high above the creek. Soon the bench and the blazes disappear but continue contouring along the hillside. After about 1 km you can descend a very narrow chute to the valley floor or continue another 0.5 km then descend along the flank of a large avalanche path.

Continue up the valley bottom for 1 km to a large cliff which bars the way. Ascend treed slopes on the left, gaining about 150 vertical metres, until it is possible to safely traverse back right above the cliff bands to regain the creek bed.

Follow the valley but do not linger while exposed to the large avalanche slide paths. The valley eventually turns right, opens up and a nice campsite can be found near a small lake.

Approaching the summit via the northeast ridge. Photo Tony Daffern

Above your campsite continue up the valley for several kilometres, then begin to swing around to the right and climb up onto the glacier. Continue up the glacier, heading westwards. Near the top swing right around to the north and climb onto the northeast crest of the mountain which is followed to the summit. Usually the last few metres are windblown and it is best to walk to the summit.

Ascending Cirrus Mountain. Mount Coleman in the distance. Photo Marc Ledwidge

Cirrus Mountain

Distance 14 km return
Height gain 1700 m
Max elevation 3270 m
Map 83 C/2 Cline River

The ski ascent of Cirrus Mountain is a demanding tour best done in the spring when the days are long. You will have to be strong and move fast to do the tour in a single day. If in doubt you can always camp along the way. Good stability is required to do this tour safely. The final climb to the summit may require a rope and a belay.

Park your car along the Icefields Parkway 22 km north of the junction with the David Thompson Highway. The route begins up the first drainage south of the famous frozen waterfall known as Polar Circus (GR 014741). Ski or carry skis depending on snow conditions (these slopes can be dry in the springtime) up the north side of the drainage, then cross the creek near treeline as you approach the large slopes above. Ski up to the lake which drains the glacier of Mount Coleman. Cross the lake, kick steps up a steep short slope, then ski northwest up the drainage to the col (GR 028772). On the north side there is a very steep slope which must be descended before you can continue north to reach the Huntington Glacier. Ascend this glacier (crevasses) to reach the south ridge. (GR 016795). Skis are left at the base of the ridge which is then ascended to the summit. Return via the same route.

Cirrus Mountain

THE LITTLE YOHO VALLEY
GEM OF THE ROCKIES

The Little Yoho Valley in Yoho National Park offers some of the best backcountry skiing in the Canadian Rockies. The terrain is excellent—there are several long and uniform descents, as well as plenty of bad weather glade skiing below timberline. Situated along the Great Divide, the valley gets deep and consistent snowfalls. Finally, the presence of the beautiful Stanley Mitchell Hut (Alpine Club of Canada) makes for a perfect combination.

The one drawback of the region is the long approach—it is 23 km one way. If trail conditions are good and your pack is not too heavy you can make it in one long day. But if the trail breaking is deep or your pack is heavy it can turn into a marathon, ending in a night under the stars. You can always break the trip in two by staying at the camp shelter at the Takakkaw Falls camp ground.

A ski experience in The Little Yoho Valley is quintessential Canadian Rockies skiing and is highly recommended. The hut is rarely crowded and anyone who can make it this far into the backcountry is usually a true mountain lover.

Maps

The Little Yoho Valley is on the edge of four topographical maps—82 N/7 Golden, 82 N/8 Lake Louise, 82 N/9 Hector Lake, 82 N/10 Blaeberry River. It is recommended that you use a composite map prepared by Murray Toft, called 'Touring the Wapta Icefields'. It is printed on waterproof, tearproof and erasable paper and has aerial photographs on the back showing the more popular tours.

History of the valley

The earliest ski trips up the Yoho Valley were undertaken by the Swiss guides to clear the snow off the roof of the Takakkaw Bungalow Camp and also to clear the roof of the Twin Falls Chalet. They would usually make this expedition once or twice each winter.

In March of 1932 A.A. McCoubrey, accompanied by Roger Neave and Major H. Westmorland made the first ski exploration of the valley. They stayed at Twin Falls Chalet and explored as far as the Yoho Glacier on skis. They liked what they saw so much that in May of the same year McCoubrey and Neave returned with Ferris Neave and Campbell Secord. Using Twin Falls Chalet as their base they made explorations into Little Yoho Valley, skied up to President Pass and scrambled up the Vice President. They also inaugurated ski exploration onto the Wapta Icefields, making ascents of Mount Des Poilus, Mount Gordon, Mount Olive and Yoho Peak.

In April of 1934 A.A. McCoubrey returned to Twin Falls Chalet accompanied by his son Alex Jr., Bob Guthrie and the photographer Nicholas Morant. In a long demanding day Guthrie and McCoubrey Jr. skied into Little Yoho Valley, ascended Isolated Peak, carried on over Mount McArthur and bagged Mount Pollinger before making an exhilarating evening descent into the valley and return to the chalet.

In 1939 the Alpine Club of Canada built the Stanley Mitchell Hut in the Little Yoho Valley. Work was supervised by A.A McCoubrey. In March of 1940 the Hut was the site of what was the third

ACC ski camp. The Little Yoho was to become the spiritual home of the club ski camps. In fact, the group was so taken with the area that they used the hut for ski camps for the next seven years in a row! A prominent figure at these camps was Ken Jones who served as guide and cook. Another unique figure was Bruno Engler who had just arrived from Switzerland and was hired as a guide at the 1941 camp. At that camp a guest broke his leg and in a marathon effort Ken and Bruno worked together to pull the injured guest on a sled to civilization at Field—there were no easy helicopter rescues in those days.

"Ken Jones got to work on the toboggan with Bruno and Mac [A.A. McCoubrey], and with a few nails, cord, two stout spruce spars, and parts of the only chair in the place, produced a very fine sledge, strong but flexible, which could be steered from behind and in which the patient could lie in his sleeping bag, well padded and wrapped up, in surprising comfort and security."

"A start was made at two am the following morning, Bruno towing, Ken steering, and three others taking turns in carrying their skis. The patient held an acetylene lamp, which was useful amongst the trees, although there was bright moonlight. Amazing progress was made by the sledging party who refused all offers of help, Bruno expending prodigious efforts on the tow ropes and Ken showing marvellous skill in steering and controlling the sledge in steep and difficult places. It was a weird cavalcade to disturb the silence of moonlight and early dawn on that wild wintery trail." [1]

[1]From 'The 1941 Ski Meet' by Squadron Leader R.S. Peill, CAJ, Vol 27, No. 2, 1940, page 220.

During the 1950's and 1960's Hans Gmoser and Leo Grillmair made extensive use of the Stanley Mitchell Hut in their ski touring program. After pulling their guests by snowmobile to the bottom of the Laughing Falls hill, they would then lead them the rest of the way to the warm and welcoming hut. For several weeks during the winter they would entertain their guests and introduce them to the joys of back country skiing. In return these two contributed a great deal of energy into maintaining the hut. In 1961 Hans and Leo built a new stone foundation for the hut and put on a new metal roof. In 1964 the two of them, assisted by some young climbers from Calgary, carried a new cook stove to the hut on foot. After removing all plates, bolts, doors and other loose objects, the stove was tied onto a frame pack. Taking turns they carried this 70 kg load step by step the 10 km uphill to the cabin!

In 1990 the Stanley Mitchell Hut was once again home to an Alpine Club of Canada Ski Camp and Ken Jones was in attendance at this Fiftieth Anniversary Camp. Although nearly 80 years old, Ken skied the 23 km to the hut carrying a 15 kg pack. At night Ken would sleep on one side of the stove and the author on the other. Every hour or two we would put several more pieces of wood on the fire so that the cabin would be warm in the morning!

The Stanley Mitchell Hut in the Little Yoho Valley has a long and rich history of ski adventure. The log walls of this beautiful cabin have heard laughter, songs and ski tales for over half a century. Today the valley offers a ski adventure little changed from those early pioneer days and a chance to experience the peace and joy of the Rockies in winter.

"The light on the mountains in the early morning, the long runs down pure white snow slopes, the silence and mystery of the great peaks and the comradeship enjoyed around the fireplace at night were the highlights of the camp".[1]

Alex A. McCoubrey

A.A. McCoubrey was a fine mountaineer who explored the Purcells extensively where he has many first ascents to his credit. He was skiing in the Selkirks as early as 1911 and 1914 and at Lake Louise in 1922. In the spring of 1932 he was one of the first to discover the joy of skiing in the Little Yoho Valley and made an ascent of the Vice-President that year. He was to explore the skiing potential of the Little Yoho almost every year until his death.

In 1936 he inaugurated the first ACC ski camp which was held at Lake O'Hara and went on to supervise the organization of the 1940 and 1941 ski camps in Little Yoho. Unfortunately, he died the following year at the age of 56.

McCoubrey was in charge of the construction of the Stanley Mitchell Hut, was editor of the Canadian Alpine Journal for almost ten years and also served as president of the Alpine Club for several years. He was for many years the leading figure with the Winnipeg Section of the ACC.

"The idea of a Club ski camp originated with the late A.A. McCoubrey, and the success of the first camps was due to his own hard work. Mr. McCoubrey was one of the pioneers who realized, many years ago, that skiing was not only a sport in itself but an interesting supplement to mountaineering." [2]

Ken Jones

Ken is the first Canadian-born mountain guide. He earned all the National Park badges—the Pony and Trail badges for outfitters, the Alpine Climbing badge and the Ski Mountaineers badge. Born and raised in Golden, BC, Ken was a skier from his childhood days. In the late 1930's Ken was for three years the Canadian cross-country ski champion. One year he was the overall Canadian Ski Champion, excelling in all disciplines—cross country skiing, slalom, downhill and ski jumping.

Ken was largely responsible for the successful functioning of the ACC ski camps and for many years would organize the camp, cook the food and do much of the guiding. Ken served the ACC and the skiing community at these camps for a total of thirteen years.

"The hard-working member of the party was Ken Jones in his triple capacity of cook, guide and instructor. However he seemed to thrive on it and after a morning or afternoon of skiing he would dash back to the hut ahead of us and have the meal practically on the table by the time the rest of us arrived." [3]

"I cannot close without a tribute to the mainstay of our last few camps, Ken Jones, who conducts simultaneously the offices of guide, ski instructor, cook and back packer. The 'dollar-a-year' man of the ski camps, Ken performs a prodigious amount of work for a very small compensation. He does it for the love of the thing and has earned the respect and gratitude of all who have been with him at our camps." [4]

---

[1]Elinor Richardson after the first ski camp in the Little Yoho Valley.

[2]Norman Brewster.

[3]Roger Neave

[4]Norman Brewster.

Cougar Milk

Cougar Milk was the backcountry skiers drink of the 1930's, 1940's and 1950's. It was originally known as Moose Milk and the recipe for this drink was displayed on the back of the bottles of Coruba Rum which was popular in those days. It's likely that Erling Strom coined the name Cougar Milk and the name stuck. After a hard day skiing the intrepid adventurers would retire to their mountain lodge and prepare this hot drink. The recipe is very simple:

In a glass combine a heaping teaspoon of Eagle Brand sweetened, condensed milk, one ounce of rum and a pinch of nutmeg. Add boiling water to taste. Simple but effective!

An Alpine Club ski camp in the 1940's.
Ken Jones standing at far right.
Photo Ken Jones Collection

Stanley Mitchell Hut

The Stanley Mitchell Hut was built in honour of one of the founding members of the Alpine Club of Canada. Stanley Mitchell was appointed Secretary-Treasurer of the club in 1907 and held this position until 1930 at which time he was elected Honorary Secretary, a position he held until his death in 1940.

The major donation of $1500 for the hut came from Helen M. Trenholme of Montreal and the project was entrusted to prominent ACC member and past president, A.A. McCoubrey. Mr. H. A. Dowler was given the contract to build the hut and it was finished by the end of the summer of 1939 at a total cost of $3200. Unfortunately, Stanley Mitchell died shortly after and did not get a chance to see this very beautiful cabin.

Carved on the mantle above the fireplace is the ACC motto 'Sic Itur Ad Astra'. A quotation from Virgil's Aeneid, it means "Thus one goes to the stars".

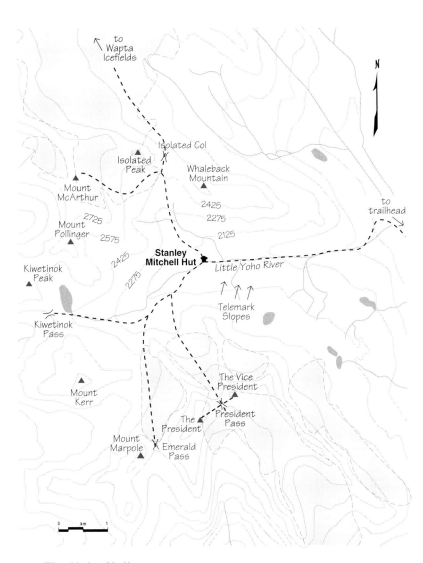

N

to
Wapta
Icefields

Isolated Col

Isolated
Peak

Whaleback
Mountain

Mount
McArthur

2425

2275

2125

to
trailhead

2725

Mount
Pollinger

2575

2425

Stanley
Mitchell Hut

Little Yoho River

2275

Kiwetinok
Peak

Telemark
Slopes

Kiwetinok
Pass

Mount
Kerr

The Vice
President

The
President

President
Pass

Mount
Marpole

Emerald
Pass

0   km   1

The Yoho Valley

Approach to Little Yoho Valley

Distance 23 km one way

Time The journey into the Little Yoho Valley can be done in one day by strong skiers but some skiers will find it necessary to overnight at the Takakkaw Falls Campground, particularly if there is deep trailbreaking. Most parties can ski back out to the highway in one day with little trouble.

Height gain 675 m from the Trans-Canada Highway to the Stanley Mitchell Hut in the Little Yoho Valley

Max elevation 2,060 m at the hut

Maps 82 N/8 Lake Louise
82 N/9 Hector Lake
82 N/10 Blaeberry River, or Touring the Wapta Icefields by Murray Toft.

Parking A large parking lot is located at the trailhead which is reached by taking the turn-off for the Yoho Valley, 4 km east of Field. If coming from Lake Louise, turn right, just after you descend the big hill from the Kicking Horse Pass and after crossing the bridge over the Kicking Horse River.

Facilities There is an enclosed camp shelter at the Takakkaw Falls Campground. Toilets are nearby and a pile of firewood is hidden under the snow.

The first half of the approach to the Little Yoho Valley follows a road to a campground located not far from Takakkaw Falls. The road begins from the east end of the parking area and is simple to follow. After about 5 km the road climbs several switchbacks. Just after the switchbacks, the road is threatened by giant avalanche paths high on Wapta Mountain. In fact, the road is often piled high with avalanche debris. Proceed as quickly as possible across these areas without stopping.

At the end of the road carry on directly into the campground. The camp shelter is located at the far end. Fire wood will be found under the snow not far from the shelter.

The trail to the Little Yoho Valley leaves from the far (north) end of the Takakkaw Falls Campground, crosses a large open area which in summer is a stream outwash, then enters the woods on the opposite side. The trail is easy to follow to begin with as it follows a wide, straight cut through the forest. After several kilometres it climbs a long and uniform hill (Hollingsworth Hill), then continues through the woods beyond. The trail can be hard to follow in this area.

After 4.5 km (from the campground) the route turns left just beyond Laughing Falls and begins its climb out of the Yoho Valley into the Little Yoho Valley. The turn-off point is sometimes hard to find, particularly if the trail signs are buried deep under the snow. Nowadays there are enough people touring in this area that the trail may be easier to follow than in the past. The trail switchbacks through open mature forest up the west wall of the valley and can be hard to follow if you are new to the area.

After about 240 vertical metres of climb, when the angle begins to ease off, the trail angles left towards the Little Yoho River. It continues along the north bank above the river into the valley. After a while the steep hillside that the trail is traversing levels off, and the trail meanders through forest and open glades to the hut. Stay on the north bank of the river throughout. Route finding can be tricky at times because the trail crosses meadows then re-enters forest on the opposite side at points that are hard to find. The hut is located in trees at the edge of a meadow, on the north side of the Little Yoho River, about 5 km from the Laughing Falls turn-off.

The return journey to the highway can be an exciting challenge for less experienced skiers. This is particularly true in the springtime when the trail can be icy. The descent of the steep hillside above Laughing Falls is not a laughing matter if you are unsure on your skis. Be careful here and take your time. The same holds true for the Hollingsworth Hill which is steep and long. For your return journey remember to get away early in the morning to allow plenty of time to reach the highway in one day.

Ken Jones at his 50th anniversary camp. Photo Keith Morton

Stanley Mitchell Hut

Map 82 N/10 Blaeberry River or preferably 'Touring the Wapta Icefield' by Murray Toft

Location The hut is located at 2060 m on the north edge of a small meadow about 100 m above the Little Yoho River, at the bottom of a steep, wooded slope (GR 303081).

Reservations ACC in Canmore

Capacity 22

Facilities A beautiful log cabin with three rooms and a sleeping loft (foam mattresses are provided). The common room has a wood stove for heat. The kitchen has Coleman stoves and lanterns and is well stocked with cooking and eating utensils.

Water A small creek, next to the Little Yoho River about 75 m from the front door of the cabin.

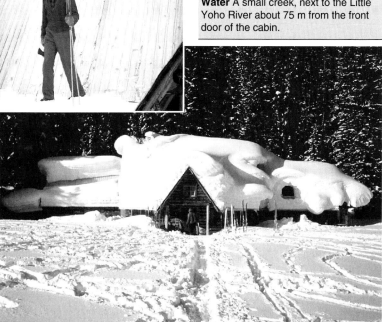

The beautiful Stanley Mitchell Hut deep in snow. Photo Keith Morton

Photo Keith Morton

President Pass between the Vice-President (left) and the President (right). The photo shows the tremendous run down President Glacier. Emerald Pass at far right.
Photo Alf Skrastins

President Pass

Distance 6 km return
Height gain 850 m
Max elevation 2910 m
Map 82 N/10 Blaeberry River

The tour to the President Pass is one of the best in the region. It offers a pleasant ski descent of about 700 vertical metres and is very popular. The tour is on a glacier which has a substantial number of crevasses so the party should carry a rope and be prepared for an emergency. It is possible to ascend both the Vice President and the President from President Pass but in both cases it is necessary to leave the skis behind and do some serious scrambling to reach the summits.

From the Stanley Mitchell Hut ski down to the creek and follow it west for about 150 m. Turn left and follow a shallow draw through the trees for about 100 m into a small bowl. Climb up and right out of the bowl, and over the crest of a moraine to reach a large open area which is the drainage from President Glacier. Now turn left and ascend a draw to the toe of the glacier. Continue up the glacier, staying generally just right of centre, to the pass located between Vice-President and the President.

The bergschrund was huge in 1995 making access to President Col difficult. Use caution on the final headwall above the bergschrund. It is steep enough to avalanche and has been the site of a fatality.

If the weather is overcast and snowy, there is good tree and glade skiing below the Vice President. The descent is generally 100-150 vertical metres. Several kilometres of skiable terrain in this area will keep you occupied for several days.

Mount McArthur

Distance 7 km return
Height gain 860 m
Max elevation 2920 m
Map 82 N/10 Blaeberry River

A highly recommended tour offering an outstanding descent of 800 vertical metres. The more adventurous can take their skis off and climb the last 50 vertical metres to the summit, but this involves some serious scrambling.

Begin this tour right behind the Stanley Mitchell Hut on the east corner above the biffy. The route traverses out right for a short distance, comes back left, then climbs steeply back and forth in switchbacks up through glades in the trees. After a steep climb of about 120 vertical metres the angle lays back.

Continue climbing through sparse trees until the terrain opens up and you can see Isolated Col at the far end of the valley. At this point you can see steep cliffs up on the left which bar a direct ascent. Continue ascending the valley until you are below the steep final climb to Isolated Col (GR 297099). At this point a bench leads out left onto the toe of the McArthur Glacier.

Traverse out on the bench to the glacier and continue working your way above. It is less steep on the left side of the glacier and after a while the angle lays back. Continue ascending under the east face of Mount McArthur. On skis, you can reach a point just north of the summit and about 50 vertical metres lower.

The run back down is excellent. You must be certain to traverse left (northeast) on the bench to regain the valley below Isolated Col. Do not attempt to ski straight down into the valley as there are cliff bands barring the way.

High on Mount McArthur, looking across to President Pass (centre) and Emerald Pass (far right). Photo Don Gardner

Ascending to Isolated Col. In the distance is Emerald Pass (centre) and Mount Marpole.
Photo Keith Morton

Isolated Col

Distance 5 km return
Height gain 460 m
Max elevation 2515 m
Map 82 N/10 Blaeberry River

The tour to Isolated Col offers a shorter day's skiing than going all the way up Mount McArthur. The final climb to the col is steep and extreme caution is advised. The descent is south facing and can be easily affected by the sun.

To reach Isolated Col follow the tour description for Mount McArthur. However, when you are below the col do not traverse out onto the McArthur Glacier but simply climb the steep slope above to reach the col (GR 298101).

Kiwetinok Pass

Distance 6 km return
Height gain 365 m
Max elevation 2425 m
Map 82 N/10 Blaeberry River

This is a very pleasant tour and is perfect for an easy day. The angle of most of the tour is quite gentle so it does not offer a lot of turns. However, the scenery is lovely and it is a nice way to get up high.

From the Stanley Mitchell Hut ski across to the creek and follow it upstream for about 150 m. Turn left and follow a shallow draw in the trees for about 100 m up into a bowl. Climb up and right out of the bowl and over the crest of a moraine to reach a large open stretch which is the drainage from the President Glacier. Cross this in a southwest direction to reach a draw along the left margin of the trees. Continue ascending, staying on the left edge of the trees in open terrain.

Near the edge of treeline there is a moderately steep slope to climb. Remain on the left side of the creek bed and ascend the slope at its lowest and least steep point. High on the left are prominent cliffs. Above the steep hill traverse out right to the creek bed, then continue climbing over open alpine terrain to reach Kiwetinok Lake and a short distance beyond, Kiwetinok Pass (GR 277073).

Emerald Pass

Distance 7 km return
Height gain 670 m
Max elevation 2730 m
Map 82 N/10 Blaeberry River

The tour to Emerald Pass (GR 296045) has long been popular and offers some good skiing. The south-facing slope on the far side of the pass offers excellent skiing of about 300 vertical metres.

From the Stanley Mitchell Hut follow the tour to Kiwetinok Pass for 1.5 km to GR 293071. To reach Emerald Pass ascend a steep looking slope on the left (use caution) then enter a draw. The route passes through a narrow canyon (Danger steep slopes above!), then ascends a slope to gain the Emerald Glacier. From here you can continue with little elevation gain 1.5 km across to Emerald Pass. Good skiing can be had on the far side of the pass (steep to begin!). Another option is to ski the lower slopes on Mount President at about GR 299057 (use caution as there is a large and dangerous mountainside above).

KANANASKIS FAVOURITES

Kananaskis Country is well-known for its cross-country track skiing and Nordic touring. It does, in addition, have some excellent trips that take you up high and offer some good potential for turns. Some of these trips are extremely popular.

To reach Kananaskis Country from Calgary drive west on the Trans-Canada Highway. After 60 km turn south on Highway 40 and continue for 45 km to the Kananaskis Lakes area. Highway 40 is closed beyond here and the road jogs right onto Kananaskis Lakes Trail. After another 2 km, turn right onto the Smith-Dorrien–Spray Trail.

To reach Kananaskis Country from the west turn off the Trans-Canada Highway at Canmore. Drive through the town, cross the Bow River, and continue up the hill past the Canmore Nordic Centre. You are now on the Smith-Dorrien–Spray Trail which continues for 60 km to join the Kananaskis Lakes Trail.

Most of the tours described here begin from parking lots along the Smith-Dorrien–Spray Trail. The tour to Mount Joffre begins at the Upper Kananaskis Lake Parking Lot.

Approaching Mount Joffre (left centre). The approach follows the ramp below the rock peak to the Mangin Glacier. On the mountain the route climbs the right side of the face.
Photo Tony Daffern

Mount Joffre

Distance 14 km one way
Height gain 1725 m
Max elevation 3450 m
Map 82 J/11 Kananaskis Lakes

The ascent of Mount Joffre is best done later in the year when snow conditions are stable. The route traverses a very threatening avalanche slope which has swept away skiers in the past. Pick the right time and be cautious.

To reach the trailhead drive Highway 40 to Kananaskis Lakes Trail. Follow the road to the end and park at the Upper Kananaskis Lakes parking lot.

Ski across Upper Kananaskis Lake to the Hidden Lake outlet (GR 287085). Continue above through relatively open trees to Hidden Lake. From here there are two variations for the next 3 km. The traditional route, while easier, is subject to serious avalanche risk. The alternative route, recommended by Don Gardner, is a much safer alternative.

Traditional route Cross Hidden Lake to the southernmost point, then work your way above through the trees until you reach open slopes (GR 285067).

Traverse up and across these open slopes to a gully leading through cliff bands. Climb up the gully until you can traverse right across the top of the cliff bands to the trees on the far side. Ski to a small lake at GR 277049, then pick your way across two drainages to Aster Creek. Follow the left bank of the creek to Aster Lake.

Alternative route Ski halfway along Hidden Lake to the inlet of Foch Creek (GR 283074). Ascend the creek for a short distance, then climb up to the right along the left margin of a large avalanche path. After gaining about 300 vertical metres where the angle begins to lay back, traverse left through open trees to reach the bench above Fossil Falls. Ascend Foch Creek then turn right up Aster Creek to reach Aster Lake where the two routes rejoin.

Cross Aster Lake, then round a corner to the left and continue up the open valley. After about 2.5 km climb up to your right onto the Mangin Glacier and ascend the glacier towards Mount Joffre. Climb as high as you can on skis, then continue on foot. The route ascends the right side of the northwest face to gain the summit ridge. Continue along the ridge a short distance to the summit.

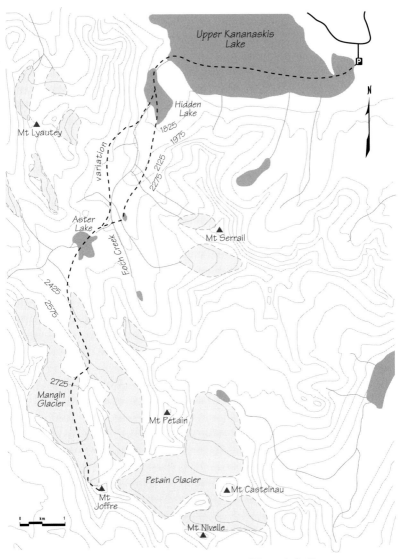

Upper Kananaskis Lake

Hidden Lake

Mt Lyautey

1825

1975

2275

2125

variation

Aster Lake

Foch Creek

Mt Serrail

2425

2575

2725

Mangin Glacier

Mt Petain

Petain Glacier

Mt Castelnau

Mt Joffre

Mt Nivelle

N

P

0   km   1

Opposite: the summit ridge.
Photo Tony Daffern

Mount Joffre

Burstall Pass

Distance 8 km
Height gain 500 m
Max elevation 2377 m
Maps 82 J/14 Spray Lakes Reservoir
82 J/11 Kananaskis Lakes

This is one of the most popular locations for making a few Telemark turns in the Rockies. The snow comes early (late November) and builds up deep over the winter.

The trip begins at Burstall Pass Parking Lot located on the west side of the Smith-Dorrien–Spray Trail, 40 km from Canmore or 20 km from the Kananaskis Lakes Trail junction.

From the parking lot follow the well packed trail across Mud Lake Dam and up a hill to the French Creek trail junction. Keep right and follow the main Burstall Creek trail for several kilometres until it descends to the right through the trees to reach the gravel flats of Burstall Creek.

Angle across the gravel flats to a point just left of West Burstall Creek where you will find the trail again. Most folks put on their skins here. Climb steeply through the forest for 150 vertical metres to where the angle lays back and you ski out into open glades. Ski across meadows (don't linger in the huge avalanche path), then ascend a draw. As you rise above timberline you will see Telemark slopes off to the right. From Burstall Pass itself (GR 146244) there is an excellent view of Mount Assiniboine to the west.

On the way back down, rather than descend the steep trail through the trees to the gravel flats, it is best to descend the gully of West Burstall Creek. It offers a good little ski run.

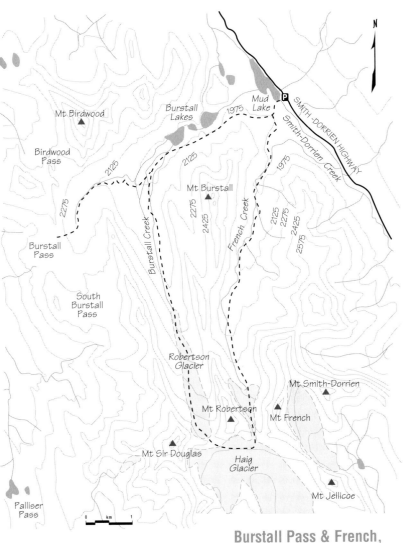

Burstall Pass & French, Haig, Robertson Circuit

Opposite: Burstall Pass. Note the Telemark slopes at lower right. Photo Gillean Daffern

Robertson Glacier

Distance 9 km to the pass
Height gain 1000 m to the pass
Max elevation 2896 m at the pass
Maps 82 J/14 Spray Lakes Reservoir
82 J/11 Kananaskis Lakes

A popular tour which takes you up a narrow valley onto a small glacier. You should be equipped with a rope and the necessary crevasse rescue equipment. The approach to the glacier is threatened by avalanche paths high above so do not linger.

The Robertson Glacier, showing the col between Mount Robertson (left) and Mount Sir Douglas. Photo Alf Skrastins

The trip begins at Burstall Pass Parking Lot located on the west side of the Smith-Dorrien–Spray Trail, 40 km from Canmore or 20 km from the Kananaskis Lakes Trail junction.

Follow Burstall Pass trail for 3 km as far as the gravel flats on Burstall Creek. Stay left and continue south up the long thin valley. Another 3 km brings you to the toe of the glacier.

The glacier itself offers some very good skiing when not wind-scoured. In fact, some entrepreneurs even installed a small ski lift at one time. If you choose you can climb all the way to the pass and have a long run. Generally, you climb the lower part of the glacier on the left and the upper part of the glacier on the right to avoid crevasses.

The steep climb above the Haig Glacier to the pass between Mount Robertson and Mount Sir Douglas. In the distance is Mount Jellicoe. Photo Alan Kane

French/Haig/Robertson Circuit

Distance 20 km round trip
Height gain 1000 m
Max elevation 2896 m
Maps 82 J/14 Spray Lakes Reservoir
82 J/11 Kananaskis Lakes

This is a terrific backcountry adventure. It gets you up high into glaciated country, offers great scenery and at the end of the day there is the potential of a good ski descent. Start early as the trip takes a full day. You should carry a rope and be equipped for crevasse rescue.

The trip begins at Burstall Pass Parking Lot located on the west side of the Smith-Dorrien–Spray Trail, 40 km from Canmore or 20 km from the Kananaskis Lakes Trail junction.

From Burstall Pass parking lot follow the well-packed trail across Mud Lake Dam, then climb a short hill up to the left to reach a trail intersection. Take the left branch and traverse south into French Creek. After reaching the creek the trail crosses onto the left bank and stays on this side for about 0.5 km. The trail is good to this point. However, it eventually disappears and you follow the creek bed. Soon it is necessary to make a short climb up a side drainage to the left. Follow the lower-angled drainage above for a short distance, then ski back right to the main drainage.

At the next step in the creekbed a poor trail contours around through the woods to the left and eventually breaks out of the forest back into the main drainage of French Creek. The route now follows this drainage until you can

Ascending the French Glacier. Mount Birdwood towers above. Photo Peter Haase

ascend up and to the left onto the slopes that lead to the French Glacier. Easily ascend the French Glacier and continue through a pass onto the névé of the Haig Glacier (GR 193201).

Turn sharply right and continue west across the Haig névé for about 1.5 km. This takes you to beneath the steep slope which leads up to another pass between Mount Sir Douglas and Mount Robertson (GR 183202). Remove your skis and climb on foot to the pass. This slope is steep and offers serious difficulties. If it is windblasted and hard you will want an ice axe. There is real potential for a fall. If the slope is covered in deep snow the risk of an avalanche is very real as well. Use caution and common sense when dealing with this slope.

From the pass traverse out right a short way and descend onto the head of the Robertson Glacier. In the upper part of the descent of the Robertson Glacier it is best to stay to the left to avoid some crevasses. Lower down the glacier you drop down a lovely ski slope to reach the right bank of the glacier which is followed to the valley floor.

From here continue along the valley through open forest to reach the gravel flats of the valley bottom as described on page 136. Ski across the flats to join Burstall Pass trail (description on page 134). You climb up to the right for a short distance to reach an old road, then follow the road for several kilometres back to your car, keeping left at the junction with the French Creek trail.

Black Prince Telemark Slopes

Distance 5 km return
Height gain 350 m
Max elevation 2300 m
Map 82 J/11 Kananaskis Lakes

Black Prince is one of the most popular Telemark destinations in the Rockies. It is advised you get there soon after a snowfall before it is skied out.

Parking for Black Prince is along the Smith-Dorrien–Spray Trail, 52 km from Canmore or 8 km from Kananaskis Lakes Trail. It is located on the west side of the highway down a short road.

From the entrance to the parking lot descend south for a short distance, cross the creek and continue uphill to the right on an old road. Climb moderately steeply for about 0.5 km to a large clear-cut swath, then branch right on a trail through the forest which descends for several hundred metres to reach the creek. Cross the creek and work your way up to the left. The trees soon begin to open up as you ascend slightly to the right to find a drainage.

Ascend the drainage for about 0.5 km until the forest begins to open up and you can climb the slope out left onto the main Telemarking hillside (GR 252194). Continue climbing for another 200 vertical metres through sparse trees, then enjoy a great run back down. Despite the presence of trees there is still significant avalanche potential and you should ski with caution.

The ridge just north of Black Prince, which faces and runs parallel to the highway (GR 250201), also offers good skiing, particularly at its south end where you can ski avalanche clearings down to the highway.

TELEMARK AREAS NEAR THE ROAD

Often you want to reach an area quickly, make a few turns and get home in time for dinner. Here are a few suggestions of where you might get a little exercise and fresh air without making a major commitment of time or energy.

Bow Summit

Distance 1 km to the base of the ski slope.
Height Gain The most popular slope is about 100 vertical metres high. From the parking lot to the highest area normally skied is about 330 vertical metres.
Max elevation 2250 on the bench above the most popular slope
2410 high in the upper bowl
Maps 82 N/9 Hector Lake
82 N/10 Blaeberry River
Touring the Wapta Icefields, Murray Toft

Bow Summit is perhaps the easiest location in the Rockies to access a few quick turns on a sunny day. It has long been a popular destination and on a spring day can be a magical spot. There is usually lots of snow, the views are excellent and the ski hill is only ten or fifteen minutes from the car. **Note:** the area may be closed to skiers in the early winter until there is sufficient snow to prevent damage to the fragile alpine vegetation.

Bow Summit has been the scene of avalanche fatalities in the past. Although the slopes are not large, they should be treated with caution.

Turn west off the Icefields Parkway at Bow Pass, 40 km north of the junction with the Trans-Canada Highway and drive up the road towards the Peyto Lake viewpoint. In winter the road is only plowed a short distance to a parking lot.

A skied-out slope at the end of the day. Photo: Alf Skrastins

From the parking lot ski up the road several hundred metres then angle out left and ski to the base of a prominent hill. This hill is one of the most popular attractions at Bow Summit, and although it is not large, many hours can be spent climbing up and skiing back down. It is highly recommended.

Higher up, some good turns can be made in a cirque. To reach this area ski along the bench which runs along the top of the hill. The trail reaches a creek drainage after about 1 km and turns right into a wild alpine cirque. Some of the slopes here are skiable but are potentially hazardous.

On rare occasions the snow is good high on the windswept shoulder above Peyto Lake viewpoint. This is a forepeak of Mount Jimmy Simpson and can at times offer a long enjoyable run.

Observation Peak

Distance 4 km return
Height gain 550 m
Max elevation 2575 m
Map 82 N/9 Hector Lake

The lower slopes of Observation Peak offer some excellent ski terrain and in less than an hour from the car you can be making turns. There are two obvious destinations, both described here.

The first location is along the north boundary of a large cirque which lies about 2 km directly south from the main summit of Observation Peak. To reach this slope, park at the Bow Summit parking lot on the Icefields Parkway, then walk back down the road and cross the road. Ski across a large meadow into trees on the other side. Start climbing and angling out right through the trees. For about 30 minutes the travel is through thick forest but it soon begins to open up. Keep climbing through the open forest and continue up to an elevation of about 2480 m and a grid reference of 370301. From here there is an excellent ski descent of about 300 vertical metres. The upper half is in the open and the lower half is through glades in the trees. You can do several runs here if you choose. On the last descent continue straight down through the forest working slightly to the right. If you find the good line it can be easy travelling through the trees. Continue over to the highway, then walk back up to your car.

The second location is not far away and actually enters the cirque. To reach this slope you should park along the highway 1.4 km south of the Bow Summit turn-off. There is a very indistinct creek drainage which crosses the highway here. With deep snow it will be tough to spot this drainage, so just do your best and head east into the forest. Keep looking around for this drainage because it soon becomes more distinct and offers an easy path through the forest. Follow the creek for perhaps 800 m, then just before the creek enters a narrow V-shaped drainage, climb up to the right through open timber (the drainage from here on is threatened by steep slopes on both sides and is not recommended). Work your way up the hillside on the right side of the drainage. The forest opens up more and more and soon you are in open terrain above the trees. Continue into the cirque, staying right of centre. It is possible to work your way quite high (GR 375299). The descent follows your route of ascent and offers good skiing terrain almost all the way back to the car. If the day is overcast and visibility is poor, the skiing at the edge of timberline can be just what you are looking for.

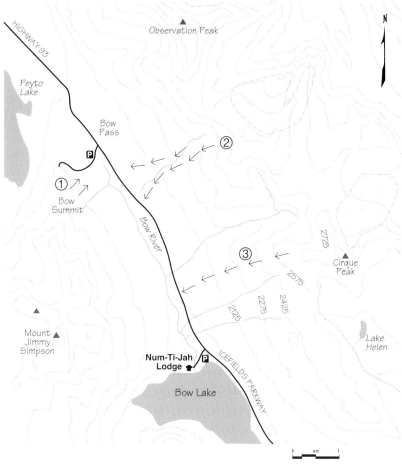

Bow Summit Area

① Bow Summit
② Observation Peak
③ Cirque Peak

*Opposite: On the west slopes of
Cirque Peak, looking out across
Bow Lake to the Wapta Icefields.
Photo Chic Scott*

Cirque Peak

Distance 6 km return
Height gain 500 m
Max elevation 2500 m
Map 82 N/9 Hector Lake

The west flank of Cirque Peak above the Icefields Parkway offers some good skiing at timberline. It is possible to ascend to the small sub peak high above timberline, but the skiing is usually windblown and hard. The views across to the Wapta Icefields are superb.

Park along the Icefields Parkway about 1.2 km north of the turn-off into Num-Ti-Jah Lodge. Ski through the woods and up the hill, heading east and slightly north. A slight drainage shows on the map (GR 381274) and that is the direction in which you should be heading. The trees along the south side of this minor drainage are quite well-spaced and offer a good line of ascent and descent. Once you reach timberline there is a large amount of skiable terrain to choose from. The descent back to the highway along the south flank of the drainage can offer some good tree skiing if you hit it right.

You can reach a small peak (GR 396277) by working your way up the slopes above and by heading south along the ridge. The view is magnificent and if the weather is good it is worth the effort. Leave your skis just short of the peak and scramble to the top.

Father south there is a major bowl and drainage (GR 388272) which looks appealing. The bowl itself and the glades at timberline do, in fact, offer some good skiing, but the forest below presents terrible skiing as the trees are very thick. This descent is one continuous bushwhack and is not recommended.

Parker Ridge

Distance 2 km
Height gain 410 m
Maximum elevation 2440 m
Map 83 C/3 Columbia Icefield

Parker Ridge is the classic Telemarking location in the Rockies. The slope is excellent, the views are outstanding and the snow is deep. The hillside starts within a stones-throw of the car and if you choose to stay overnight, there is even a hostel right at the bottom of the run. Because the snow comes early and stays late, it is a favourite autumn and springtime ski hill. **Note:** the area may be closed to skiers in the early winter until there is sufficient snow to prevent damage to the fragile alpine vegetation.

Parker Ridge is avalanche country. There have been a number of fatalities here over the years. Ski with caution, and use all avalanche safety procedures.

Parking is available in a lot on the north side of the Icefields Parkway overlooking Hilda Creek, about 3 km south of Sunwapta Pass.

From your car, walk across the highway and continue a short distance east along the highway until it is possible to put your skis on and ski up to the hostel which is located just south of the road. From the hostel make your way up through the trees for a short distance, then angle off to the right at about the point where you break out of the trees. Above you on your left the slope steepens. Ski a short distance to your right to where the angle of the hillside lays back, and there is a poorly defined drainage.

Climb the hillside at the lowest and safest point to reach the bench above.

Now begin to work your way to the southeast, climbing very gradually to Parker Ridge. Once you reach the ridge you can continue climbing along the crest for another 150 vertical metres. Most people stop about this point where the ridge becomes narrower and admire the incredible view.

The safest descent is to return along the route you climbed. There are, however, many alternative lines of descent if conditions are adequately stable.

Hilda Ridge

Distance 2.5 km
Height gain 410 m
Max elevation 2440 m
Map 83 C/3 Columbia Icefield

This is an enjoyable alternative to Parker Ridge and will often be in shape when Parker Ridge is either skied out or windblown.

Park your car as for the Parker Ridge tour and make your way to Hilda Creek Hostel.

Ski west beyond the hostel through the trees to Hilda Creek. Continue up the creek bed for a short distance, until it appears reasonable to begin climbing the hillside on your right (north). Work your way up through the trees for about 180 vertical metres until you break out of the forest onto the crest of a ridge. Continue working your way up the ridge for another 100 vertical metres.

From here you can descend to Hilda Creek a number of different ways. The 200 vertical-metre descent straight down to Hilda Creek is the obvious line. Use caution!

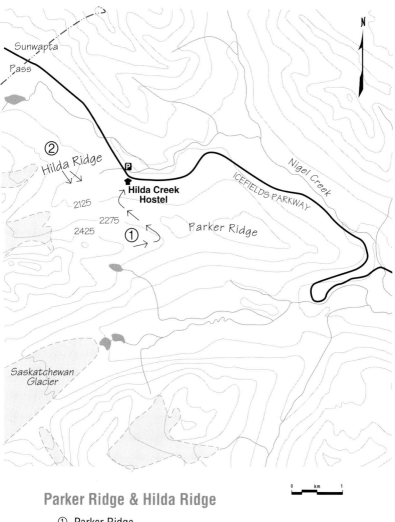

N

Sunwapta
Pass

② Hilda Ridge

P
**Hilda Creek
Hostel**

2125

2275

2425

① Parker Ridge

Nigel Creek

ICEFIELDS PARKWAY

Saskatchewan
Glacier

0   km   1

Parker Ridge & Hilda Ridge

① Parker Ridge
② Hilda Ridge

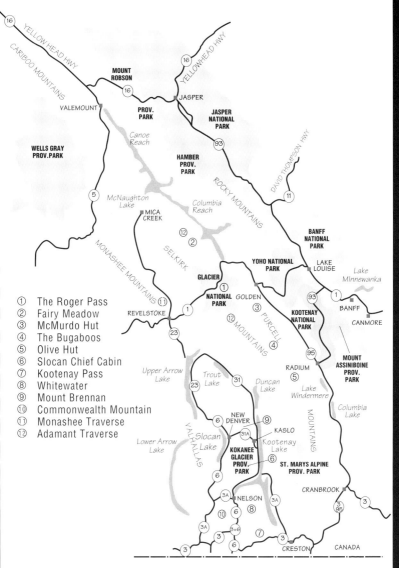

① The Roger Pass
② Fairy Meadow
③ McMurdo Hut
④ The Bugaboos
⑤ Olive Hut
⑥ Slocan Chief Cabin
⑦ Kootenay Pass
⑧ Whitewater
⑨ Mount Brennan
⑩ Commonwealth Mountain
⑪ Monashee Traverse
⑫ Adamant Traverse

UNITED STATES

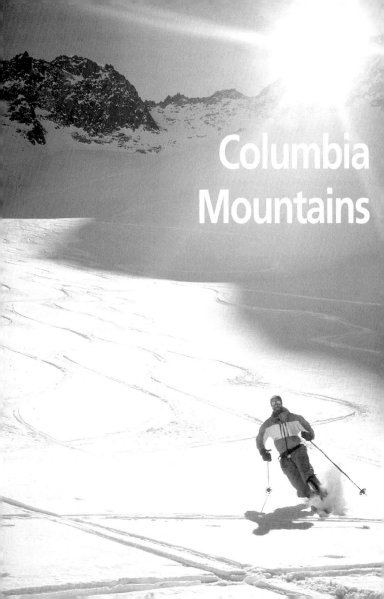

Columbia
Mountains

THE ROGERS PASS

The Rogers Pass offers some of the finest powder skiing in North America. Situated on the crest of the Selkirk Mountains, the pass receives up to 10 metres of snowfall per year. The mountains rise steeply almost 2000 vertical metres above the pass and the ski runs themselves normally offer about 1000 vertical metres of descent.

Most of the skiing is up side valleys with varying lengths of approach to the runs. The three main areas of activity are the Asulkan Valley, the Illecillewaet Valley, and Connaught Creek.

Area History

The Rogers Pass was discovered in 1881 by Major A.B. Rogers. He was searching for a route through the Selkirks for the proposed transcontinental railway. In 1885 the Canadian Pacific Railway was completed, linking the eastern cities with the Pacific Coast of Canada. But the surveyors and construction crews were only familiar with Rogers Pass during the summer and were unaware of the extent of snowfall and the consequent avalanches during the winter.

For a number of years, at great expense and difficulty, the railway through the pass was kept open during the winter. Often avalanches from surrounding peaks would bury the line and in 1910 a massive avalanche swept down and killed 62 workers who were already digging out the tracks from a previous avalanche. In 1916 the CPR was forced to reroute the line through a giant 8 km-long tunnel.

Previous page: Skiing at Fairy Meadow. Photo Peter Tucker

During the 1890's and the early part of this century the Rogers Pass became known as a centre for mountaineering. In fact, the pass was the birthplace of Canadian mountaineering. In 1887 the Canadian Pacific Railway opened a luxurious hotel called Glacier House not far from the summit of the pass and in 1899 began importing trained Swiss guides to lead the guests up the mountains. Glacier House was a bustling mountaineering hub for many years. Eventually the hotel was torn down in 1929.

There was little skiing activity in the pass until 1947 when the Alpine Club of Canada built a log hut not far from the old site of Glacier House. The hut was named for the founder of the club, A.O. Wheeler. During the late 1940's and 1950's keen skiers would take the train to a small stop called Glacier Station just west of the pass, then ski back to the hut. Activity, however, was still minimal.

In 1962 the Trans-Canada Highway was completed through the pass and this was to open the area for ski tourers. Over the years the popularity and fame of the Rogers Pass as a powder ski destination has spread around the world. Today, this is perhaps the premier ski mountaineering location in Canada.

Nowadays, you stay at either Glacier Park Lodge or the Wheeler Hut. Not far away across the Ilecillewaet Icefield is another hut, the legendary Glacier Circle Cabin which has been home to mountaineers for many years.

"The Glacier Circle Cabin was built about 1920 [for the CPR] by Mr. Fred Pepper of Field, British Columbia, who mushed in over the Illecillewaet glacier with a dog team. With him were his wife

and baby daughter. Their experiences, camping out at the Circle in a tent for several weeks while Fred constructed the cabin, would in itself make an epic story. At one time during a severe blizzard Fred was forced to descend to the Beaver River Valley in search of provisions as their stock was about exhausted. His wife held the fort while he was gone for several days. He finally returned with provisions which he had procured from a trapper further up the Beaver. These enabled them to carry on until the cabin was completed, when they returned to Glacier by way of the Great Glacier." [1]

During the 1920's and 1930's the cabin was used by parties led by the Swiss Guides attempting mountain climbs in the area. But by the 1960's the cabin had fallen into complete disrepair–half the roof had caved in and one wall had fallen down. The lease had been abandoned and the cabin had reverted from the CPR back to the crown. In 1972 Bill Putnam, Dave Jones and a number of their friends put a tremendous effort into reconstructing the hut. Much of the hut was completely rebuilt and the work was jointly paid for by Parks Canada and donations from members of the American Alpine Club.

Maps

The Rogers Pass area is on the corner of four topographical maps—82 N/3 Mount Wheeler, 82 N/4 Illecillewaet, 82 N/5 Glacier, 82 N/6 Blaeberry—which is very inconvenient. You need the composite map, 'Touring at Rogers Pass', prepared by Murray Toft which encompasses all of the skiing described in this book. All ski routes are marked and there are photographs on the reverse side. It is available in most of the local outdoor shops for about $15.

[1]From "A Short History of Glacier National Park British Columbia", National Parks Branch, Glacier National Park, Revelstoke, mimeographed, p. 10.

Access

You really need a car. However, you can reach the pass by Greyhound bus. There are several scheduled each day, both eastbound and westbound.

Glacier Park Lodge

Located adjacent to the highway at the summit of the pass, this fully modern hotel offers very comfortable accommodation. Some years they offer terrific skier specials. For more information phone (250) 837-2126. Service station adjacent.

The Illecillewaet/Asulkan Parking Lot

This parking lot is located on the south side of the Trans-Canada Highway about 3.5 km west of Glacier Park Lodge. It is the starting-off point for tours up the Illecillewaet and Asulkan valleys and also for the Wheeler Hut. If you are approaching from the east it is difficult to access as there is a giant concrete barrier in the middle of the road. It is best to continue several hundred metres to a turnoff to the right (railway access) and here, where the road is straight and visibility is good, you can more safely reverse your direction and approach the parking lot from the west.

Winter route to Wheeler Hut

From the east end of the Illecillewaet/Asulkan parking lot climb steeply through the trees for about 50 vertical metres to reach an old road. There are usually lots of old tracks to show the way. Turn left and follow the old road and railway grade for about 1.5 km. After 1 km you pass an historic monument and the junction with a trail on the right which is the start of all ski tours up the Illecillewaet and Asulkan valleys. The Wheeler Hut is on your left a short distance further along the trail (GR 657791). In winter, the hut is usually entered through the rear door.

The Wheeler Hut on a sparkling winter morning. Photo Chic Scott

Wheeler Hut

Map 82 N/6 Blaeberry
82 N/5 Glacier
Location About 1.5 km from the highway at the entrance to the Illecillewaet Valley.
Reservations ACC in Canmore, at (403) 678-3200. The door to the hut is locked with a combination lock. When you phone and make a reservation they will trade you the combination number for your Visa or Mastercard number.
Capacity 24
Facilities Coleman stoves, lanterns and all the necessary pots, pans and dishes. There is an axe, wood heating stove and foam sleeping mattresses.
Water from a small creek just north of the hut

Wheeler Hut

The Wheeler Hut is a beautiful log cabin set far enough back from the road so that you cannot hear the roar of the traffic. Sometimes in the winter the cabin tends to be a bit gloomy because the snow builds high around the windows, but on a starlit night, standing outside the hut, smelling the wood smoke in the air, it is truly a magical place. Once you get the fire going the hut is warm and cosy.

The hut is about 1.5 km from the road. Although it is an easy ski, it is suggested you put your skins on and get your pack in order before you head off. It is longer than you think when you are carrying a case of beer under each arm.

Parking for the Wheeler Hut (and all the tours in the Illecillewaet and Asulkan Valleys) is at the 'Hotel Gun Site' parking lot.

Special Regulations

Because avalanche conditions threaten the safety of visitors on the Trans-Canada Highway, Parks Canada is involved in avalanche control in some areas of the park. Heavy artillery fire is used to achieve this control. Both the artillery fire and the avalanches which result can present real danger to unwary visitors. Areas affected by these control measures are closed to the public.

Other closed areas are test slopes or snow profile sites which must not be disturbed because of their importance to avalanche forecasting. Any disturbance of these areas could reduce the effectiveness of the avalanche control program.

Closed Areas

The following areas may be closed to public travel on a day to day basis during the avalanche season. To ski these areas you must obtain a permit at no cost from the Rogers Pass Information Centre.

- all slide paths facing the Trans-Canada Highway
- Cougar Valley
- Hermit Trail and area
- Marion Lake and all slopes above the lake
- all areas on Mount Fidelity
- Rogers Pass from the Northlander Hotel to Illecillewaet campground

Any trail or area in the park may be closed on occasions when particularly high avalanche hazard exist.

Trip Registrations

There no longer is mandatory registration; it is now optional. Registration is advised and you should check in with the Rogers Pass Information Centre for the weather report and the snow stability forecast. There is a $6.00 per person per day park use fee for ski touring. A yearly pass is $42.

Parking

To ensure there is no interference with snowplowing or artillery fire, parking is never permitted on the Trans-Canada Highway or in gun positions. A number of areas that are not gun positions have been plowed alongside the highway for parking. The locations of these parking areas will be identified by the information service when you register out.

When you return to your car from a trip there may be an avalanche control program underway along the section of the highway where your car is parked. At these times, a card informing you that the road is closed will be placed on your windshield. Stay with your car until the card is removed by the warden service.

The ski trails in the park are neither groomed nor packed. Deep and heavy snow is normal. Most skiers find that light, cross-country ski equipment is not suitable for these conditions. Heavier ski-touring or ski mountaineering equipment and techniques are far more practical.

Rogers Pass Centre

The Rogers Pass Centre is located at the summit of the pass next to the Glacier Park Lodge. It is open in winter from 7:00 am to 5:00 pm, seven days a week. Here you can receive up-to-date information, purchase park passes, register out, study snow stability reports and weather reports. The warden office is located across the highway in the highway maintenance compound, but often wardens are out in the field so it is best to visit the Rogers Pass Centre. For information phone (250) 837-7500.

Illecillewaet Tours

Each tour up the Illecillewaet Valley is an extension of the previous one.

Practice Slopes

Distance 4 km return
Height gain 400 m
Max elevation 1700 m
Maps 82 N/3 Mount Wheeler
82 N/5 Glacier

At the head of the Illecillewaet Valley, near the toe of the glacier are several good locations to practice your technique or spend a short day. Both of the locations are also recommended when visibility is poor—these two hills have enough trees to give some reference in a whiteout.

Park at the Hotel Gun Site parking lot and proceed up the trail towards the Wheeler Hut to the location of the old Glacier House Hotel (there is a historic display here). See page 150 for the route from the highway. The trail now turns to the right, crosses a meadow and climbs up into the forest. Follow this trail for 0.5 km, passing a trail junction which branches left to 'The Meeting of the Waters'. Do not take this branch but continue straight ahead, climbing through the forest for another 0.5 km to reach another trail junction. Turn left here and follow the trail towards the Illecillewaet Glacier. In about 50 m it crosses a bridge over Asulkan Creek, then works its way through the forest, climbing over into the Illecillewaet drainage. Eventually, the trail breaks out into the open valley bottom of the Illecillewaet River and ascends easily towards the toe of the glacier.

The two practice slopes are located toward the end of the valley. The first area is on the left in the trees between two giant avalanche slopes. If snow stability is good you can also consider skiing the lower slopes of the avalanche paths themselves, however, it is like playing on the railway tracks—you must be certain no trains are coming. The second is straight ahead and is a triangular-shaped slope at the very end of the valley. There is a crest along the left margin, a steep rock cliff at the top, and small trees dotting the hillside. Both these locations offer very enjoyable skiing and you can choose between steeper pitches or more gentle slopes depending on your inclination and snow stability. Despite the fact these are called practice slopes there is still significant avalanche potential and you should ski with caution and follow all safety procedures.

Lookout Notch

Distance 8 km return
Height gain 880 m
Max elevation 2120 m
Maps 82 N/3 Mount Wheeler
82 N/5 Glacier

The descent into the Illecillewaet Valley from Lookout Notch is a good run, offering 700 vertical metres of skiing over varied slopes, rolls and benches. The slope faces northeast and consequently keeps powder conditions longer than some other slopes. Because of the complexity of the terrain good visibility is required. Somehow this tour feels like an easy day and is, therefore, an option when you have a late start or a slower group.

Begin by skiing up the Illecillewaet Valley (see the trail description to reach the practice slopes). At the end of the valley you climb steeply over rolls and bumps along the west side of the headwall, staying well back from the steep slopes of

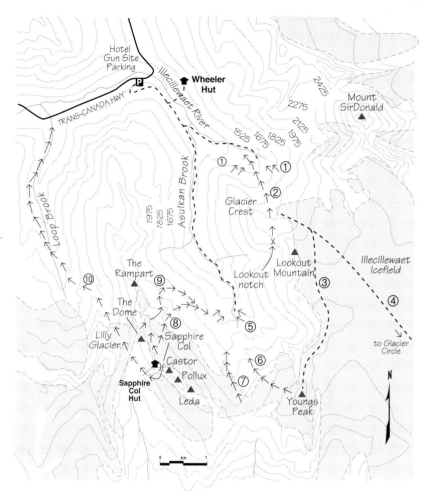

① Practice Slopes
② Lookout Notch
③ Youngs Peak
④ Glacier Circle route
⑤ Practise Slopes
⑥ Seven Steps of Paradise
⑦ Asulkan Pass

Illecillewaet &
Asulkan Valleys

⑧ Sapphire Col
⑨ Dome Glacier
⑩ Lily Glacier

Glacier Crest. This is an intricate ascent and it requires routefinding skills to work your way through the complex terrain. The last part of the tour climbs more gently to reach the col between Glacier Crest and Lookout Mountain (GR 680760). The tour to this point does not cross any glaciers and is not exposed to crevasses. From the notch the view to the southwest across the head of the Asulkan Valley is excellent; a superb vantage point for all the tours in that valley (see photo on page 161).

The descent back into the Illecillewaet Valley is delightful and varied. Be careful before committing yourself over steep rolls and treat the steep slopes of Glacier Crest with respect.

There is a short-cut back to the main trail which joins your ascent route not far from the Wheeler Hut. This short-cut descends the Illecillewaet Valley, staying high up on the right bank above the river. If you feel like exploring you can search for it and often there will be old tracks showing the way. If you want to play it safe, you can always follow your track of earlier in the day.

Youngs Peak

Distance 15 km return
Height gain 1575 m
Max elevation 2820 m
Maps 82 N/3 Mount Wheeler
82 N/5 Glacier

The traverse of Youngs Peak is one of the finest tours of the Rogers Pass. It offers great views and great skiing in a magnificent high mountain setting. It is highly recommended and should be saved for one of those sparkling clear days. The descent back into the Asulkan Valley down the Seven Steps of Paradise is an outstanding run. However, the upper pitch, right at the top of the descent, is very steep and should only be descended if you are certain of its safety. Because there is no way around this pitch you should only undertake this traverse during periods of optimal snow stability. Remember, it is always possible to ascend the Asulkan Valley and ski the Seven Steps of Paradise and leave out the final pitch if you are uncertain.

The tour begins by following the trail to the practice slopes at the head of the Illecillewaet Valley (see page 152). Continue following the description of the tour to Lookout Notch (see page 152). Do not follow the slope out toward the notch, but, at an altitude of about 2060 m traverse up and left out onto the Illecillewaet Glacier (caution—crevasses here!).

Climb steadily up onto the flat of the névé. It is big country up here and you need good visibility. As well it is farther than you think over to Youngs Peak. Ski past a small rock peak on your right, then continue along a crest with several rolls and bumps (watch for cornices on your left). Ski down into a notch, then climb steeply up the other side. It will probably be necessary to take off your skis to break through the cornice at the top. From here ski along the crest, staying well back from the cornices. The last few hundred feet to the top are best climbed on foot.

Cross the peak, then descend a short distance down the other side to locate the descent (to the right) down the Seven Steps of Paradise. A short steep pitch to a bench is followed by a very long steep pitch to more moderate terrain.

Glacier Circle

Distance 26 km return
Height gain 1360 m (each way)
Max elevation 2600 m
Maps 82 N/3 Mount Wheeler
82 N/5 Glacier

The tour over to Glacier Circle is a serious trip and should only be considered if you are experienced at glacier travel and are well prepared. It is a very long day and unless you are familiar with its location you will most likely have trouble finding the cabin. When it comes time to return to the highway the weather may be completely socked in and it is then not advisable to try to find your way across the Illecillewaet Icefield. You are advised to wait for better weather or to consider skiing down the valley to the east to reach the Beaver River, then follow the trail along the river for 25 km to reach the highway. It is a long and boring trip but it is better than getting into trouble in a whiteout on the glacier.

To reach Glacier Circle begin by following the previous three tours in this book (Practice Slopes, Lookout Notch and Youngs Peak) to the Illecillewaet Glacier just east of Lookout Mountain at about GR 693755. Continue southeast, gradually gaining elevation up onto the névé of the icefield. The flat icefield is crossed in a south-southeasterly direction. Be careful not to get sucked into the drainage of the Geikie Glacier if there is limited visibility. Just west of Mount Macoun at about GR 722716 begin descending in a southwest direction out onto the flat area just northeast of The Witch Tower (GR 707702). From here the descent into Glacier Circle under the east flank of the Witch Tower

is challenging skiing and towards the bottom of the glacier you are exposed to some risk of falling ice. To reach the cabin stay along the right flank of the forest for a way before heading into the trees to look for the hut (GR 726689).

Glacier Circle Cabin

Map Mount Wheeler 82 N/3
Location GR 726689 at an elevation of 1800 m
Reservations The fee for using this cabin is $10/person/night and reservations can be made by phoning (250) 837-7500.
Capacity 8
Facilities foam mattresses, stoves, lanterns and utensils

Asulkan Hut

Map Mount Wheeler 82 N/3
Location Built in the mid '90s by Parks Canada, this hut is located at the top of the tree triangle below the Seven Steps of Paradise. GR 673735
Reservations The cost is $20/person/night and reservations can be made through the Alpine Club of Canada (403) 678-3200.
Capacity 12
Facilities propane lights, stoves and heating

Previous page: High on the Illecillewaet Glacier, looking across a sea of clouds covering Rogers Pass to Cheops Mountain.
Photo Roger Laurilla

Tours From the Asulkan Valley

Some of the finest skiing in the Rogers Pass is to be found up the Asulkan Valley. All the tours follow the same route as far as the practice slopes.

Practice Slopes

Distance 10 km return
Height gain 725 m
Max elevation 1970 m
Maps 82 N/3 Mount Wheeler
82 N/5 Glacier

At the head of the Asulkan Valley there are some slopes lower down, near the valley floor, which can offer some good skiing on those days when visibility is poor. To reach these slopes takes about 90 minutes following a usually well packed and easy-to-follow trail.

Park at the Hotel Gun Site parking lot and proceed up the trail towards the Wheeler Hut to the location of the old Glacier House Hotel (historic display). See page 150 for the route from the highway. Turn right, ski across a small meadow and follow the trail as it climbs up into the forest. Ascend the trail for about 1.0 km, staying to the right at the turn off to 'The Meeting of the Waters' and to 'The Great Glacier'. The trail then levels off and continues through the forest for 0.5 km to reach a bridge across Asulkan Brook. Cross the bridge and continue along the left bank through the forest for about 3 km until the trees thin out and the valley narrows considerably. You are now approaching what is called 'The Mouse-trap'. The route stays along the left flank of the brook and climbs up through the narrow valley until it opens up again.

All around you are steep slopes and high above to your left is a huge avalanche path. Do not stop here but continue climbing until you are in a safer location.

There are now two slopes to choose from. You can either climb up to the right side of the valley and ski along the left margin of the forest amongst sparse trees. Or you can work your way straight above and to the left towards a large wedge of trees. Good skiing can be found in both these locations. The small trees give good definition on those overcast days and there is actually a large amount of terrain to work with where you can find untracked snow.

The Seven Steps of Paradise

Distance 14 km return
Height gain 1575 m
Max elevation 2820 m
Maps 82 N/3 Mount Wheeler
82 N/5 Glacier

This is one of the finest tours in the area, the descent offering about 1000 vertical metres of excellent skiing down alternating slopes and benches where you can take many different lines.

To reach the top of the run, follow the route up the Asulkan Valley which leads to the practice slopes. Beyond 'The Mousetrap' begin climbing steeply above, working your way out left toward the wedge of trees. Ascend through the trees traversing back and forth until you break out of the trees, then ascend a short steep slope (use caution here) and level out beside the Asulkan Hut. Work your way up open slopes above the hut toward Youngs Peak until you are below the last steep climb immediately below the peak. Many people stop here, particularly if they are unsure of the stability. It is possible to climb straight above to reach the summit of Youngs Peak. However, it is a very steep slope and you must be absolutely certain of snow stability. Enjoy the descent!

Asulkan Pass

Distance 14 km return
Height gain 1060 m
Max elevation 2300 m
Maps 82 N/3 Mount Wheeler
82 N/5 Glacier

This is another popular tour, and offers a more gentle angle of descent which might be appreciated by less experienced ski mountaineers. There is an impressive view from the pass of the Dawson Range to the south.

Follow the route up Asulkan Brook as described for the practice slopes. Beyond 'The Mousetrap' climb above and work your way out left towards the wedge of trees. When you reach the slope below the crest of trees you can work your way back to the right and follow a bit of a draw up towards the toe of the Asulkan Glacier. Ascend some steepish rolls then work your way up along the left margin of the glacier to the pass. For this tour it is a good idea to carry a rope and be prepared to do a crevasse rescue if needs be. The years when the crevasses are more open than normal you can stay well to the left edge of the glacier and not set foot on the ice until almost at the pass.

The run back down is quite gentle most of the way and is perfect for less experienced skiers.

Sapphire Col

Distance 16 km return
Height gain 1330 m
Max elevation 2575 m
Maps 82 N/3 Mount Wheeler
82 N/5 Glacier

The tour to Sapphire Col is a real classic. It can be done as a day trip or as an overnighter by staying in the small hut in the pass. From Sapphire Col you really have three options for your descent—you can return basically the way you climbed to the col (as described here), descend via the Dome Glacier (see page 159) or descend via Lily Glacier and Loop Brook (see page 160).

To reach Sapphire Col begin by skiing up Asulkan Brook to reach the practice slopes as described on page 157. Beyond 'The Mousetrap' climb up and to your right across open slopes to reach the edge of the forest. Continue climbing up through sparsely-treed slopes along the left margin of the forest until near the upper limit of the trees, then work your way out to the right. Climb up and to the right through the trees until the forest disappears and you are on open slopes again. Continue traversing across to the right to eventually reach the prominent rock buttress at the bottom of a shoulder which descends from the Dome (GR 655745). Keep this cliff on your right and climb straight up, generally following a groove or trough. Eventually this groove peters out and it is necessary to traverse up to the left across a large slope to reach more gentle terrain above. At this point you are about level with the top of the shoulder which separates the Dome Glacier descent and the normal route to Sapphire Col. From here the route climbs gently in a southerly direction to reach Sapphire Col. The small bivouac shelter is right in the col (GR 652729) and can accommodate six comfortably.

The descent back down to Asulkan Brook offers some excellent skiing and the route followed is usually the same as the ascent route.

Photo Keith Morton

The Sapphire Col Hut

This hut was the first of the 'modern' high altitude huts erected. It was built on August 15, 1964 by the Alpine Club of Canada and was turned over to the Government of Canada. It was the first of many huts designed by mountaineer and architect, Philip Delesalle.

Map 82 N/3 Mount Wheeler
Location On Sapphire Col at an elevation of 2590 m. GR 651730
Reservations The fee for using this cabin is $10/person/night and reservations can be made by phoning (250) 837-7500.
Capacity 6
Facilities minimal
Access See the tour on page 158.

The Dome Glacier

Distance 15 km return
Height gain 1300 m
Max elevation 2545 m
Maps 82 N/3 Mount Wheeler
82 N/5 Glacier

This tour offers one of the finest ski descents in the region. The slope faces northeast, is protected from the wind and consequently is one of the most likely locations to find powder snow when conditions are poor. The best part of the descent is only about 500 vertical metres high but, of course, it is always possible to climb back up for a second run if conditions are good.

To reach the Dome Glacier follow the tour up Asulkan Brook to the practice slopes (see page 157), then continue following the directions for Sapphire Col (see page 158) until you reach the rock buttress at the end of the shoulder which descends from The Dome (GR 655745). From here continue traversing north under the rocky crag into the next bowl between The Rampart and The Dome. Once you are in this bowl you angle up to your left and begin climbing back up to the west. After 200 vertical metres of ascent the route climbs up a slope on your left to reach the top of the shoulder which descends from The Dome (GR 653743). Continue climbing up the broad crest till it flattens below the pass. If you like you can climb right up to the col from the bottom of the north ridge of The Dome (GR 647742).

The descent follows the line of ascent and normally traverses to the right under the rocky buttress to follow the up track back into the Asulkan Valley. However, if conditions are good and you know where you are going it is possible to find a route which heads down and to the left directly into the valley. I have not described this route since the skiing is very challenging and it is possible to get into trouble on it. If you are a strong skier talk to some of the locals and check this one out.

The top of the Dome Glacier can be reached from Sapphire Col by simply descending gently down from the hut in a northerly direction, then traversing across a moderately steep slope to gain the crest of the shoulder below The Dome. It is also possible to climb the Lily Glacier then cross the high pass (GR 647742) at the north end of The Dome to reach the top of the Dome Glacier descent. Steep step kicking is necessary on the west side of this pass.

The Lily Glacier

Distance 7 km descent (one way)
Height gain 1180 m
Max elevation 2425 m (Top of the Lily Glacier)
Maps 82 N/3 Mount Wheeler
82 N/5 Glacier
82 N/4 Illecillewaet

The Lily Glacier offers an excellent ski descent. Often skiers climb to Sapphire Col from Asulkan Brook, then descend the Lily Glacier to exit via Loop Brook. It is possible, however, to ascend Loop Brook to the top of the Lily Glacier and return the same way.

To descend the Lily Glacier from Sapphire Col it is first necessary to descend steep slopes immediately below the col to the southwest. In certain conditions these slopes could present an extreme hazard so caution is urged. After de-

scending about 150 vertical metres begin contouring to your right, staying as high as possible and traverse out into the pass at the head of the Lily Glacier, between Mount Swanzy and The Dome (GR 645734). From here a pleasant ski descent of about 700 vertical metres brings you to the edge of a very sharp moraine. Ski with caution as there are some open crevasses on this descent. Continue descending the trough on the right flank of the moraine. As you reach the edge of tree line do not follow the apparent route straight down the valley but cross to the left bank of Loop Brook and traverse through the trees, remaining high above the valley floor. Contour around the corner and enter the creek drainage which descends from the west below Mount Green. Staying high, cross this drainage, then gradually descend towards the valley over a distance of 1.5 km, staying high above Loop Brook. At the end of this descending traverse a large avalanche path takes you into the valley bottom. From here, work your way down the creek bed to the highway. There is a parking lot at the east end of the bridge over Loop Brook where a car can be left.

If you chose to ascend this valley to the Lily Glacier the route followed is the same as the descent route described.

Opposite top: The view from Lookout Notch. Looking across the Asulkan Glacier to Sapphire Col (centre right). Photo Murray Toft

Opposite bottom: Looking across to the upper part of the route to Sapphire Col (tracks). The hut is just out of sight to the right. Photo Roger Laurilla

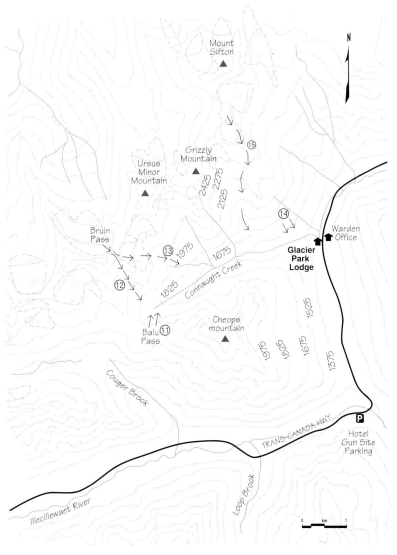

Connaught Creek Area

① Balu Pass
② Bruins Pass

⑬ Ursus Minor Basin
⑭ Grizzly Shoulder
⑮ Little Sifton

Tours from Connaught Creek

Connaught Creek is perhaps the best area for touring at Rogers Pass, with tours for both novice ski tourers and experts.

Balu Pass

Distance 10 km return
Height gain 725 m
Max elevation 2030 m
Map 82 N/5 Glacier

This is one of the favourite destinations at the Rogers Pass. It has a moderately long approach (about 5 km) along Connaught Creek but at the end you are rewarded with some terrific skiing. The slope on the north side of the pass is not high but is a very pleasant and consistent angle. This is an excellent location for newcomers to the area or beginner backcountry skiers. On a sunny day the view from the pass towards Mount Bonney is outstanding.

To reach Balu Pass begin immediately behind Glacier Park Lodge. Angle up to your right across an open slope to reach the large trail that ascends along the left bank of the creek. Follow this trail, climbing gradually. After a short distance the trail narrows, then crosses the creek on a small bridge. Continue up the creek along the right bank and soon the valley begins to open up. From here one simply continues up the valley, either keeping to the right bank or following the creek bottom itself. You must cross several very large avalanche paths and it is best not to linger in these exposed locations. The ski slopes are at the head of the valley below Balu Pass. (Note that Cougar Valley on the south side of Balu Pass is closed to ski tourers).

Bruins Pass

Distance 10 km return
Height gain 1180 m
Max elevation 2480 m
Map 82 N/5 Glacier

Another excellent tour which offers an unbroken descent of 700 vertical metres on a slope of intermediate steepness. This southeast-facing slope has the potential to avalanche after fresh snowfall. However, it can also offer great corn snow skiing in the spring.

Begin the tour as for Balu Pass and follow Connaught Creek almost to its end. Begin the climb to Bruins Pass (GR 592831) by one of two routes. You can either ascend to Balu Pass, then climb the ridge above until it is possible to traverse out right into a bowl which is ascended to Bruins pass. Or it is possible to turn back right on a bit of a bench part way up the slope towards Balu Pass and work your way out into the bowl which is then ascended to Bruins Pass.

From Bruins Pass an option is to descend into Ursus Minor Basin (see inset photo on p 164).

Ursus Minor Basin

Distance 9 km return
Height gain 1180 m
Max elevation 2480 m
Map 82 N/5 Glacier

Another of the great classic tours in Rogers Pass. It offers 800 vertical metres of fine skiing on open slopes and through light trees. Like the descent from Bruins Pass this is a southeast-facing slope and can be greatly influenced by the sun.

Follow the tour for Balu Pass for about 3 km. On your right is the bottom of a twisting avalanche path which descends in a final steep pitch from above (GR 613827). Climb up this avalanche path to gain the bowl above it. It is a bit of a grunt to climb the initial 150 vertical metres up into the bowl. Above you are many possible ways to ascend and many hectares of snow to leave tracks in. It is possible to work your way along the left flank of the bowl and climb right up to Bruins Pass (GR 592831).

Grizzly Shoulder

Distance 4 km return
Height gain 500 m
Max elevation 1800 m
Map 82 N/5 Glacier

This tour offers some excellent glade skiing and is a favourite location for those overcast days. It also makes a good destination for a short day or for a late start. Although you are skiing glades in the trees on Grizzly Shoulder, there is serious avalanche potential and you should not be lulled into a false sense of security. You should also be very careful to ski within the bounds set by the park wardens. The south flank of the shoulder more or less facing into Connaught Creek is open for skiing but the east flank of the shoulder facing the highway is closed.

The tour up Grizzly Shoulder begins at Connaught Creek behind Glacier Park Lodge (See the tour to Balu Pass on page 163). There are several different approaches to the shoulder. Some people

Opposite: Ursus Minor Basin offers some of the finest skiing at Rogers Pass.
Inset: The descent into the basin from Bruins Pass. Both photos Roger Laurilla

cross Connaught Creek right at the bottom and climb through the trees up Grizzly Shoulder. The advantage to this approach is that you now have an up-track in place and can make several runs. Other folks continue up Connaught Creek for about 30 minutes to the first large avalanche path which descends from the right. They then climb the edge of the avalanche path for about 100 vertical metres, then cut back to the right into the forest. From here they traverse, gradually gaining elevation, until they are above their line of choice. No matter what route you take there are many lines of descent that you can take on this shoulder and you can spend a whole stormy day playing here.

Little Sifton

Distance 7 km return
Height gain 1425 m
Max elevation 2725 m
Map 82 N/5 Glacier

The tour to Little Sifton (GR 614861) is complex, a major outing. Save it for a day with good visibility and good stability.

The tour begins up Connaught Creek behind the Glacier Park Lodge. (See the tour to Balu Pass on page 163). After about 0.5 hour you reach a large avalanche path descending from the right side of the valley. Ascend the right margin of this large path for about 100 vertical metres, then cut right into the trees. Ascend through glades in the forest for another 600 vertical metres. The route then traverses left into the bowl, and ascends up to the right onto the shoulder (GR 621849). From here continue north over open terrain towards the peak of Little Sifton.

Fairy Meadow

The skiing at Fairy Meadow is superb and consequently this area has become a favourite destination with many back country skiers. It must be remembered that this is big country and skiers must be prepared. You should be able to navigate on glaciers in any conditions, perform a crevasse rescue if necessary and deal with any of the other hazards of the high mountains in winter.

Access In winter all hut users fly in. Be prepared for delays owing to adverse weather conditions. The cost of the helicopter flight is included in the hut rental, which is $550/person/week (ACC members) or $600/person/week (non members). You must reserve either half the hut (10 people) or the whole hut (20 people). Reservations should be made six months in advance.

The only reliable communication from the hut to the outside world is through a private logging channel. It is for emergency use only with a charge of $100/week if used. You must provide your own programmable FM radio. Radios can be obtained through Gen Com Communications in Banff at (403) 762-4396.

Hut History The Adamants and Fairy Meadow were a summer climbing destination for a number of years but only became a ski destination with the construction of the hut in 1965. Americans Bill Putnam and Ben Ferris had often climbed in the area and recommended the site to the Alpine Club of Canada. The club obtained the lease of occupation for the land and paid for about half the cost.

Sentinel Peak

Fairy Meadow Hut

Maps 82 N/13 Sullivan River
82 N/12 Mount Sir Sandford
Location at 2050 m (GR 394352)
Reservations Alpine Club of Canada.
Due to the hut's popularity, you must
phone early to reserve a ski week.
Capacity 20
Facilities Two-storey wooden structure, with several rooms for sleeping on
the second floor (foam mattresses provided). Coleman stoves and propane
stoves for cooking and Coleman lanterns. Wood burning heating stove. Hut
users must provide their own propane,
white gas and toilet paper.
Water from the creek south of the hut.

Fairy Meadow Hut.
Photo Alf Skrastins

*Below and p 168: The Adamants. Looking
across the upper Granite Glacier from Mount
Sir William. Photo Phil Janz*

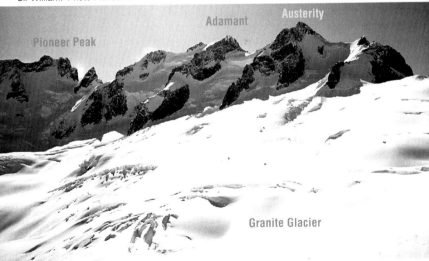

Pioneer Peak   Adamant   Austerity

Granite Glacier

Climbing to Friendship Col, one of the most popular tours. Photo Roger Laurilla

Mount Unicorn

of the hut. Putnam and Ferris, aided by the Harvard Mountaineering Club, paid the other half of the costs and actually undertook the job of construction of the building. Soon people were using the hut as a winter ski destination because of the outstanding terrain available.

It was soon discovered that the roof was not adequate for the tremendous snow loads encountered. Consequently in 1973, a major rebuilding was done. A second floor and new roof were completed and a new custodian's wing was added. The costs for this rebuilding were jointly borne by the ACC and Bill Putnam.

It was originally agreed upon by the ACC, with serious misgivings, that in return for his tremendous contribution,

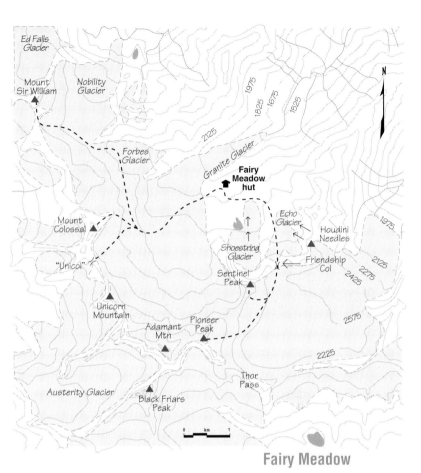

Fairy Meadow

Putnam would have certain rights over the cabin and in particular the custodian's quarters. It was found that this arrangement made for difficulties with other hut users and within a few years the arrangements was terminated, unfortunately with some bitterness and acrimony. Over the years the situation has mellowed and Putnam was awarded by the ACC both the Distinguished Service Award and an Honorary Membership for his contributions to the club.

Under the direction of Mike Mortimer, Chairman of the ACC Huts Committee, the Fairy Meadow hut has received a tremendous amount of attention in recent years and several major work parties have significantly added to its comfort.

Ski Tours

The Fairy Meadows Hut is perhaps 'the' backcountry ski destination in Canada. The snow is deep, the runs are excellent and the hut very comfortable.

Some of the more popular tours are:

- **Practice Slopes** There are excellent 'practice slopes' about 200 vertical metres high right outside the door of the hut immediately to the south. These slopes are deceptively big and should be treated with respect.

- **Tree Skiing** There is limited tree skiing a short distance east and down slope from the hut.

- **Friendship Col and Sentinel Peak** Sentinel Peak (GR 399328) makes an excellent tour. The tour climbs above the hut to the south to reach the Echo Glacier which is followed to Friendship Col (GR 406333). From Friendship Col continue across the icefield, curving around to the right to reach the south ridge of Sentinel Peak. The last few metres to the summit are easy scrambling. This is a good tour for early in your holiday as you can get an excellent view of the area and plan your week to come. The ski descent back to the hut offers generally moderate skiing.

- **Pioneer Peak** This peak (GR 388316) offers another excellent ski tour, much like the ascent of Sentinel Peak. Ascend the Echo Glacier to Friendship Col, then cross the icefield in a southerly direction and climb up to the right, ascending the east face of Pioneer Peak. Some easy ridge scrambling at the top leads to the summit. An excellent run on generally moderate terrain takes you back to the hut.

- **The Shoestring Glacier** This glacier, located south of the hut above the Bunny Slopes, offers a steep run and in stable conditions, excellent skiing.

- **The Houdini Needles** There are several very steep chutes which descend from the Houdini Needles. These are skiable in the right condition but offer expert skiing and serious avalanche risk. Use extreme caution.

- **'Unicol'** Between Mount Unicorn (GR 365326) and Mount Colossal (GR 361343) is a pass sometimes known as 'Unicol' (GR 361335). This is a good destination and offers some enjoyable moderate skiing. There are serious crevasse problems on this tour, and the bergschrund below the pass can present problems in low snow years.

- **Mount Colossal** This mountain makes an exciting but not too difficult ascent. Ski up the Granite Glacier to the bottom of the northeast ridge. Leave your skis behind and kick steps up the ridge to the summit.

- **Mount Sir William** It is a long tour across the Granite, Forbes and Nobility Glaciers to reach Mount Sir William (GR 347374). It is best left to the springtime when the days are long and glacier travel can be much easier.

- **Getting onto the Granite Glacier** The north side of the moraine between the hut and the Glacier is very steep and a direct descent is not recommended. It is possible to ski along the crest of the moraine to its upper end to reach the glacier. A safe but tiresome alternative is to descend to the lower end of the moraine then descend a bench onto the glacier.

Opposite: The summit ridge of Pioneer Peak. Mount Sir Sandford in the background. Photo Vance Hanna Inset: Nearing the summit of Mount Colossal. Photo Peter Haase

Great Cairn Hut

A number of people are now using the Great Cairn Hut as a base for a ski holiday. The cabin is truly a gem and is just the right size for a cozy holiday with some good friends. The scenery is outstanding and the massive peak of Mount Sir Sandford towers above the hut. The skiing in the vicinity is not as extensive as Fairy Meadow but there are some decent runs. There is good touring and exploration in the area.

Access Often skiers will make a side trip from the Fairy Meadow Hut to the Great Cairn Hut. This route passes through Friendship Col, Thor Pass and Azimuth Notch. It is a serious mountaineering trip. See the Northern Selkirks Ski Traverse (page 247) for more information. You can also fly directly to the hut by helicopter from Golden. Contact Canadian Helicopters, Golden.

It is now possible to access the Great Cairn Hut on foot. Begin by driving up the Goldstream River from the west for about 40 km, travelling along logging roads with steep and muddy sections. A four wheel drive vehicle is needed. From here, ski to Moberly Pass, ascend the Goat Glacier, then descend the Haworth Glacier to the hut. The trip from the road end takes about 12 hours in good conditions.

Hut History On a rainy day in August, 1953, a group from the Harvard Mountaineering Club, exploring the area near Mount Sir Sandford, passed the day by erecting a giant cairn, 20 feet high. Ten years later Bill Putnam and Ben Ferris were struck with the idea of erecting a small hut at the same location. They offered to pay half the cost of the materials if the Alpine Club of Canada would pay the additional costs. The ACC secured a licence of occupation from the BC Government and the following summer, in July 1964, Ben Ferris, assisted by his family and several friends, built this beautiful cabin using the stones of the great cairn.

Great Cairn Hut
Map 82 N/12 Mount Sir Sandford
Location North of Mount Sir Sandford in the Northern Selkirks at 1800 m. (GR 393263)
Reservations Alpine club of Canada
Capacity 6
Facilities wood heating stove, foam mattresses, Coleman lantern and stove.
Water Snowmelt

The Great Cairn Hut below Mount Sir Sandford. Photo Chic Scott

McMurdo Creek

The Spillimacheen Range southwest of Golden is rapidly becoming a centre for backcountry skiers. The snow is deep, access is not difficult and the McMurdo Hut makes a comfortable base.

The McMurdo Hut is located on the north slope of the Spillimacheen Range at the head of McMurdo Creek. It was once part of a mining camp. Originally there were three cabins, but there is now only one cabin standing and the remains of one other.

Access The hut is accessible both by helicopter from Golden and by snowmobile. If you choose to fly contact Alpine Helicopters in Golden (see page 28). The average cost for a return flight with a minimum of 3 people is about $200. If the visibility is poor when it comes time to fly out, the pilot can follow the valleys to reach the cabin in almost any weather and if you are prepared to pay the additional cost (for the longer flight required) the pilot will guarantee your return flight.

McMurdo Hut

Map 82 N/3 Mount Wheeler
Location on the edge of a meadow on the north slope of the Spillimacheen Range at the head of McMurdo Creek. (GR 896554)
Reservations Book one month in advance through BC Forest Service in Invermere. Phone (250) 342-4200.
Capacity 5
Facilities wood cooking stove and a wood heating stove, table, chairs, foam mattresses, Coleman lantern and stove, axe, pots and pans and utensils
Fee No charge but donations are gladly received by the Columbia Valley Hut Society, Box 922, Invermere, BC, V0A 1K0. Phone (250)-342-3509

McMurdo Hut. Photo Chic Scott

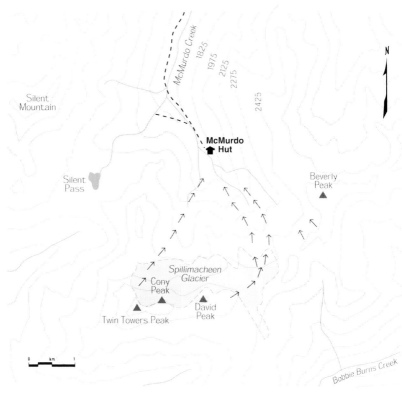

McMurdo Creek

If you choose to go in by snowmobile contact the Crestbrook Forest Industries in Parsons (phone (250) 348-2211) about the state of the road and if active logging is going on that day. The road is usually plowed for a substantial distance, often up to km 28. It is another 30 km to the cabin which takes about 2.5 hours on a snowmobile.

The road up the Spillimacheen River leaves Parsons (which is located on highway #95, 35 km south of Golden)

about 200 m north of the office of Crestbrook Forest Industries. The road crosses the Columbia Valley, then after about 2 km starts to climb steeply. It makes four switchbacks, then continues south climbing up the hillside. The road crosses the crest of the ridge at km 13, then swings west and drops into the drainage of the Spillimacheen River. Continue along this main road, ignoring any turn-offs, to a plowed parking area at km 28.

From here the travel by snowmobile is generally easy and flat for the first 18 km along the road on the north flank of the Spillimacheen River. At km 46 take a branch road to the left which is the McMurdo Creek Road. It immediately crosses the river to the south side. The road now begins to climb more steeply up McMurdo Creek and crosses several bridges which can offer a little trouble. After about 10 km the road swings right in a clear cut, but the way to the hut climbs up the narrow road straight ahead through the trees. The last kilometre to the hut is very steep much of the way. When the trees open up into a meadow the hut can be found on the left side (east) a few metres into the trees.

Other users This area is very popular with the snowmobile crowd which means that the road to the hut will most likely be very well packed and offer easy travelling. This area is also used for heli-skiing, so you may find your peaceful day in the mountains interrupted by the arrival of a load of skiers in a helicopter.

Skiing Only three runs are described here but, of course, there is a lot of other terrain to play with.

• One of the finest runs descends from the shoulder of David Peak. Begin this tour by following an old mining road which starts about 40 metres southeast of the cabin. The road climbs the hillside a few metres above a creek. When the road swings off to the right after about 0.5 km continue directly south up the creek bed towards the east branch of the Spillimacheen Glacier. Ascend the creek for several hundred metres (some steep steps) until you come out into a basin with steepish slopes toward the upper end. Ski up into this basin, then work your way up the left flank onto a wooded shoulder. Climb the shoulder until the trees end and you can head up into open terrain. Carry on in a southerly direction over gentle open terrain towards the pass over into the Bobbie Burns drainage. As you approach this pass climb up onto the shoulder on the right toward David Peak. Climb as high on this shoulder as you can to reach a point just under the rocks. From here you have a great descent back down to the cabin.

• Another fine run begins from Twin Towers Peak. It starts high on the shoulder of the peak (GR 878527) and descends the west branch of the Spillimacheen Glacier. Between 2420 m and 2570 m elevation it is necessary to follow a ramp through steep broken glacier terrain. The last part of the run to the meadow at about GR 894548 descends a steep drainage through the trees. To reach this descent one can ascend as described in the tour to David Peak, then traverse west beneath David Peak and Cony Peak to reach Twin Towers Peak.

• A more advanced run descends from a small sub peak (GR 920538) down the northwest facing slopes into a creek bed which leads directly back to the cabin. Lower down, the run descends some steep chutes which have serious avalanche potential, so only ski this run when you are certain of the snow stability.

P 176 top: Touring above McMurdo Hut. The tour to David Peak shows the great terrain. P 176 bottom: Touring at the head of the Vowell Glacier. Both photos Stan Wagon

The Bugaboos

The Bugaboos are world famous as a helicopter ski destination. It is also possible for the average ski tourer to enjoy this wonderful area. However, without a helicopter it is difficult to access the sort of terrain that has made the Bugaboos famous.

It is still a fine place to have a magical ski vacation, touring and turning amongst the impressive towers of Bugaboo, Snowpatch and Pigeon Spires. The Howser Towers above the head of the Vowell Glacier are truly a wonderful sight on a glittering sunny day.

Conrad Kain Hut This is a large modern hut, built in 1972. It sleeps 50 and although it is not heated it is reasonably comfortable as long as the temperature is moderate. Most groups use the hut only in April and May when it is not too cold.

Access Although most folks fly with Canadian Mountain Holidays to the hut, BC Parks discourages this and prefers that you access the hut via the Bugaboo Road. The road is normally plowed in winter for about 17 km. From there it is another 25 km on skis or by snowmobile to the CMH Bugaboo Lodge. A ski ascent of 700 vertical metres and 5 km up the Bugaboo Glacier takes you to Conrad Kain Hut.

Skiing Skiing near the hut is limited. There is some good skiing above the hut below the east faces of Snowpatch and Bugaboo Spires. A very good ski run can be had down the Bugaboo Glacier, starting along the left side of the glacier and finishing on the right side into the valley. For another very pleasant tour climb steeply through Bugaboo/

Snowpatch Col , then ski at the head of the Vowell Glacier surrounded by the Howser Towers, Pigeon Spire and the west face of Bugaboo Spire. There is definitely enough skiing here to keep a group busy for a week. There is no tree skiing in the event of bad weather.

Conrad Kain Hut

Map 82 K/10 Howser Creek
Location at timberline (2195 m) above the Bugaboo Glacier near what is called Boulder Camp (GR 166204)
Reservations The Conrad Kain Hut has been hit twice in the past by avalanches and is officially closed in winter. The door is not locked, however, and skiers can still use the hut at their own risk. For up-to-date information phone the East Kootenay District Office at (250) 422-4200
Capacity 50
Facilities Foamies, propane for lights & cooking but no pots, pans or utensils and no heating (April & May recommended).

A summer shot of the Conrad Kain Hut. Photo Chic Scott

Catamount Glacier

This area is in some ways like a compact Wapta Icefield with peaks to climb, excellent shorter runs (150-300 m) and several good long runs. There is no tree skiing so if the weather is poor there is not much to do. Because of adjacent heliski operations, you may not have the area to yourself. The Olive Hut is a delightful little cabin named after Peter and Debbie Olive who were killed in helicopter accidents.

Access You can fly with Frontier Helicopters from Invermere at a cost of $400 per flight. The helicopter can carry 3 passengers with heavy baggage or 4 passengers with light baggage. You can also access the hut via Forster Creek—a 20 km ski up the creek, or more likely a ride on a snowmobile followed by a steep climb up to the Catamount Glacier. This climb involves slopes which could present serious avalanche risk, and in certain conditions could be impassable.

Skiing
- From Mount Griffith descend to Thunderwater Lake and Forster Creek. Return via the hut approach.
- From the col northeast of Gwendoline Mountain (GR 316074) ski down the North Star Glacier to Forster Creek. Return via the hut approach.

Olive Hut

Map 82 K/10 Howser Creek
Location Starbird Range in the Purcell Mountains on the west flank of the Scotch Peaks at 2640 m (GR 313088).
Reservations Book one month in advance through BC Forest Service in Invermere. Phone (250) 342-4200.
Capacity 6
Facilities Foamies, a Coleman stove and lantern, pots, pans, utensils and a wood heating stove.
Fee No charge but donations are gladly received by the Columbia Valley Hut Society, Box 922, Invermere, BC, V0A 1K0. Phone (250)-342-3509

Photo Martha McCallum

Kokanee Glacier Provincial Park

Kokanee Glacier Park is renowned as one of the absolutely best destinations for powder skiing in Western Canada. There is lots of snow, a great variety of runs to choose from and tree skiing—everything you could want.

Access Groups normally fly in to the Slocan Chief Cabin, then at the end of the week they ski out. The helicopter bringing in the next group usually takes out the heavy baggage and any garbage from the previous week's group. The cost of the flight is somewhat variable depending on the size of your group and the amount of baggage but is normally about $150/person (Canadian Helicopters, Nelson or High Terrain Helicopters, Nelson. See p 28).

Maps 82 F/14 Slocan
82 F/11 Kokanee Peak

Slocan Chief Cabin

Map 82 F/14 Slocan
Location (GR 873128)
Reservations Lottery system through Kokanee Glacier Mountaineering, RR#1, Site 3, Comp. 32, Nelson, BC, V1L 5P4.
Capacity 12
Facilities bunks, foam mattresses, wood heating and propane cooking
Fee $15/night/person or $1,260/week for 12

Rangers A ranger is stationed in the nearby rangers cabin and is in contact with the outside world.

Cabin History This large cabin was originally built for the Smuggler Mining Company in 1896, with ore shipped from this area as late as 1928. The area was made into a provincial park in 1922.

Photo Clive Cordery

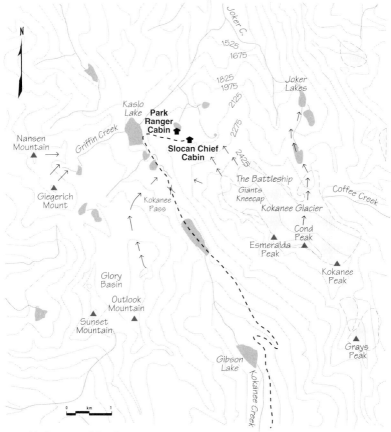

Kokanee Glacier

In the early years the cabin was regularly used by local clubs and mountaineering groups, but it eventually fell into a state of disrepair. By 1962 BC Parks was contemplating burning the cabin to the ground until a group of local mountaineers headed by Helen Butling spent much of that summer rehabilitating the cabin. In 1964 additional repairs were undertaken and for the next ten years the Kootenay Mountaineering Club took care of the cabin. In 1974 it was taken over by B.C. Provincial Parks.

The use of the cabin is now closely controlled and is allotted on a lottery system. Groups must apply before October 1st, giving several dates they would prefer to use the cabin. Names are then selected and all applicants, successful or not, are soon contacted.

Skiing Here are a few of the more popular ski descents.

- The large northwest facing slope below the Battleship (GR 883116) and the Giants Kneecap (GR 888112) back down to the Slocan Chief Cabin is a popular run. (600 vertical metres).

- One of the finest runs is to ski north from the summit of Esmeralda or Cond Peaks down the Kokanee Glacier to an unnamed lake (GR 898122), then further down to Joker Lakes (GR 902131). (800 vertical metres).

- Another good run can be had from the north summit of Outlook Mountain (GR 863096). Head north, then curve down to the right to reach Kokanee Pass. (550 vertical metres). The approach to this peak is up Outlook Creek to Lemon Pass where the way above is blocked by a short steep section. It is possible to climb this obstacle by a narrow crest just above Lemon Pass (GR 852111).

- Good skiing can be found from the crests of Nansen Mountain and Mount Giegerich into the basin of Griffin Creek. (250 vertical metres).

- If it is overcast a good location for skiing with a few trees for visibility is along the west flank of Smuggler's Ridge, and near the bottom below the ridge towards the cabin. Smuggler's Ridge is the crest which descends northwest from The Pyramids (GR 883111) to about GR 867124).

- Many summits can be reached at Kokanee Park. It is possible to ski to the top of The Pyramids, Esmeralda Peak, Cond Peak, and Kokanee Peak. You can walk out onto the crest of The Battleship but the trip to reach the summit of The Giant's Kneecap requires a rope and some technical climbing.

The tremendous ski run below the Battleship and the Giants Kneecap.
Photo Clive Cordery

Kokanee Peak

Cond Peak

Esmeralda Peak

High on the Kokanee Glacier.
Photo Peter Tucker

Ski Out Most folks ski out from the Slocan Chief Cabin rather than take the helicopter. It is a long way (8.5 km to Gibson Lake, then another 15 km down the road), and normally takes from 4-6 hours. However, if there is deep trail breaking it could take considerably longer. Leave a car at the bottom of the trail at Kokanee Creek Provincial Park. The Rangers or the helicopter personnel can advise you on the safest location to leave the vehicle.

The ski-out descends from the Slocan Chief Cabin to Kaslo Lake. Continue past Garland Lake and Keen Lake to Kokanee Pass. Continue along the centre of the valley to Kokanee Lake, then ski across the lake to the far end. At this point climb up a shoulder on the left to the top of a small hill–do not attempt to descend directly down the creek.

From the hill top descend gradually along a bench, following the line of the summer trail shown on the map. Be careful not to descend too quickly. Ski through what is called Esmeralda Notch (which is a small ravine-like feature), then continue out onto semi open and avalanche path terrain. Lose elevation gradually along benches and through woods and across avalanche paths. Descend about 200 vertical metres to reach the end of the road shown on the map (GR 888086). Descend the road in several large switchbacks to Gibson Lake.

At Gibson Lake there is a large enclosed shelter with a stove and firewood which would be comfortable in the event of emergency. From here ski down the road for 15 km to Highway #3A at Kokanee Creek Provincial Park. The road comes out to the highway 1 km east of Kokanee Creek. The descent down the road can be very fast if conditions are icy but can take much longer if you are breaking trail.

Opposite: Ascending towards the Battleship.
Outlook Peak lies across the valley.
Photo Clive Cordery

Silver Spray Cabin

The Slocan Chief Cabin is so popular that another cabin in Kokanee Glacier Provincial Park has been made available for winter bookings. The original cabin was constructed by the Violet Mine Company as a bunkhouse in the early 1920's.

The new Silver Spray Cabin is located in Clover Basin at an elevation of 2330 m above Woodbury Creek. The new 16' x 28' cabin, constructed from Douglas fir and cedar, has big windows, a porch and propane lighting, heating and cooking. It is operated the same way as the Slocan Chief Cabin, with a lottery system being used for reservations (see box to right).

Access By helicopter (Canadian, Nelson or High Terrain, Nelson) at a cost of about $150/person. Visitors normally ski out down Silver Spray Creek then along Woodbury Creek to a waiting car at Highway #31.

Skiing There is a mix of tree skiing and alpine skiing at the Silver Spray Cabin. The cabin is located above timberline so if the weather is overcast the skiing is below the cabin.

• The longest run starts from just above the hut and continues down for about 400 vertical metres into Clover Basin. This run is mostly in the trees so it is your bad weather skiing.

• Good skiing can be found in a basin southeast of Sunrise Mountain (GR 940190). The runs, however, are short (150 vertical metres).

• Another popular destination is the bowl below the Caribou Glacier (GR 926198). To reach this bowl ascend above the hut to a pass (GR 930193), round the corner to the west to the Caribou Glacier, then descend to the small lake below. The runs here are short as well (150 vertical metres).

Silver Spray Cabin

New 16' x 28' timber frame cabin with big windows and a porch.
Map 82 F/14 Slocan
Location Clover Basin above Woodbury Creek, at an elevation of 2330 m (GR 934187)
Reservations Lottery system Dec. 1-Jun. 1 through Kokanee Glacier Mountaineering, RR#1, Site 3, Comp. 32, Nelson, BC, V1L 5P4.
Capacity 8-11
Facilities Propane lighting, heating and cooking. Foam mattress. Radio for emergency communication.
Fee 187/week/person

Photo Clive Cordery

Photos: Silver Spray Cabin and nearby ski slopes. Photo Dave Campbell

TWO COLUMBIA HAUTE ROUTES
A MONASHEE TRAVERSE

Over a period of seven days in May of 1993, Ruedi Beglinger led a group across a splendid and challenging ski traverse in the Monashee Mountains. The route traversed about 25 km of icefield in the Jordan Range northwest of Revelstoke. Along the way the group made a number of ascents including Pyrite Peak (GR 887852), the main summit of Cat Peak (GR 936847), Schrund Peak (GR 923800), the 'Egg-Horn' (GR 932802), Bastion Peak (GR 901773), Glacier Peak (GR 906766), Glissade Peak (GR 921749) and the Tour Ronde (GR 906723). In addition, they enjoyed many thousands of metres of fine ski descents. This is indeed an alpine traverse and requires a high level of mountaineering skill and good judgement. It should be attempted by experienced ski mountaineers only.

A helicopter was used to access and exit this traverse. The helicopter placed food drops on its approach flight from Revelstoke, then ferried the group into the first camp at the Bourne Glacier (GR 899877) from a staging area on Highway #23, 55 km north of Revelstoke (just before the Downie Creek Loop). At the end of the traverse the group was picked up by helicopter from high in the drainage of Bews Creek (GR 900696), then flown 8 km out to Perry River.

The route travels from the drop-off point up the Bourne Glacier, traverses a saddle (GR 933847) just west of Cat Peak (20 metre rappel required), then descends to a camp (GR 952824) on the glacier at the head of the Big Eddy Creek. The route continues to a high pass (GR 929803) just east of Schrund Peak, then descends to a camp (937769) on the glacier at the head of Frisby Creek. From here the route is very complex. It begins by ascending directly south to a col (GR 928751), then traverses the southeast flank of Glissade Peak to the ridge (GR 923743) directly south of the summit. Continue south and west along the crest of the ridge, then descend steeply to a pass at the head of the Jordan River (GR 907729). Descend a steep couloir to the west, then traverse at about 1820 m to reach the upper of two lakes. From here climb a final steep couloir to a ridge (GR 893711) where the Beglinger group placed their final camp. From this point the route traversed across a steep bowl to another ridge (GR 897709), then continued out onto the south face of the Tour Ronde (GR 906723). After climbing climbed to the summit of the peak the group enjoyed a fall line ski descent of about 600 metres. It is necessary to traverse left at the 2030 m elevation for about a kilometre to avoid steep slabs before descending the drainage to the lake below.

Maps
82 M Seymour Arm (1:250,000)
82 M/1 Mount Revelstoke
82 M/2 Parry River
82 M/7 Ratchford Creek
82 M/8 Downie Creek

Reference
Beglinger, Ruedi, "The Monashee Ski Traverse", CAJ, 1994, p.96.

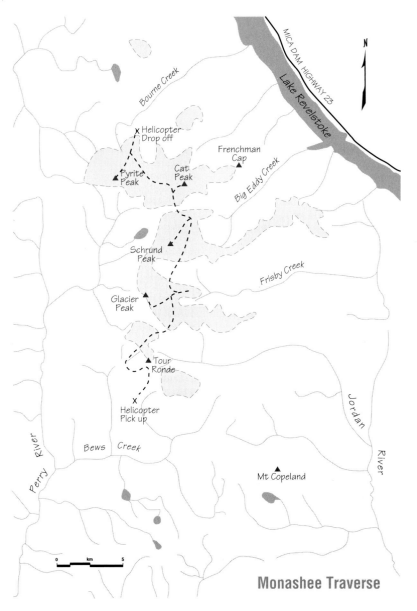

Monashee Traverse

Two Columbia Haute Routes 187

THE ADAMANT TRAVERSE

This is a tour which Ruedi Beglinger led over a period of seven days in 1994. He described it as the best traverse he has ever done (including the European Haute Route) and graded it as difficult to very difficult. The route traverses about 45 km of exceptionally wild and beautiful high alpine terrain where it is possible to make ascents of numerous peaks along the way.

This traverse is also accessed by helicopter. Ruedi and his group drove from Revelstoke up the Mica Creek Highway (Highway #23), then continued up the Goldstream River on good logging roads to the junction with Stitt Creek (near the CMH Adamant Lodge). From here a helicopter flew the group up Stitt Creek, through Austerity Pass, and dropped them off at the edge of timberline high above Austerity Creek.

On their first day the group ascended a small glacier above their camp site to a col (GR 343374), then continued to their right along a ridge to an unnamed summit (GR 346374 - known as Mount Sir William on older versions of the map). From here a ski descent down the east face took them to the glacier. The group then ascended to the south to another unnamed summit (GR 356354 - known as Enterprise by many skiers). Finally, they descended to the Granite Glacier and continued to the Fairy Meadow Hut (GR 394352).

The second day was spent touring from the Fairy Meadow Hut. An ascent was made of Ironman (GR 369320) via the Ironman/Turret Col. This is a serious alpine day with many large crevasses.

On the third day they climbed to Friendship Col (GR 406333) and on to the summit of Pioneer Peak (GR 389316). A descent down the east face took them out onto the head of the Gothics Glacier where they set up camp.

Day four required a very early start as south-facing slopes had to be negotiated. The group took a new route here, and instead of using Thor Pass, climbed to a col just south of The Gothics (GR 395308), made an ascent of The Gargoyle (GR 392307), then descended to the Adamant Glacier. They crossed the Adamant Glacier, then forgoing Azimuth Notch, climbed steeply to a high point on the ridge (GR 383287) northwest of Azimuth Notch. From here they could reach Silvertip Glacier with some

Left: At Friendship Col. Photo Chic Scott
Opposite: Crossing Granite Glacier below the Adamants. Photo Roger Laurilla

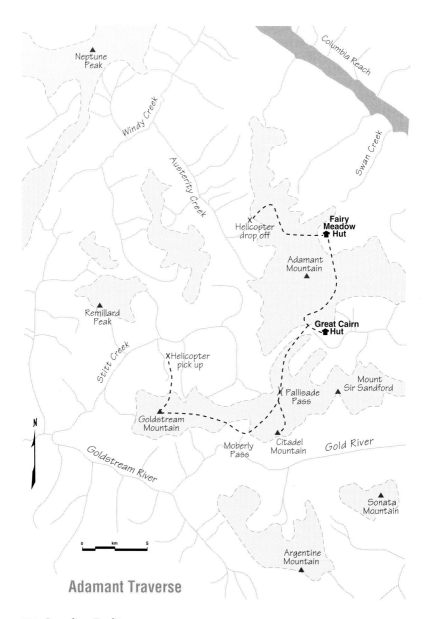

Neptune
Peak

Columbia Reach

Windy Creek

Austerity Creek

Swan Creek

X
Helicopter
drop off

**Fairy
Meadow
Hut**

Adamant
Mountain

Remillard
Peak

**Great Cairn
Hut**

Stitt Creek

X Helicopter
pick up

Mount
Sir Sandford

Pallisade
Pass

N

Goldstream
Mountain

Moberly
Pass

Citadel
Mountain

Gold River

Goldstream River

0   km   5

Sonata
Mountain

Argentine
Mountain

Adamant Traverse

At Palisade Pass looking towards Citadel Mountain (left) and Sir Sandford Pass (centre right).
Photo Chic Scott

steep climbing and descend to the Great Cairn Hut (GR 393263).

On day five the group stayed at the Great Cairn Hut and made an ascent of the Footstool (GR 422231).

Day six was a moving day again. The group ascended the Haworth Glacier, crossed Palisade Pass to the Sir Sandford Glacier, then ascended the northeast ridge of Citadel Mountain (GR 355204). The route then continued to Sir Sandford Pass and descended the heavily crevassed Goat Glacier to a campsite (GR 328196).

On the last day the group climbed to the northwest onto the Goldstream névé and continued to the summit of Goldstream Mountain (GR 268218). A last ski descent to the northeast took the group into the valley to a helicopter pick-up at an elevation of about 1670 m (GR 288248). A short flight and they were back at the CMH Adament Lodge.

Maps 82 N Golden (1:250,000)
82 N/13 Sullivan River
82 N/12 Mount Sir Sandford
82 M/9 Goldstream River

For more information on the Monashee and Adamant Traverses contact:

Ruedi Beglinger
Selkirk Mountain Experience
Box 2998,
Revelstoke, B.C.
V0E2S0
Phone: (250) 837-2381
FAX: (250) 837-4685
e-mail: selkirk@junction.net

For helicopter support contact:

Gerald Richard
Selkirk Mountain Helicopters
Phone: (250) 837-2455
FAX: (250) 837-8022

For ground transportation contact:

Revelstoke Taxi
(250) 837-4000

NELSON CLASSICS

Tours Near Whitewater Ski Resort

Whitewater Ski Resort, located about 30 minutes from Nelson, is reached by driving 11 km south on Highway #6 towards Salmo, then turning left up the access road. The resort is another 10 km along this road. The access road is steep so you should have good snow tires on your vehicle.

This area gets lots of snow and the Whitewater Resort is becoming a bit of a destination for serious 'ski bums' who are looking for steep powder. Although there are a number of tours in the immediately vicinity of the resort, I have included just three of the most popular. Two of them actually begin on lifts from the resort.

For more information on this area please refer to:

"Cross Country and Ski Touring in the West Kootenays (South)", by Trevor Holsworth. Copies can be purchased for $8 from Kootenay Experience, 306 Victoria Street, Nelson, B.C., V1L 4K4. Phone (250) 354-4441.

White Queen

Distance 4 km return
Height gain 600 m
Max elevation 2170 m
Map 82 F/6 Nelson

This is a short and pleasant tour easily reached from the ski resort.

The tour begins by riding the Silver King chairlift to an elevation of 1910 m. A one way ticket can be purchased for $5.50. From the top of the chairlift traverse out right on the packed slopes for a short distance to the top of the Little Mucker run. Then climb through trees and glades above, gaining about 100 vertical metres to a small col between White Queen and Mount Ymir (GR 907767).

Turn left and climb along a broad ridge crest. The route climbs about 50 vertical metres over a minor peak, then drops about 50 vertical metres into a notch. A final climb along a broad ridge crest, gaining 150 vertical metres over about 1 km, takes you to the summit of White Queen.

You have three descent options:

- You can follow the route of ascent back down to the ski resort.

- You can make your way northwest to Hummingbird Pass (GR 875789) by following a shallow draw on the north side of the ridge crest. From Hummingbird pass make your way back to the Whitewater Access Road by reversing the tour to Evening Ridge.

- If conditions are very stable it is possible to ski the trees and glades along the left margin of the large avalanche slope on the southwest face of White Queen. The descent begins about GR 895779, several hundred metres east of the summit of White Queen. Note that this descent is expert terrain with high avalanche potential. A good snow cover is required due to alders at the bottom of the run.

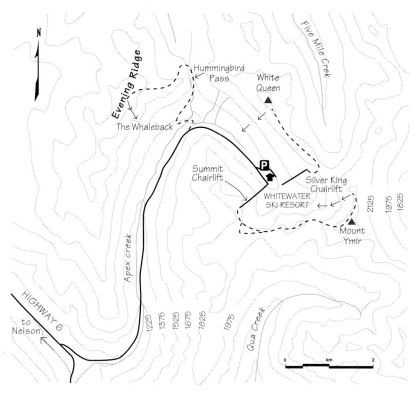

Whitewater Resort Area

Evening Ridge

Distance about 5 km
Height gain 600 m
Max elevation 2075 m
Map 82 F/6 Nelson

This is an excellent tour, and if snow conditions are stable the descent down "The Whaleback" is outstanding.

The tour to Hummingbird Pass and up Evening Ridge starts from a point about

8 km along the Whitewater Ski Resort access road (GR 876776). Immediately below the ski resort road is an old logging road which is marked accurately on the map. Follow this road which heads northeast below the Whitewater Road, then curls around almost 180 degrees. In the course of this curve it crosses Apex Creek (which descends from the ski resort) and also the small, unnamed creek coming down from Hummingbird Pass. Only several hun-

dred metres after leaving the car, the road has crossed two creeks and curved around so that you are now heading west.

The road continues west for several hundred metres without gaining any elevation, then it turns up to the right and begins to climb steeply. After gaining about 75 vertical metres, strike out right on an indistinct old mining road which can be difficult to find. Follow this old mining road through the trees, gradually climbing for about 0.5 km until the road reaches and crosses the unnamed creek draining Hummingbird Pass.

From here follow the creek bed for another 0.5 km up to Hummingbird Pass. There are some large and potentially dangerous slopes above you at one point so be aware.

Ski through the pass for about 50 m and just as the hill begins to descend on the other side near a big rock, begin to work your way up onto the left shoulder. Continue working your way up the hillside, heading back south. Gain about 150 vertical metres up to the crest of the ridge. Along here you are in open glades which makes for excellent, safe skiing. Once you reach the crest of the ridge (GR 875785), simply follow it along for another 100 vertical metres up to the first summit (GR 871784).

Here you should reassess snow stability and decide whether or not to continue. If conditions are unsafe return the way you came. However, if conditions are safe you can continue up to Evening Ridge proper and consider skiing 'The Whaleback'. From the first summit descend about 75 vertical metres then continue climbing up to the west, gaining about 150 vertical metres to GR 862782.

From this point a superb 700 vertical metre descent called 'The Whaleback' leads down to Apex creek. This ski descent takes you into 'big country' and is surrounded by avalanche terrain. You must find your way carefully and skilfully.

The descent follows a broad rounded ridge which shows up on the map as a large white area. The upper Whaleback is open and rounded with a few trees. To either side are the steep start zones of major avalanche paths. The middle section of the Whaleback offers some tree skiing where you must pick your way through openings and glades for a short distance. At the bottom the descent opens up again and there is terrific skiing all the way down to Apex Creek.

Climb a short distance up the hillside on the other side of Apex Creek to the road, then walk back to your car.

Mount Ymir

Distance about 6 km
Height gain 720 m
Max elevation 2380 m
Map 82 F/6 Nelson

The highly recommended tour up Mount Ymir yields an excellent summit with good views followed by a fine ski descent. The tour does offers some avalanche risk and you must also be careful of cornices.

Begin the tour by taking a ride up the Summit Chairlift (a single ride ticket can be purchased for $5.50). From the top of the chairlift descend the packed run down to the left for about 100 m to the start of the traverse out into Catch Basin.

Traverse out into Catch Basin and continue traversing to reach the west ridge of Mount Ymir at GR 895753. Alternatively you can climb steeply above for about 100 vertical metres in a southerly direction to reach the west ridge of

Mount Ymir at about 2060 m (GR 888754). From here you descend to the east for about 75 vertical metres to reach the point where the Catch Basin traverse reaches the ridge.

The route then follows the west ridge of Mount Ymir up to the summit. It climbs fairly easily over treed slopes, gaining about 150 vertical metres and crossing a small bump (GR 902755). The route then descends about 50 vertical metres into another notch where you get a good view to the left out into Ymir Bowl.

The final climb of 270 vertical metres to the summit is steep. The routefinding is complicated by many steep wind rolls, very dangerous cornices on your left and towards the top a large, steep and potentially dangerous slope on your right. Good routefinding skills are required for climbing this section. After the first 150 vertical metres of steep ascent the angle eases somewhat.

Mount Ymir from the summit of White Queen. The route ascends the righthand ridge to the summit. The descent route follows the lefthand ridge for a short distance, then descends the bowl below the summit. Photo Chic Scott

From the summit the best descent is down the north ridge for about 75 vertical metres into a notch (GR 915760), then down left into Ymir Basin. Note that there are three ridges converging on the summit and you want to descend the north ridge, not the east ridge. In poor visibility there is potential for a mistake here.

The initial descent down the north ridge is done on foot for a short distance until you can put your skis on and continue to the pass. The 600 vertical-metre descent to the ski resort down Ymir Bowl is outstanding. The skiing is open, set at a good angle all the way and the slope is north facing. It is, however, potential avalanche terrain so use caution.

The area in and around Stagleap Provincial Park, which is located at the summit of Kootenay Pass, offers excellent ski touring. The area gets a heavy snowfall and deep powder snow is the norm. The runs are not long but access from the road is quick.

Highway #3 between Salmo and Creston passes directly through the pass and there is an avalanche control program operating to keep the highway open. The road is often closed for short periods of time while they shoot down avalanches with 105 mm artillery. You should be aware of some rules and operating procedures associated with this avalanche control program. The following information is taken from the brochure: "Safety During Avalanche Control at Kootenay Pass".

- There is a sign posted at the Bridal Lake parking lot which provides information about the avalanche control program and identifies areas which are hazardous to back country users during explosive control.

- The area north of the highway will be closed without notice to backcountry recreation during avalanche control activity.

- At these times the Caribou Loop trail and slopes above and around Bridal Lake will also be closed to the public.

- While avalanche control is underway or anticipated, the gate at the trail head will be closed.

- Observe the avalanche closure gate at the Bridal Lake parking lot and other backcountry access points.

- Avoid the hazardous areas identified in the brochure and on the public information sign; avalanche control can commence without warning at any time.

- Use the areas on the south side of the highway when the park north of the highway is closed.

- If you are unsure about safe access to the park, contact the Ministry of Transportation and Highways Regional Radio Room at (604) 354-6742 for current road and weather conditions.

Skiing at Kootenay Pass

Most of the good skiing is located north of the highway. Two of the finest runs are located on the east flank of what are known locally as Buz's Ridge and Wolf Ridge. These descents are about 400 and 500 vertical metres respectively, and the approaches to both runs are reasonably short. These are only two of the classic runs. There is, of course, plenty of other good skiing in the area

The skiing south of the highway is of the touring variety although there are many possibilities for short ski descents. A nice idea is to ski up to Ripple Cabin for the night and do a little touring at the same time.

The map for all the tours described in this book is 82 F/3 Salmo.

Looking across Kootenay Pass towards Cornice Ridge (centre). Buz's Ridge is to the right of Cornice Ridge.
Photo Dave Smith

Wolf Ridge

Distance 10 km return
Height gain 700 m
Max elevation 2150 m
Map 82 F/3 Salmo

Park at a plowed parking area on the north side of the highway about 5 km east of the summit of the pass. The approach to Wolf Ridge follows along a logging road/power line heading back up the unnamed valley to the west. Follow this road for several kilometres but as you approach Lost Creek Pass do not attempt to climb steeply along the power line route. Instead, take a line more to the north, roughly along the gas transmission line shown on the map. Climb over a small summit (GR 964372), then continue north up the crest to the summit of Wolf Ridge (GR 960379).

There is an excellent descent down the east flank of Wolf Ridge back into the unnamed valley. Return to your car via the road and power line.

Cornice Ridge/Buz's Ridge

Distance 3 km return
Height gain 360 m
Max Elevation 2120 m
Map 82 F/3 Salmo

Park at Bridal Lake Parking area at the summit of the pass. Start at the warming hut. Do not continue if the avalanche closure gate is down. Work your way up the steep hillside above the lake to reach the ridge at about GR 968343. This ridge is called Cornice Ridge on the map but to all the locals and to the avalanche control team it is known as NoName Ridge. Continue climbing along the ridge, passing over a small summit. Descend into a col then climb to the crest of Buz's ridge (GR 963355).

The descent to the southeast from the summit of Buz's ridge is avalanche terrain and considered an expert run. If you want a more mellow descent you can start from the col between Cornice Ridge and Buz's Ridge (GR 960351). Both these descents finish straight down the drainage to the highway.

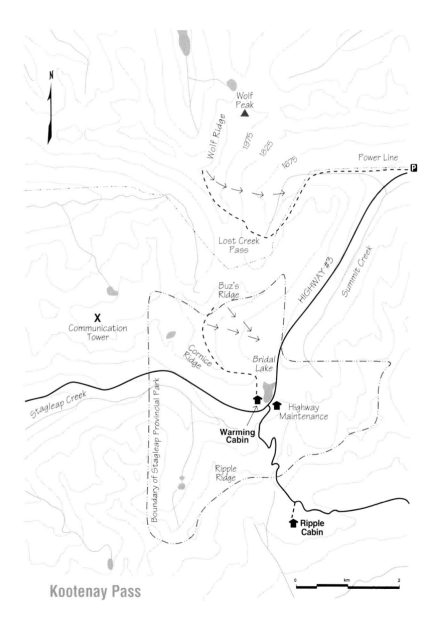

Kootenay Pass

Ripple Cabin

Distance 2.5 km to the hut one way
Height gain 200 m
Max elevation 1970 m
Map 82 F/3 Salmo

This is an easy overnight touring destination. At the moment there are two cabins. However, this may change in the future. The older cabin, built and maintained by the Creston Nordic Ski Club, has a stove and bunks for about twenty. Its future is in doubt at the moment. The BC Forest Service has built a new cabin which sleeps about six. Unfortunately, it is not adequate for the usage the area gets.

Park at the Bridal Lake Parking area. Cross the highway and head up the road/trail to the south. This trail is a wide road which climbs steadily for 2 km to a pass. At this point you leave Stagleap Provincial Park. From the pass continue for about 300 m along the road. Just as the road turns to the left and begins to descend steeply, break off to the right along a trail through the trees and continue along the crest for a short distance to the Ripple Cabins.

There is good touring in the vicinity of the cabins. From the pass it is pleasant to ski to the southwest along the crest of Ripple Ridge towards what is called Lightning Strike on the map. To return to your car, rather than ski back along the road a nice variation is to traverse below Baldy Rocks towards The Crags, ski through a pass (GR 986331), descend into a basin, then work around the corner back to Bridal Lake.

For more information on this area refer to: "Cross Country and Ski Touring in the West Kootenays (South)", by Trevor Holsworth. Copies can be purchased for $8 from Kootenay Experience, 306 Victoria Street, Nelson, B.C., V1L 4K4. Phone (250) 354-4441.

Other tours near Nelson

Mount Brennan

Distance 8 km
Height gain 1880 m
Max elevation 2280 m
Map Roseberry 82 K/3

This is a major ski ascent with a tremendous amount of relief. It is recommended that the trip be done over two days so that you can time your passage through exposed areas for early in the day. Good skiing can be found on the descent but it is possible in the springtime to find some difficult skiing conditions as well.

On Highway #31A between Kaslo and New Denver is the small settlement of Retallack. This is where the tour begins. A plowed turnout where you can leave your vehicle will be found just east of town on the south side of the highway .

Follow a logging road which begins at GR 898432 right in Retallack. Ski behind the old abandoned mine buildings, then travel west for a short distance before you curve around and head back east. There is quite a maze of these logging roads and you should follow the BC Forest Service signs for Lyle Creek which are posted at the junctions. Follow these logging and mining roads

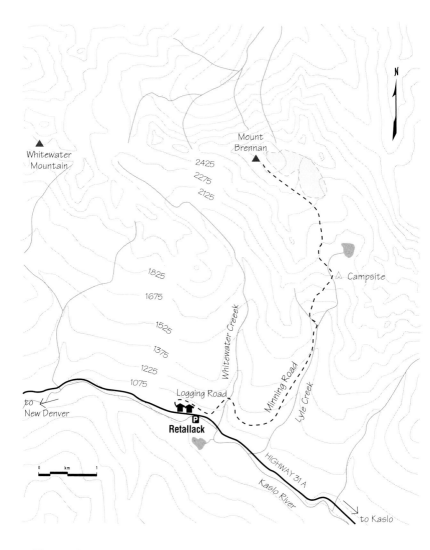

Mount Brennan

Mount Brennan offers a terrific ski descent. Lyle Peak in the background. Photo Paul Heikkila

back to the east, crossing the drainage of Whitewater Creek, then curve around a shoulder to enter the drainage of Lyle Creek. The first 4 km of this tour follows good roads with posted signs but at GR 924447 the road fades and you find yourself below a steep headwall. You want to reach this point quite early in the day so you can climb the headwall while it is safe.

The route ascends a treed ramp, threatened by avalanche slopes the entire way, that climbs up and right to the top of the headwall.

At the top of the headwall there is a lovely camp site overlooking the valley, not far from a small lake (GR 927458). It is a good idea to spend the night here in order to avoid poor late afternoon snow conditions.

Above the campsite there is another headwall to climb. Though short, it presents avalanche hazard. Most groups ascend a gully (GR 925462) for about 150 vertical metres.

From here route choices abound and a moderate ascent offering no serious difficulties takes you to the summit. Simply work your way northwest over open terrain to the peak.

Commonwealth Peak

Distance 16 km round trip
Height gain 1545 m
Max elevation 2340 m
Map 82 F/6 Nelson

Commonwealth Peak is another popular tour in the Nelson area. This is a long trip so give yourself plenty of time.

Between Nelson and the town of Ymir along Highway #6 is a small settlement called Porto Rico (GR 825640). This is the starting point for a long and interesting tour to Commonwealth Peak. Park in a plowed turn-around area on the west side of the highway, about 100 m north of the highway bridge over Barrett Creek.

Begin by following a road for 3 km along the north side of Barrett Creek, then at GR 799638 turn north on a road along Lost Creek. The Lost Creek Road climbs steeply for about 600 vertical metres up to the ridge crest overlooking Keno Creek (GR 798670). From here, the road turns west, climbs up the ridge, then traverses over to Lost Lake (GR 777668).

Looking from upper Barrett Creek towards Commonwealth Peak. Ascent route follows the righthand skyline ridge. Photo John Carter

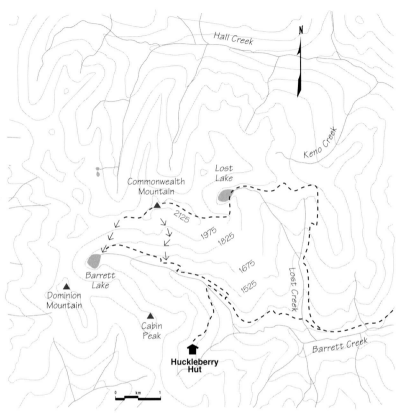

Commonwealth

The route now ascends the east ridge of Commonwealth Peak above Lost Lake. Use caution as there is some avalanche hazard in the lower section of the climb. An ascent of about 370 vertical metres from the lake takes you to the summit of the peak.

You can then traverse the peak to a sub-peak (GR 758664). From here you can descend southeast down excellent ski slopes for about 250 vertical metres until it begins to get steep. Traverse a short distance out to the right to slightly easier terrain, then descend steeply through the trees for another 250 vertical metres to the Barrett Creek Road. (As an alternative you can traverse farther along the summit ridge to about GR 751663, then descend somewhat easier terrain down to Barrett Lake).

You will most likely find the road along Barrett Creek packed by snowmobile tracks which makes for a fast trip back to your waiting car.

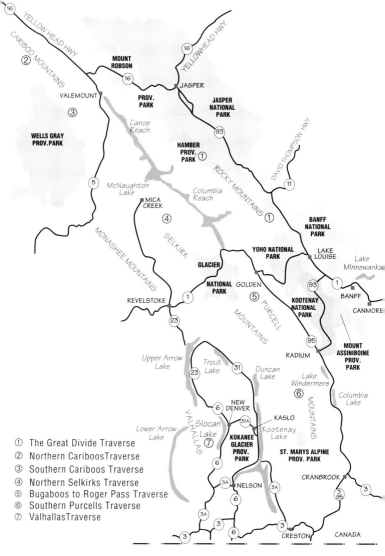

① The Great Divide Traverse
② Northern Cariboos Traverse
③ Southern Cariboos Traverse
④ Northern Selkirks Traverse
⑤ Bugaboos to Roger Pass Traverse
⑥ Southern Purcells Traverse
⑦ Valhallas Traverse

UNITED STATES

the Grand Traverses

Western Canada has a number of wilderness ski traverses which cross the icefields of the Rockies, Selkirks, Purcells, Cariboos and Valhallas. These traverses have been pioneered over the last 40 years and are gradually becoming more and more popular. Some of them are now done every year.

They are major ski adventures, up to 300 km in length, and present the problems of any large expedition. Thankfully, they do not involve the hassles associated with expeditions to foreign lands. The problems to be dealt with here are only those presented by the mountains themselves.

In this section seven of these traverses are described. To begin with there are some general tips on how to successfully complete one of these adventures, then each trip is described in detail complete with a little history and some planning notes specific to each traverse.

Good luck if you attempt one of these 'Grand Traverses'. Do not take them lightly; they are major undertakings. While you do not have to be an expert mountaineer or a super skier to complete a traverse, you must be well organized, experienced and committed.

Equipment

Most everyone who has skied these traverses has used a Nordic style backcountry ski with a cable binding and a sturdy pair of backcountry touring boots.

This type of equipment has been found to be lighter than the randonee skis and plastic boots, but still provides adequate control for the downhills. Remember that you will be skiing with a heavy pack many miles from the highway and getting down the hill safely and cautiously will be the goal, not aggressive turns. In addition, the large majority of the time you are ascending or traversing long icefields and wilderness valleys. Downhill skiing makes up a relatively small percentage of the trip.

Be prepared to deal with winter conditions and temperatures of perhaps minus 20°C. Tents and sleeping bags should be of high quality and should be very comfortable because you may have to wait out bad weather for long periods of time.

Planning

Meticulous planning is the key to a successful expedition. If all your gear functions well, if the food caches are properly placed and if you know the route well, then it is simply a matter of several weeks of enjoyable skiing. Of course, you must have some luck with the weather, but given a normal season you can expect to ski about two days out of three. If you look individually at each day then it's not too difficult. It is just a matter of putting a lot of these days together.

You should study the route in detail beforehand, using maps, air photos and any written reports available. If possible talk to someone who has done the trip. The better you know the route the more confident you will feel and the easier it will all seem. Know your escape routes in the event of an emergency.

Begin planning as early as possible and try to come up with a compatible team of friends. Four is a good number–any less and the trail breaking could be difficult.

Previous page: The Northern Cariboos Traverse. Ascending the Niagara Glacier. Photo Scott Duncan

Pay great attention to weight of your equipment and try to keep your pack as light as possible.

The best time to tackle any of these traverses is late April when the days are long, sunny and warm. However, they have also been successfully completed in both March and May. To a great extent, how late you can travel depends on how heavy the snowfall has been the previous winter. These traverses are definitely not advised in January and February when it is dark, cold and the snow is very powdery.

Place your caches very carefully with an eye to animals and ease of location. Food should be placed inside plastic bags which are themselves inside 5 gallon pails. The pails should then be taped shut. Caches should be hung high in a tree near some well defined landmark. Put a piece of flagging around the tree. If you do lose a cache you are in real trouble and will probably have to abort your trip.

As a general rule travel only when there is good visibility. During whiteouts it is best to sit in your tent, read and rest. Travelling by map and compass is difficult, very slow and the possibility of errors is high.

Steve Smith and Friends

Over the years a number of ski mountaineers have put a great deal of energy into skiing these great traverses. Donnie Gardner was an early pioneer as were Dave Smith and Ron Robinson. A second wave of adventurers including Bob Saunders, Mel Hines, Errol Smith, Phil Smith and Scott Duncan skied many of the 'Grand Traverses' through the late 1970's and 1980's However no one has shown greater dedication and commitment to these traverses than Steve Smith. Over a brief period of seven years he skied almost all of them, some twice and in addition completed some other outstanding ski adventures. The following is a summary of Steve's achievements during this very active period.

- 1977 the Southern Rockies Traverse (Columbia Icefield to Lake Louise).
- Over two seasons (1977 and 1978) the Bugaboos to Rogers Pass Traverse with Errol Smith (no relation), Mel Hines and Bob Saunders.
- 1978 the Northern Rockies Traverse (Jasper to the Columbia Icefield) with his brother Phil and Scott Duncan.
- 1979 over a period of 49 days Steve and his companions skied to Mount Logan pulling sleds, climbed the mountain, circumnavigated the mountain, then skied out to civilization. He was joined on this trip by Bob Saunders, Mel Hines, and Errol Smith. (Note this was the first time since 1925 that Mount Logan was climbed without air support.)
- 1980 the Southern Rockies Traverse (Columbia Icefield to Lake Louise) with Phil, Scott, Archie Ellis and Mark Dahlie.
- 1981 the Northern Selkirks Traverse with Phil and Scott.
- 1982 the Southern Purcells Traverse with Bob Saunders.
- 1982 the Northern Cariboos Traverse with Phil and Scott.
- 1983 the Southern Cariboos Traverse with Bob Saunders.

Photos on page 210: Alf Skrastins climbing to the Gilmour Glacier from Tete Creek (Southern Cariboos Traverse). Photo Tony Daffern
Left inset: Descending Butters Creek (Bugaboos to Rogers Pass Traverse). Photo Steve Smith
Right inset: Grass skiing (Northern Selkirks Traverse). Photo Chic Scott

Steve Smith and friends

Bob Saunders (left) and Mel Hines.

Errol Smith. Photo Chic Scott

Top: left to right Phil Smith, Steve Smith, Scott Duncan. Photo Tom Duchastel

Steve Smith and friends

Ron Robinson. Photo Chic Scott
Top: Dave Smith. Photo Chic Scott

Chic Scott. Photo Don Gardner
Top: Don Gardner. Photo Chic Scott

It's not all skiing!

THE GREAT DIVIDE TRAVERSE
JASPER TO LAKE LOUISE

Along the crest of the Rockies between the Yellowhead Pass and the Kickinghorse Pass stretches a wilderness of ice. There are nine icefields, each of which is surrounded by a sea of glistening peaks and separated by deep valleys filled with forests of spruce, fir and pine. Luckily, all of this beautiful mountain paradise is protected as national park. There are almost no roads, hotels, parking lots, clear cuts or huts. It is still almost real wilderness.

There is a line which connects these icefields into one beautiful and adventurous ski traverse. It has been skied in its entirety twice, in 1967 and in 1987, and in both cases the trip took 21 days. The northern half of this traverse from Jasper to the Columbia Icefields has been done perhaps half a dozen times. The southern half, from the Columbia Icefields to the Kickinghorse Pass has been done

perhaps 15-20 times and, in fact, has been done twice as a guided trip.

The traverse was conceived and first attempted in 1954 by a group from Eastern Canada. They made extensive preparations for their attempt, but when they actually came to grips with the adventure they progressed only a short distance before they realized the magnitude of what they were undertaking, and called it quits. However they had sowed the seed and started a great dream.

"Let us get our skis ready, our minds set on a great adventure and travel through a mountain range with huge glaciers and snowfields, wonderful powder snow and long ski runs. Mind you, there are no overnight shelters and no places to buy food along the way. We have to carry everything on our backs. It is not as difficult and strange as it may seem." Hans Gmoser

Hans Gmoser and team on the Lyell Icefield, 1960. Photo Phillip Delesalle

In April of 1960, ski adventurer and mountain guide Hans Gmoser attempted the route. This time the team was strong and experienced—Neil Brown, Kurt Lukas, Pierre Garneau, Pat Boswell and Philip Delesalle. Despite meticulous preparations they still managed to cover only the southern half of the traverse, as far as the Columbia Icefield, and it took them 25 days at that. After days of storm, lost food caches and deep trail breaking, the group abandoned their attempt.

They had, however, inspired another young skier, Don Gardner. Don began dreaming and planning for an attempt of his own some day. Seven years later, in May of 1967 Don led his group successfully along the full length of the traverse. His team was composed of Charlie Locke, Neil Liske and Chic Scott.

For seven months before attempting the traverse, this group had prepared carefully, studying every detail of the route on air photos and maps. Of particular note was their use of Nordic touring equipment which had to be purchased directly from Norway. This expedition awakened in many others the potential for Nordic skis above tree line and most subsequent high glacier traverses have been done on this type of equipment.

The traverse has since been repeated only once in its entirety despite a number of attempts. On this occasion the group was made up of Peter Tucker, Rory MacIntosh, Steve Langley and Charlie Eckenfelder.

This traverse is indeed one of the great ski adventures in the world. Because there are virtually no huts and the national parks prohibit helicopter landings, it should remain so. It is a trip that requires good planning and organization, and an experienced, strong and committed team. It is a good way to have a major adventure for a minimum of expense and hassle. Simply place your food caches and go.

Hans Gmoser and team ascending the Lambe Glacier, 1960. Photo Phillip Delesalle

**The First Traverse
Party of 1967**

Top: Neil Liske, Charlie Locke, Chic Scott.
Inset: Charlie Locke, Neil Liske and Chic
Scott at Fortress Cabin.

Bottom: left to right Don Gardner, Chic Scott,
Neil Liske, Charlie Locke at Castleguard River.
All photos taken by Don Gardner in 1967

Length of the traverse about 300 km
Vertical height gain 10,000 m
Approximate time 20-30 days

The traverse is normally skied from north to south and is described so here. It is not described in great detail as it is presumed that only experienced ski mountaineers will attempt the route and they will be able to work out the fine points for themselves.

In 1967 the group approached the Hooker Icefield up the Whirlpool River. Two and one half days of valley skiing brought them to the toe of the Scott Glacier. However, a more aesthetic line would begin via the Tonquin Valley. You could ascend Portal Creek or the Astoria River, and after a break at the Wates-Gibson Hut continue south by one of several routes into the Whirlpool River valley.

In 1974 a group did just this. They reached the Wates-Gibson Hut via the Astoria River, then continued south up the Eremite Valley and over an unnamed Pass (GR 183315) into the drainage of the Whirlpool River. In 1991 another party skied an even more direct line. They reached the Tonquin Valley via Portal Creek and Maccarib Pass, then continued south. They first crossed the Fraser Glacier and descended into Simon Creek. They found this quite reasonable except for a narrow, treed canyon about 3 km long in Simon Creek. They then turned south again at GR 172255, crossed an unnamed pass (GR 188214) and descended into the Middle Whirlpool River. This section went well and the descent was good. Finally, they climbed from the Middle Whirlpool River up an unnamed creek to cross a shoulder at GR 212155. The shoulder was crossed just about 0.5 km south-

west of a small pass. They then descended the drainage on the far side to the gravel flats of the Whirlpool Valley where it joins the 1967 route at Scott Creek.

The Scott Glacier is ascended to reach the Hooker Icefield. In 1967 a moraine along the east margin offered easy access onto the glacier, but this has now changed and easy access is no longer the case. The 1991 party found the moraine breached by a gully so it is now necessary to climb directly up under seracs of the Scott Glacier, then work your way up left, climbing steeply up the moraine until you can gain the glacier above. The Hooker Icefield is crossed in a southerly direction and the south slopes of Serenity Mountain traversed to reach the Serenity Glacier which the 1967 party descended to reach the Wood River. The 1991 party descended directly into the Wood River valley in a southwest direction from Serenity Mountain, aiming for the Clemenceau Icefield, but they found the descent extremely difficult and got into steep cliffs and rappels.

The 1967 party then ascended the Wood River, crossed Fortress Lake and followed the Chaba River to the toe of the East Chaba Glacier. The East Chaba Glacier itself is extremely broken, but you can avoid the difficulty by climbing a small glacier just to the east (GR 533848) to reach a pass just east of Chaba Peak (GR 551833). From there, easy travel in a southeasterly direction across flat icefields leads to a small col (GR 616780) several kilometres west of Mount King Edward. There are several little passes here; take the one farthest left.

An alternative way to reach this point is to descend the Wood River for several kilometres to the west from its junction with Serenity Creek, staying on the right bank. Then turn south (GR 340988) and ascend Clemenceau Creek to reach the Clemenceau Icefield. (There may be difficulties crossing to the south side of the Wood River.) Both the Smith party of 1974 and the Enagonio party of 1991 ascended Clemenceau Creek along the east flank about 100 vertical metres above the creek itself. Higher up, you get out of the trees and travelling becomes good. You can now make a side trip to the Lawrence Grassi Hut to rest for a few days and perhaps pick up a food cache. To reach the hut ascend the Tusk Glacier, cross the Tusk névé, descend to the Cummins Glacier and continue to the hut which is located on Cummins Ridge at GR 320813.

After a few days of eating and resting at the hut the traverse continues by crossing the Clemenceau Icefield in a southeasterly direction to rejoin the 1967 route. Begin by retracing your steps across the Cummins Glacier and the Tusk Glacier to reach the Clemenceau Glacier. Climb the Clemenceau Glacier along the left flank, then cross a pass about 1 km south of Apex Mountain (GR 443844). Continue skiing east to another small pass (GR 488830) which is not obvious from below. This puts you above the head of the East Chaba Glacier.

Descend easily out onto the névé and continue in an easterly direction under the south flank of Chaba Peak. Ascend to a pass southeast of Chaba Peak (GR 550828). On the east side of this pass there is a cliff band which it is necessary to rappel. There are several pitons in place for anchors. A 25-metre rappel

Crossing the Clemenceau Icefield. Photo Doug McConnery

takes you down the cliff band but leaves you on steep snow above a bergschrund from where you must downclimb. The 1991 party found that a 50-metre rappel took them over the bergschrund as well, but the same party a year later in 1992 found that the bergschrund was lower and even a 50-metre rappel left them above the bergschrund which necessitated some steep down climbing to reach easier ground. At this point the variation across the Clemenceau Icefields joins the 1967 route again.

From the col west of Mount King Edward (GR 616780) continue traversing southeast under the slopes of Mount King Edward towards Mount Columbia. From here the 1967 party descended into the head of the Bush River directly south of Mount Columbia (GR 697715). They then descended the creek a short distance and climbed with difficulty back up through steeply wooded slopes on the east side of the creek to reach alpine meadows above. From here they worked their way back up northeast to reach a small col on the long ridge which descends southeast of Mount Columbia (either GR 728714 or 725731). They crossed the col and descended to the glacier which flows out of the Columbia Icefields into the head of Bryce Creek. They ascended this glacier back up in a northerly direction to reach the main body of the Columbia Icefield. Most parties have since followed this route.

A group in 1992 managed to find a way to traverse directly across to the Columbia Icefields high above the head of the Bush River. The route is quite technical and requires good weather and excellent snow stability. The route is described in detail in the 1992 CAJ.

Gaining the Columbia Icefield from the west. Mount Castleguard to left. Photo Don Gardner.

Escape! When you are way back on the west side of Mount Columbia you are very remote and escape in the event of bad weather or injury is a real problem. The 1991 party were forced to descend logging roads to the west and were eventually picked up and taken to civilization. These logging roads have penetrated the valley and have reached a point high on the ridge south of Mount Columbia between the two forks of the upper Bush River at an approximate Grid Reference of 708676. Remember, it is about 125 km to the Trans-Canada Highway along these logging roads and about 50-60 km to the logging camp at Bush Harbour!

Once on the main névé of the Columbia Icefield traverse east, descend into the big dip then climb back out again onto the centre of the icefield. Turn south and continue traversing around the west side of Mount Castleguard. Descend the Castleguard Glacier. At the edge of treeline it is best to work out right onto steep treed slopes and descend these to the Castleguard River. Do not attempt to follow the creek itself into the valley.

Continue easily down the Castleguard River along open gravel flats until the river becomes enclosed by cliffs. Then, ski up onto the right bank and continue through the trees. Turn the corner to the right into the headwaters of the Alexandra River and camp on the edge of the trees before the open gravel flats.

Cross the gravel flats and round a small lake to the toe of the East Alexandra Glacier. Begin the mammoth ascent on the right. Climb up a short distance then traverse left to gain the glacier. You are exposed here to serac fall for a short time.

Once on the glacier climb straight up, negotiating crevasses where necessary, then cross the flat bench towards the upper icefall which is negotiated well to the right near the edge of the rocks. Above the steep section work your way out left onto another flat bench, negotiating crevasses where necessary. Then continue up the centre of the glacier to the col between Mount Farbus and Mount Lyell (GR 918559).

Remove your skis and climb directly above the col for about 150 vertical metres. Once you reach the bench above and the angle lays back, put on your skis and continue the ascent. Angle out left around Lyell 3 (Ernest Peak) to reach the Lyell 2-3 col (GR 933562).

This climb is a major crux of the traverse and unless you have been there before it is almost impossible to negotiate in a whiteout. Because the climb reaches 3380 m it is often in the clouds. You are advised to have a good cache of food, complete with some goodies, at the bottom of the ascent. Then, if necessary, you can relax in comfort until visibility is good.

From the Lyell 2-3 col, descend onto the icefield below. There are some crevasses straight down so traverse out right to avoid them. Cross the Lyell Icefield in a southeasterly direction towards Division Mountain. To get around Division Mountain also requires reasonable visibility as there are some slopes with avalanche potential. From the edge of the Lyell Icefield climb for a short distance along the ridge of Division Mountain. Descend the steep slopes to the west where appropriate, then traverse south to gain the Mons Icefield.

The Alexandra Glacier. This 2000 m ascent is a major crux of the traverse.
Photo Richard Priddy

The Mons Icefield and Mons Peak.
Photo Alf Skrastins

Cross the Mons Icefield in a southeasterly direction, then continue east onto the West Glacier to a small col (GR 017442) above the valley between Golden Eagle Peak and Cambrai Mountain. The descent from here follows steep snow slopes for about 75 vertical metres, then descends over a steep cliff to easy ground below. On the right as you descend you will find two bolts on a large ledge near the top of the cliff. From here to the snow at the bottom of the cliff is 50 vertical metres. You can continue farther down the snow gully to the very edge of the cliff where several pitons will be found. The drop from here is 25 vertical metres (see photo).

From the bottom of the cliff it is a pleasant ski descent for quite a distance to the edge of treeline. However, the final descent to the valley floor is steep, difficult tree bashing.

Looking up at the rappel from the Mons Icefield. Photo Doug McConnery

Turn west and ski up Forbes Creek to just short of Bush Pass. Turn south and climb up into a high bowl. At the top of the bowl it is necessary to take off your skis and climb steeply for about 150 vertical metres to Niverville Col (GR 034377). Descend easily out onto the Freshfield Icefield. In the event of unstable snow conditions this steep and potentially dangerous climb can be avoided by skiing down Forbes Creek to the east for 8 km, then turning the corner to the right and climbing back up onto the icefield via the Freshfield Glacier.

Cross the Freshfields in a southeasterly direction towards Mount Lambe, then climb up the southwest facing slopes to the col just west of this peak at GR 119317. This climb offers serious avalanche potential and should best be done early in the day. Round Lambe Mountain to the north, then turn back south to reach the Lambe Glacier which is descended easily. However, it is often tricky to negotiate the crevasses and steep slopes at the toe of the glacier.

Once off the glacier, descend easily down open slopes. Near tree line work your way out right onto sparsely treed slopes until forced to descend into the Blaeberry Valley. Continue down the valley, thrashing through the alders along the left bank until you reach the junction with Wildcat Creek. A logging road and clearcuts will be found here.

The climb up Wildcat Creek begins easily up a logging road. However, after a large clear-cut the road ends. Carry on straight ahead along a trail near the creek for a short distance until it crosses a bridge over the stream to the right bank. Soon the trail begins to climb very steeply through the trees (blazes on the trees) up to the base of a rock cliff. Traverse under the cliff and around the corner to gain easier ground. Continue

climbing through the forest, following a bit of a trail to reach Mistaya Lodge (GR 254274) on the shores of a small lake. Unless prior arrangements have been made it will not be possible to stay here (see page 280).

From Mistaya Lodge climb easily up the Baker Glacier to the col between Mount Baker and Trapper Peak. Below you stretches the Wapta Icefields. Descend out onto the Wapta and continue via the Balfour Hut and the Scott Duncan Hut to Kickinghorse Pass at the Trans-Canada Highway. Refer to page 32 for route descriptions to the Wapta Icefields.

Another route to the Wapta Icefields from the Blaeberry River was found by the 1987 party. After descending the Lambe Glacier and Lambe Creek to the junction with the Blaeberry River, turn left upstream for a short distance. Then

Chic Scott and Charlie Locke climbing to Niverville Col in 1967. Photo Neil Liske

Top: Crossing the Freshfield Icefield.   Photo Doug McConnery
Bottom: Camped on the Wapta Icefields.   Photo Clive Cordery

from a point midway between Lambe Creek and Ebon Creek climb up onto the east flank of the valley above the Blaeberry. The terrain soon becomes rolling benches with open forest and the travelling is very pleasant. The route traverses southeast at an elevation of about 1880 m, crosses Breaker Creek, then continues at about the same elevation south to Parapet Creek.

Ascend Parapet Creek to the east, climbing up to 2575 m on the shoulder of a peak (GR 258329) then traverse out south onto the head of the Barbette Glacier. Cross the Barbette Glacier, contouring to keep your altitude in a southeast direction to reach a col northeast of Barbette Mountain (GR 283307). Cross the pass onto the Delta Glacier. Note that the steep terrain indicated by the contour lines on the map does not exist and the way onto the Delta Glacier is very easy. Cross the Delta Glacier, skiing southeast to Cauldron Lake. From Cauldron Lake contour around the shoulder at about 2360 m elevation to reach the Peyto Glacier. Note that this is a dangerous traverse and an avalanche on this shoulder would carry you over large cliffs. Extreme caution is advised.

On the Wapta Icefields you follow the Wapta Traverse to West Louise Lodge on the Trans-Canada Highway at Kickinghorse Pass (see page 47).

Treat yourself to a beer at the hotel.

Planning Notes
Possible placements for caches are:

- Inside the Lawrence Grassi Hut on the Clemenceau Icefield
- If the above is not possible, ski up the Athabasca and Chaba Rivers to Fortress Lake and leave a cache at the junction of Serenity Creek and the Wood River.

- On the edge of the forest below the East Alexandra Glacier (put some goodies in this one in the event of a long stay).

Additional places for caches could be Forbes Creek or the Blaeberry River.

Maps
1:50,000
83 D/16 Jasper
83 D/9 Amethyst Lakes
83 D/8 Athabasca Pass
83 C/5 Fortress Lake
83 C/4 Clemenceau Icefield
83 C/3 Columbia Icefield
82 N/14 Rostrum Peak
82 N/15 Mistaya Lake
82 N/10 Blaeberry River
82 N/9 Hector Lake
82 N/8 Lake Louise

1:250,000
83D Canoe River
83C Brazeau
82N Golden

Further reference
Gmoser, H.: "High-level Ski Route From Lake Louise to Jasper", Canadian Alpine Journal, 1961, p 1.

Scott, C.: "The Great Canadian High Level Ski Tours", Canadian Alpine Journal, 1978, p 1.

Scott, C.: "Odyssey in the Canadian Icefields", Nordic World, Volume 7, No. 6, February, 1979, p 36.

Scott, C.: "High Level Ski Tours", Polar Circus, Volume 1, 1986, p 15.

Trouillot, Eric: "Heads or Trial", Canadian Alpine journal, 1992, p.68.

Enagonio, B.: "Rethinking the Clemenceau Icefield Traverse", Canadian Alpine Journal, 1993, p. 93.

Scott, C.: "Across the Great Divide: The Rockies Icefields Traverse", Alberta Nordic Skier, 1993-94, p. 10.

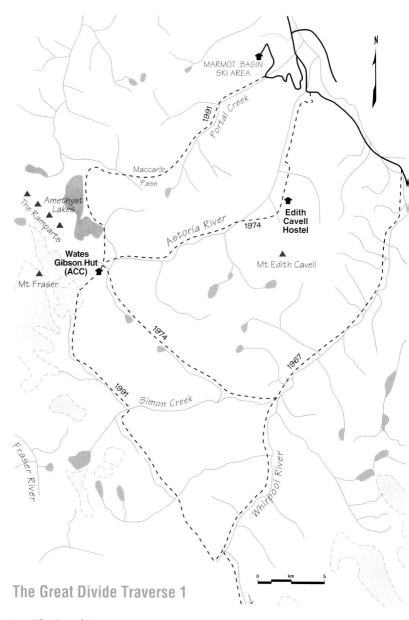

The Great Divide Traverse 1

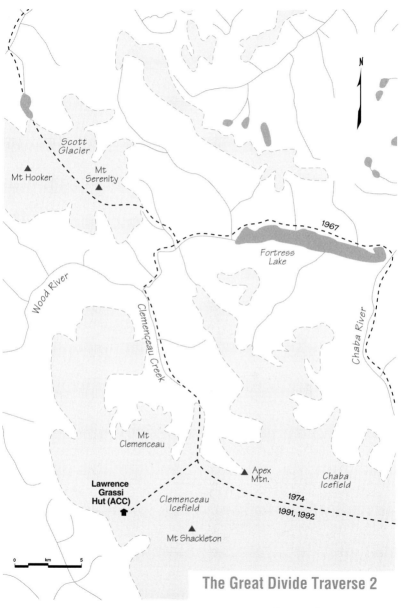

Mt Hooker

Scott
Glacier

Mt
Serenity

1967

Fortress
Lake

Wood River

Clemenceau Creek

Chaba River

Mt
Clemenceau

Apex
Mtn.

Chaba
Icefield

**Lawrence
Grassi
Hut (ACC)**

Clemenceau
Icefield

1974
1991, 1992

Mt Shackleton

0   km   5

The Great Divide Traverse 2

The Grand Traverses 225

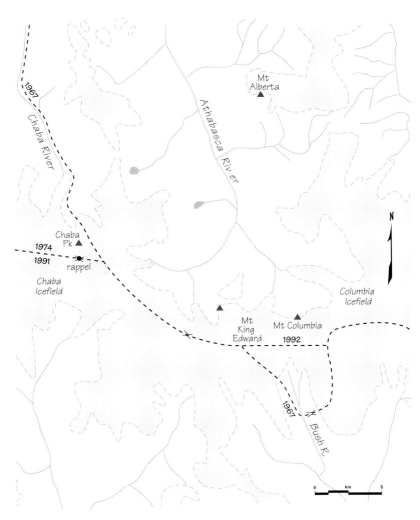

The Great Divide Traverse 3

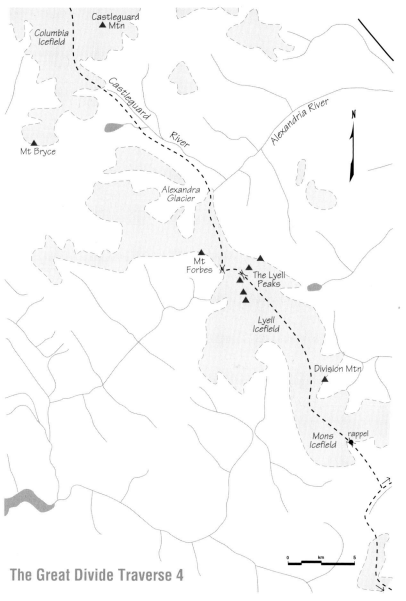

Castleguard Mtn

Columbia Icefield

Castleguard River

Alexandria River

Mt Bryce

N

Alexandra Glacier

Mt Forbes

The Lyell Peaks

Lyell Icefield

Division Mtn

Mons Icefield

rappel

0   km   5

The Great Divide Traverse 4

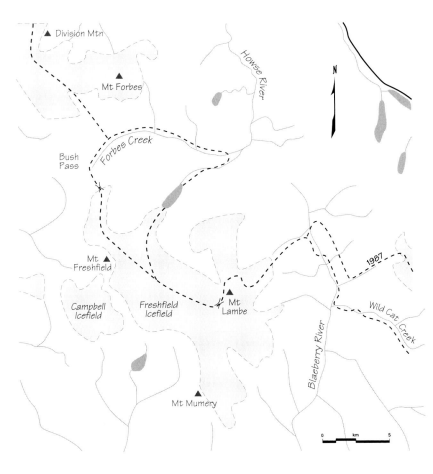

The Great Divide Traverse 5

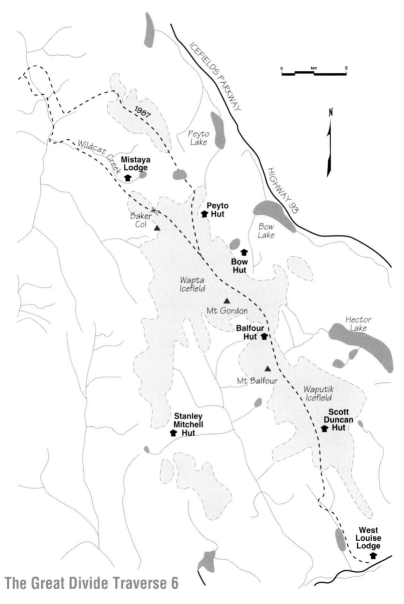

The Great Divide Traverse 6

THE NORTHERN CARIBOOS TRAVERSE

This traverse, which has only been done once, is highly praised by those who completed the trip. It stays high most of the way, travels through tremendous wilderness mountains and is truly a major undertaking when completed by linking with the Southern Cariboos traverse. It is characteristic of this traverse that many of the peaks and glaciers are still unnamed.

The traverse was completed by Steve Smith, his brother Phil and Scott Duncan in May of 1982. The trip took 15 days and much of the time they battled poor weather.

Length of the traverse about 110 km to the junction with the Southern Cariboos Traverse. The trip could be completed by skiing north through the Premier Range (an additional 40 km), south to Miledge Creek (60 km), or you can ski out logging roads along the North Thompson River (50 Km).
Vertical height gain 7500 m
Approximate time 14-21 days
(depending on finish)

The traverse begins along Highway #16, about 4 km north of the town of McBride, at the point where the road crosses the Doré River. Ski along logging roads up the Doré River for about 9 km then turn left up the south fork at GR 808049. Follow the south branch for about 15 km to GR 746909 where you turn left again and climb into a higher valley. Ski to the end of the valley then ascend open slopes to reach a pass (GR 729853) just south of a small lake. Descend the slope on the west side, angling south to reach a small lake (GR 717844).

Ski south about 1 km towards a larger lake then begin ascending slopes in a southerly direction to reach the toe of an unnamed glacier. Continue ascending the glacier for about 6 km to reach another col (GR 696763), then descend steeply down the south side to another unnamed glacier.

Continue south across the glacier and work your way around the shoulder of Mount Lunn at GR 701737 into a basin on the south flank of the mountain. Continue south across this basin, then ascend to the shoulder of an unnamed peak (GR 712719). After skiing east across the south face of this peak you descend to the south, avoiding heavy crevasses, to reach a col at GR 730707. Take your skis off and climb on foot up the corniced ridge to the south to reach the top of an unnamed summit (GR 734704). From here a descent to the south takes you into an unnamed creek which is then followed down to the valley of Niagara Creek (GR 781635).

The Niagara Valley is a beautiful wilderness area. It is as yet unlogged and the snow is said to be covered in animal tracks. (Castle Creek to the north, however, has a logging road in it and in the event of emergency would provide a route of escape.) Follow the valley for about 7 km to the bottom of a very impressive icefall (Niagara Glacier). Climb along the crest of a lateral moraine on the north flank of the icefall until it is possible to traverse out onto the glacier above the worst of the crevasses. Continue ascending, staying on the north flank of the glacier near the edge of the ice. This is very impressive

Beneath the northeast flank of Mount Pierrway. Photo Scott Duncan

terrain. When you are up on the névé of the icefield continue skiing to the east and round some small peaks to the north (GR 906663). Descend to the south into the basin of another unnamed glacier, then ascend to the southeast along the east flank of Mount Pierrway to reach a high shoulder (GR 945616). From here descend south and slightly east, angling across steep terrain to reach a pass at the edge of timberline (GR 960580).

From the pass climb southeast along a bench on the west flank of the crest. Round a corner beneath an unnamed peak to reach the edge of a glacier (GR 988560). Continue ascending the icefield in a southeast direction to cross a ridge (GR 005521), then ski out into the bowl above another glacier. After crossing this bowl you round the shoulder of a small peak (GR 000498) out onto the

south flank of this peak. Descend in a southeast direction to reach the edge of another large glacier (GR 977478).

Ascend the glacier in a southerly direction to a col just east of a small peak (GR 986451). Turn east and ascend to a high summit crest (GR 998450). Along here you will find that the map is incorrect and there are actually two small peaks immediately to the south of you which are not shown on the map. Descend southeast along the crest for a short distance, then descend to the east, contouring around the north flank of a small peak to another pass (GR 012450). Descend a short distance to the south onto another glacier. Contour around the basin at the head of Fred Wells Creek to reach the crest of a ridge descending from an unnamed peak (GR 040424). Cross the south flank of the ridge on a bench to gain another glacier.

Opposite: Near the top of the Niagara Glacier. Photo Scott Duncan
Top: Above Fred Wells Creek at about GR 995453. Looking west towards an unnamed peak. Photo Scott Duncan

Ascend this glacier to a col (GR 065410), then descend the southeast flank to Azure Pass (GR 092394).

To finish the traverse ascend in an easterly direction to a broad pass (GR 132388) from where you have three choices:

- You can end the trip fairly quickly by descending Ella Frye Creek to the North Thompson River, and following logging roads back to Highway #5.
- You can turn north to reach the Raush Glacier, then continue through the Premier Range of the Southern Cariboos Traverse as described on pages 237-246.
- You can turn south, make your way to McAndrew Lake and pick up the south portion of the Southern Cariboos Traverse as described on pages 237-246.

Planning Notes

Talk to the Forest Service in McBride about the state of the logging roads before you set out. Unless you can carry very heavy packs you will likely have to place a cache by helicopter.

Maps
1:50,000
93 H/8 McBride
93 H/1 Eddy
93 A/16 Mount Winder
93 A/9 Hobson Lake
83 D/12 Azure River

1:250,000
83D Canoe River
93A Quesnel Lake
93H McBride

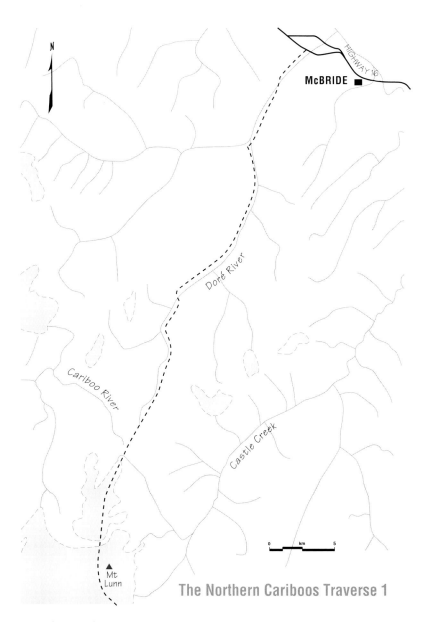

The Northern Cariboos Traverse 1

McBRIDE

HIGHWAY 16

Doré River

Cariboo River

Castle Creek

Mt Lunn

N

0   km   5

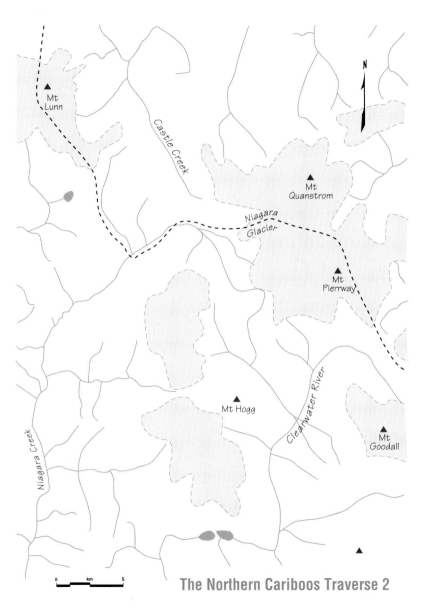

The Northern Cariboos Traverse 2

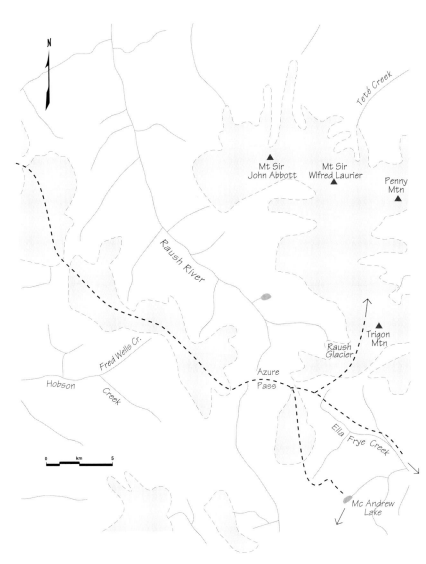

N

Teté Creek

Mt Sir
John Abbott

Mt Sir
Wlfred Laurier

Penny
Mtn

Raush River

Fred Wells Cr.

Hobson

Creek

Raush
Glacier

Trigon
Mtn

Azure
Pass

Ella Frye Creek

0   km   5

Mc Andrew
Lake

The Northern Cariboos Traverse 3

THE SOUTHERN CARIBOOS TRAVERSE

This tour was first done in May, 1980 by Allan Derbyshire, Alf Skrastins, Tony Daffern and Murray Toft. Since then it has become a real classic and has been repeated many times. It has also been guided several times by Al Schaffer.

The tour is really divided into two distinct halves. The first section takes you through the Premier Range and is very rugged and glaciated. It is big country. The second half of the trip, south of McAndrew Lake, is much gentler and there is less glaciation. Most of the time you are far from the highway, so escape in the event of an emergency is problematic. There are no huts on this traverse.

The team after the first traverse of the Southern Cariboos in 1980. Left to right: Alan Derbyshire, Murray Toft, Alf Skrastins, Tony Daffern. Photo Alf Skrastins

Crossing the névé at the head of the Gilmour Glacier in 1980.
Photo Alf Skrastins

Length of the traverse 100 km
Vertical height gain 5000 m
Approximate time 10-14 days

The original party began the route by bushwhacking for two days up Tete Creek to the Gilmour Glacier. Since then most parties simply fly by helicopter from Valemount to the head of the Gilmour Glacier. The drop-off point is about 2 km northwest of Mount Arthur Meighen (GR 265545).

If you do the traverse in 'pure' style by skiing up Tete Creek you should begin by following logging roads on the southeast side of the creek. The narrow canyon formed by the lower creek is very difficult and unpleasant. The logging roads lead to the creek bed which is then followed for about 8 km to its junction with Gilmour Creek. The toe of the Gilmour Glacier is heavily crevassed and it is best to follow a lateral moraine on the left. About 4 km later

the upper Gilmour Glacier is also heavily crevassed and is negotiated by following a ramp to the right of centre which leads to the upper icefield not far from the helicopter drop-off point.

From here the route traverses west towards Gunboat Mountain underneath the south slopes of Mount Stanley Baldwin. From a small pass just south of Gunboat Mountain (GR 226542) the route continues southwest, passing through two more passes (GR 223537 and GR 217529), then descends out onto the head of the Tete Glacier just north of Penny Mountain. This section offers some serious avalanche potential and should be treated warily. The climb to the last of the three passes, called

Opposite: Ascending the South Canoe Glacier. Photo Alf Skrastins

Bottom: Traversing towards Mount Mackenzie King at the head of the North Canoe Glacier. Photo Alf Skrastins

Penny Pass, offers a 100 vertical-metre lee slope of about 35-40 degrees, often overhung by a large cornice!

An alternative which might possibly be less exposed to avalanche hazard is to descend from the col on the shoulder of Gunboat Mountain (GR 226542) down a small glacier (crevasses) in a west and slightly north direction, then climb steeply to reach a shoulder at about GR 203544. Ascend back south up the shoulder, then traverse out onto the head of the Tete Glacier below Penny Mountain. This alternative is only marginally safer.

Traverse southwest across the head of the Tete Glacier and cross the crest of the ridge to enter the drainage of the North Canoe Glacier. It is best not to ski directly through the pass but to take a higher second notch (GR 194518).

The route then traverses around the head of the North Canoe Glacier, gradually descending a bench, then climbs to reach a basin below the east face of Mount Sir John Thompson. Continue across the basin in a southerly direction to reach a broad pass (GR 177465) overlooking the South Canoe Glacier.

The descent for about 200 vertical metres into the basin at the head of the South Canoe Glacier can be very tricky and exposed to ice fall. There are numerous large crevasses which make route finding a challenge. It is worth your while to spend some time here scouting the way before heading down.

From the basin (GR 184457) continue south, climbing a ramp below a steep mountain wall which leads you to another pass (GR 184441). This section is impressive, the route winding amongst giant crevasses and overhung by imposing ice-covered cliffs. From this pass a steep descent is required to reach the upper Raush Glacier. Most parties climb a short distance east towards a small peak then descend steep slopes on foot to the glacier below.

Traverse south across the Raush Glacier beneath Trigon Mountain, then descend along the left flank of the glacier and traverse to a small pass (GR 163397). Ski through the pass and descend about 150 vertical metres to a lake below. From the lake work your way west up open rolling terrain to reach another pass (GR 133387). From here, ascend straight south and cross almost directly over a small peak (GR 127376). The route then continues for 5 km along the east flank of the divide, above a tributary of Ella Frye Creek. It crosses briefly onto the west flank of the divide (GR 128330), then after only 1 km it crosses back onto the east flank (GR 128323). The route now turns east and for 2 km traverses the north flank of a small peak to reach a pass at GR 146324. From here a pleasant descent takes you to the shores of McAndrew Lake.

The southern half of the traverse is much less rugged. There is less glaciation and the scale is much less imposing. The tour from here on is very pleasant and enjoyable, and is characterized by many small glaciers and passes.

Ascend McAndrew Creek directly south of the lake. At an altitude of about 1970 m work your way west over an awkward shoulder into another drainage (GR 155285). Ascend this drainage, cross a pass (GR 158278), then descend to a small lake at the head of St. Julien Creek (GR 152263). Continue south for 4 km to another pass which is crossed on the right shoulder (GR 163228). After descending about 300 vertical metres, contour around the head of Knutson Creek at about 1970 m to another lake (GR 192212).

Ascending the South Canoe Glacier. The descent into the basin (see tracks) from a point on the photo below Mount Sir Wilfrid Laurier is threatened by icefall. Photo Murray Toft

Traversing below Trigon Mountain at the head of the Raush Glacier. The route crosses the pass (GR 163397) in the middle of the photo. Photo Alf Skrastins

Near the head of Angus Horne Creek. Looking northwest to col GR 195175 (1980 variation). Photo Alf Skrastins

From here there are two variations: 1. Climb gently to the south for 2 km, then cross a pass (GR 200193) into the head of Stormking Creek. Contour the head of the drainage across east-facing slopes to reach another pass (GR 215173). 2. Follow the 1980 route which ascends to a col at GR 195175 (see photo) and descends southeast to a tributary of Angus Horne Creek. Both routes now continue south to a small glacier and ascend to another pass (GR 225142). From here descend steeply to the lake below (GR 231128).

Contour south around a treed shoulder and out to a trio of lakes (GR 228110). Ascend the glacier above, gradually swinging east, and cross the icefield to the shoulder of an unnamed peak (GR 273181). Descend to the east out onto the icefield below. From here climb to the south to a high pass (GR 290056). Remaining high, traverse to the southeast, then descend to a small lake at the head of Lempriere Creek (GR 321016).

Traverse east across north-facing slopes and round a shoulder into another small drainage (GR 350005). The route continues east to a col (GR 366002), then descends south to a small lake (GR 367996).

From here there have been several different endings—none of them completely satisfactory. The original party continued traversing southeast to the head of a drainage (GR 398970) which they descended to reach the Thunder River which was then followed to the highway. Al Schaffer has descended a small glacier north to reach the head of Miledge Creek (GR 398012) which he followed for 7-8 km until he reached logging roads. This route is not recommended due to the difficult nature of the creek bed. So far, the best finish to this trip descends north on a small glacier to Miledge Creek (GR 398012), then traverses south-facing slopes high above the creek to reach a lake on a high plateau (GR 431011). Continue southeast across this plateau to its edge (GR 444996,) then descend steeply to the east to a subsidiary creek where logging roads are reached. It has been reported that this descent is made much easier by a large clear-cut. Once the logging roads are reached it is a further 5-10 km on old snowmobile tracks to the Yellowhead Highway.

Planning Notes

There is need for only one cache of food and fuel on this traverse and the best place is at McAndrew Lake. This cache can be placed by helicopter or possibly by snowmobile up the North Thompson River (it would be necessary to ski the last few kilometres up to McAndrew Lake).

Yellowhead Helicopters out of Valemount should be contacted for placing caches and for the initial approach to the Gilmour Glacier. They can be reached at Box 18, Valemount, B.C. V0E 2Z0. Phone (250) 566-4401.

Maps
1:50,000
83 D/14 Valemount
83 D/13 Kiwa Creek
83 D/12 Azure River
83 D/5 Angus Horne Lake
83 D/6 Lempriere

1:250,000
83D Canoe River

Further reference:
Toft, M. "Two (more) High Level Ski Tours", CAJ 1982, p. 27.
Scott, C.: "High Level Ski Tours", Polar Circus, Volume 1, 1986, p 15.

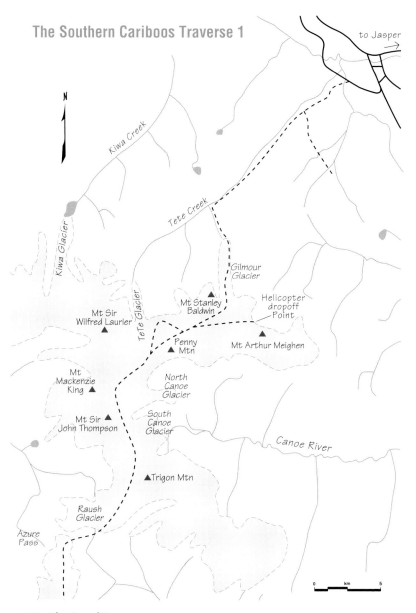

The Southern Cariboos Traverse 1

to Jasper →

N

Kiwa Creek

Tete Creek

Kiwa Glacier

TeTe Glacier

Gilmour Glacier

Mt Stanley Baldwin

Helicopter dropoff Point

Mt Sir Wilfred Laurier

Penny Mtn

Mt Arthur Meighen

Mt Mackenzie King

North Canoe Glacier

South Canoe Glacier

Canoe River

Mt Sir John Thompson

▲Trigon Mtn

Raush Glacier

Azure Pass

0   km   5

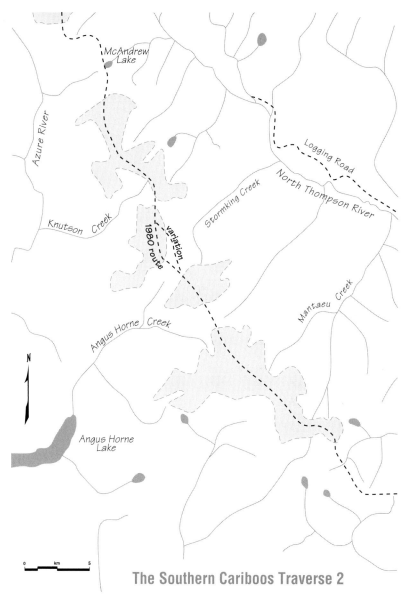

The Southern Cariboos Traverse 2

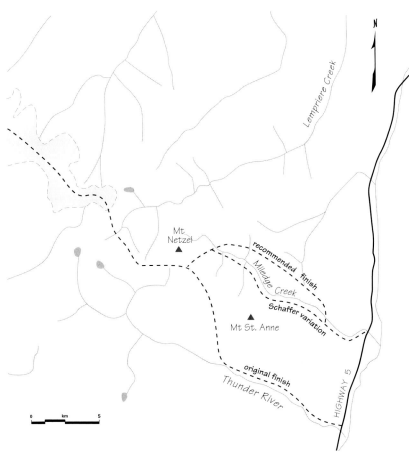

The Southern Cariboos Traverse 3

Opposite: The first traverse party in 1976.
Ron Robinson, Dave Smith and Don Gardner
enjoy a campfire and some dry ground in
Bachelor Creek. Photo Chic Scott

THE NORTHERN SELKIRKS TRAVERSE

This ski adventure was first done in 1976 by Don Gardner, Dave Smith, Ron Robinson and Chic Scott. Over a period of fifteen days of perfect weather the group traversed from Mica Creek at the northern end of the Selkirks to the Rogers Pass. The route has rarely been repeated, probably due to its length and committing nature.

The route crosses a number of major and minor icefields, dropping into deep valleys in between. There are only two huts along the way–the very comfortable Fairy Meadow Hut and the delightful Great Cairn Hut. Both of these are located about half way along the route. For most of the way escape would be difficult and would involve a long, long slog down a side valley to a road.

Length of the traverse about 200 km
Vertical height gain 11,000 m
Approximate time 15-20 days

The traverse was originally skied from north to south and is described that way here. Climb the hillside above the town of Mica Creek, then work your way down and back to reach Mica Creek itself. Follow the creek for about 10 km. Travel is not too difficult despite the tight nature of the drainage. At the head of the valley turn northeast and climb very steeply through the trees along the left flank of a creek to gain a high open bowl. Ascend this bowl to reach a small col (GR 045607).

Mount Chapman at the head of Louis Lee Creek. Photo Chic Scott

Descend the other side of this col and ski out into the meadow along Yellow Creek. Contour around the north flank of a small peak and traverse into Anemone Pass. After skiing through the pass you traverse high around the head of Louis Lee Creek to reach a small icefield (GR 118588). Climb a steep hill to gain the icefield, then traverse it in a southeasterly direction to reach a broad pass (GR 135576). From here descend the glacier to the south. Although the descent is relatively steep throughout, it is not too difficult. Once you reach treeline stay on the left flank of the creek and work your way down through the forest into Bigmouth Creek.

Turn east and ski up Bigmouth Creek for about 2 km, then take the right hand branch of Bigmouth Creek. After about 2 km there is a canyon which is rounded on the left. Continue for another 2 km up to the head of the valley. From here climb steeply through the trees straight ahead to reach a lovely hanging valley (GR 190486). Ski easily up this valley for several kilometres, then climb a steep slope for about 700 vertical metres to a very small col overlooking a small icefield (GR 225484). Descend steeply to reach the icefield, and ski out east for about 2 km onto the flats. Descend steeply down the huge slope to the south towards Windy Creek. This descent can offer good skiing, but it also offers very serious avalanche potential as well. Follow the creek down to Windy Creek, avoiding a gorge at the end by staying high on the left above the creek.

Avalanche debris in Austerity Creek.
Photo Steve Smith

Turn left up Windy creek and follow it along the right bank for about 2 km to the junction with Austerity Creek. Turn right and continue up Austerity Creek for about 10 km until you are directly west of the Adamant Range, then turn east and climb steeply for almost 1500 vertical metres to a small col (GR 358347) which opens onto the Adamants. Ski through the pass and descend gently for 200 vertical metres before turning right around the end of Collosal Mountain and traversing onto the Upper Granite Glacier. Ski down to the Fairy Meadow Hut (GR 394352). (See page 166.)

From the Fairy Meadow Hut the route travels through three passes (Friendship Col, Thor Pass and Azimuth Notch) to the Great Cairn Hut. Begin by climbing the hillside to the south of the hut and continue up past the Echo Glacier and on to Friendship Col (GR 406333). From Friendship Col continue south across the icefield to

Top: Looking across the Granite Glacier towards the Adamants. Photo Steve Smith
Bottom: At Thor Pass there's a tremendous view of Mount Sir Sandford. Photo Chic Scott

Thor Pass (GR 398307), then descend steeply to the Adamant glacier. Cross the glacier and climb to Azimuth Notch (mislabelled on map, GR 385286). From the notch descend, traversing right, to reach Silvertip Glacier which is descended to the toe of the Haworth Glacier, then continue down to the hut (GR 392268). This is a magical spot and the views of Mount Sir Sandford are magnificent.

From the Great Cairn Hut ski back northwest to reach the Haworth Glacier, then turn southwest and ascend the glacier to Palisade Pass between Palisade Mountain and Alpina Dome. From here ski onto the upper reaches of the Sir Sandford Glacier and continue southwest to Sir Sandford Pass. Carefully descend the Goat Glacier, avoiding crevasses and icefalls, and continue on down to Moberly Pass.

From Moberly Pass head south to reach the Bear Glacier then travel southeast along the slopes of Pyrite Ridge, passing south and west of Centurion Mountain. Climb to a high pass (GR 351104), then descend in a southwest direction towards Bachelor Creek. The final descent to Bachelor Creek from the hanging valley is extremely steep tree bashing interspersed with cliffs.

When the 1976 group reached this point the weather had been sunny for almost two weeks, the rivers were raging and the snow was disappearing fast. They opted to take the quickest route to finish the trip. This is described below. It may also be possible to ski a high line above Mountain Creek which would include the icefields in the vicinity of Iconoclast and Nordic Mountains.

Follow Bachelor Creek upstream for about 2 km, then turn left and climb steeply for 1000 vertical metres to reach a small pass (GR 404029). From here you descend into the valley of Mountain Creek which is followed for almost 20 km. The valley bottom travel is easy but the big difficulty is the eventual crossing of Mountain Creek itself and the crossing of tributaries which join it from the south.

Eventually, the route turns south and ascends Ursus Creek for about 5 km. Turn southwest (at GR 570867) and climb steeply up a small tributary to ultimately reach Bruins Pass (GR 592831). Descend to Connaught Creek (see page 163), and continue down to Glacier Park Lodge in the Rogers Pass.

Treat yourself to a beer or two.

Planning notes

Leave a vehicle at Glacier Park Lodge for the completion of the trip, then drive up the road to Mica Creek in a second vehicle.

During the winter have a cache placed at Fairy Meadow Hut.

Maps
1:50,000
83 D/2 Nagle Creek
82 M/16 Kinbasket Lake
82 N/13 Sullivan River
82 N/12 Mount Sir Sandford
82 N/5 Glacier

1:250,000
83D Canoe River
82M Seymour Arm
82N Golden

For further reference

Scott, C.: "The Great Canadian High Level Ski Tours", Canadian Alpine Journal, 1978, p. 1.
Scott, C.: "Odyssey in the Canadian Icefields", Nordic World, Volume 7, No 6, February, 1979, p 36.
Scott, C.: "High Level Ski Tours", Polar Circus, Volume 1, 1986, p 15

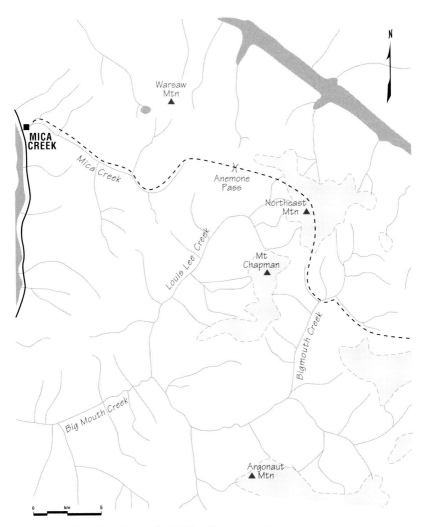

The Northern Selkirks Traverse 1

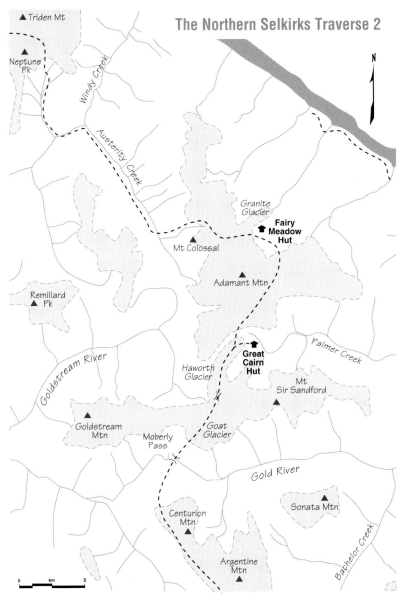

The Northern Selkirks Traverse 2

▲ Triden Mt

▲ Neptune Pk

Windy Creek

Austerity Creek

Granite Glacier

🏠 **Fairy Meadow Hut**

▲ Mt Colossal

▲ Adamant Mtn

▲ Remillard Pk

Goldstream River

Haworth Glacier

🏠 **Great Cairn Hut**

Palmer Creek

▲ Mt Sir Sandford

▲ Goldstream Mtn

Moberly Pass

Goat Glacier

Gold River

▲ Centurion Mtn

▲ Sonata Mtn

Bachelor Creek

▲ Argentine Mtn

N

0 ___ km ___ 5

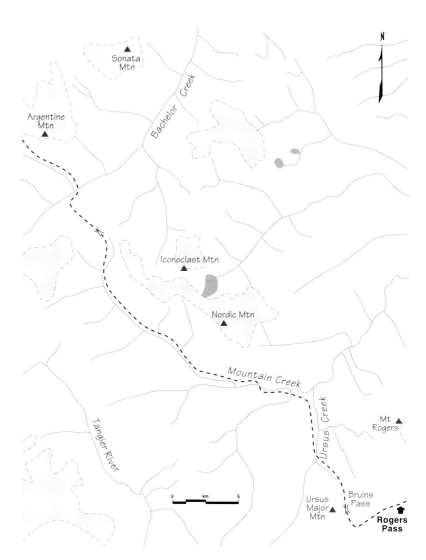

The Northern Selkirks Traverse 3

BUGABOOS TO ROGERS PASS

This tour, which takes you through some of the most spectacular mountain country in western Canada, is perhaps the most popular of all the icefields ski traverses. The peaks are wild and rugged and for much of the way the glaciation is extensive.

The traverse was first done in 1958 by a group of American skiers—Bill Briggs, Bob French, Sterling Neale and Barry Corbet. In a remarkable nine-day effort they successfully traversed from south to north, along the spine of the Purcells and the Selkirks. A brief account of their trip appears in the CAJ and an article which was written for Summit Magazine.

In 1973 another party made the traverse, this time from north to south. Don Gardner, Ron Robinson, Dave Smith and Chic Scott skied the route over a period of 15 days in May, their progress being held up by a five-day storm mid-route. Nothing was written about this trip until the CAJ of 1978.

Since then the trip has become deservedly famous and popular. It has been skied successfully perhaps 20 times over the intervening years and was successfully completed as a guided outing in 1990.

The route is described here from south to north as that is the most convenient way to ski the route.

The Desperados: Ron Robinson, Dave Smith, Don Gardner and Chic Scott at Glacier Circle Cabin in 1973.
Photo Chic Scott

The view from just east of Climax Col. Crystalline Pass (centre right) and the Conrad Icefield stretching out to the left to below Mount Thorington. Photo Chic Scott

Length of the traverse 130 km
Vertical height gain 10,000 m
Approximate time 10-15 days

From Bugaboo Lodge ski to the toe of the Bugaboo Glacier. Approach the glacier via slopes to the left, then traverse out right to gain the glacier. Climb up and right across the glacier to reach the Conrad Kain Hut (GR 166204). Some groups when they fly into the Bugaboos choose to fly directly to the hut.

From the hut ascend the glacier above, then climb steep snow slopes to the Bugaboo/Snowpatch Col. Ski out onto the Vowell Glacier. Curve to the north and descend the glacier onto the large névé which is crossed in a northwesterly direction to a small pass (GR 122232). Descend steeply for about 250 vertical metres into a deep glaciated basin surrounded by ice, then climb up the far side, staying to the right to avoid large crevasses. When the angle eases off continue in a northwesterly direction and drop into another deep basin

(the Malloy Glacier). A small fibreglass igloo is located on the right bank of the glacier at GR 104262.

The direction of travel now turns southwest for a short distance and you climb for about 500 vertical metres out of the basin to reach the Conrad Icefield. From here travel is straightforward for about 10 km as you cross the icefield, travelling northwest below the peak of Mount Thorington. Ski down off the icefield to Crystalline Pass (GR 992295).

From here the route traverses the slopes of Tetragon Peak and Crystalline Mountain in a northerly direction to reach Climax Col (GR 970336), misnamed Hume Pass on old maps. Late in the day or if avalanche hazard is high, this route is not recommended and it would be best to follow the valley.

The descent off the west side of Climax Col is very steep and is potential avalanche terrain. Once below Climax Col, descend the glacier for a short distance, then climb easily up to the right to reach the shoulder of Deluge Mountain. Descend a short distance to the west to reach Hume Pass (GR 955334). Continue north, descending into the valley bottom. Ski down the valley for a short distance before climbing steeply up the west side of the valley to reach Snowman Lake. Above the lake climb gentle slopes to a small pass (GR 961388). Descend the other side (cornice) and ski out into The Valley of the Lakes towards Syncline Mountain. Climb from the lakes up to Syncline Pass (GR 965423).

From here there are two variants. It is possible to ski over the top of Mount Syphax, but the way is steep and tricky on the north side of the peak and good visibility and conditions are required. A more reasonable way to reach the

head of Malachite Creek is to descend the glacier east of Syncline Mountain towards Azurite Mountain, then cross the shoulder of Mount Syphax into the head of Vermont Creek. Traverse the east slopes of Mount Syphax to a small col immediately northeast of the peak (GR 978454), then descend northwest into the head of Malachite Creek.

Make a very steep climb for about 200 vertical metres to gain Malachite Col on the north shoulder of Malachite Spire (GR 955474) (see photo). If the snow is unstable this is an extremely dangerous slope! Round Malachite Spire to the north, then cross the Carbonate Icefield in a westerly direction to a ridge that descends north from International Peak (GR 933474). Take your skis off and scramble down off this ridge to easier ground below.

Traverse around the head of Bobbie Burns Creek, then head north along very complex benches to reach a pass on the shoulder of David Peak (GR 910528). Many little cliffs and steep slopes can be problematic. Use caution. From the shoulder of David Peak a lovely descent to the north takes you to McMurdo Hut (GR 896554). (See page 173 for more information). This is a good place to rest and dry out before tackling the last half of the traverse.

If you are going straight through and choose to bypass McMurdo Hut it is possible to simply traverse west across the Spillimacheen Glacier beneath David and Cony Peak, then descend steep slopes into the creek which leads down to the Duncan River.

The ascent to Malachite Col (far right) is problematic. In unstable conditions this slope is very dangerous. For added security camp below the slope and ascend in the early morning. Photo Chic Scott

From the McMurdo Hut it is best to descend for about 1 km along a trail to the northwest to the valley floor, then at a large clear-cut turn up to your left and climb to Silent Pass (GR 870550). Do not attempt to take a short cut around the shoulder of the peak to the pass. From Silent Pass descend the creek to the west to reach the Duncan River not far from the Beaver-Duncan Divide.

There are a number of ways to finish the traverse. The most complete and aesthetic is to ascend the narrow valley of Butters Creek for about 5 km, then turn north and climb for about 1,000 vertical metres to a small col just west of Beaver Mountain (GR 764538). From here descend onto the névé of the Beaver Glacier, cross it in a north direction, and climb a ridge up onto the shoulder of Sugarloaf Mountain (GR 755558). This ascent can be tricky in high avalanche hazard. Traverse around to the north and west of a subpeak (GR 754557), then descend from here, continuing north onto the head of the Grand Glacier. Ascend the glacier to beneath Grand Mountain. A steep climb up a snow gully takes you to a small col on the shoulder of Grand Mountain (GR 734596). From this col descend northeast out onto the Deville névé.

The route just described is very mountainous and tricky and requires skill coupled with good weather. If conditions dictate, it is possible to short- cut this section by taking one of three variations.

• You can ski up the Duncan River (huge clearcuts for the logging fans), then turn west and ascend Beaver Glacier to the shoulder of Sugarloaf Mountain.

• You can ski up the Duncan River, continue over the Beaver-Duncan divide, then descend the Beaver River. Turn west and ascend Grand Glacier up to below Grand Mountain, then climb the gully over the shoulder of the mountain and descend onto the Deville névé.

• It is also possible to cut out the climb over Grand Mountain by climbing north from below the Grand Glacier up steep slopes onto the Deville névé just west of Beaver Overlook. The ascent begins at GR 765610 and reaches the glacier at GR 756623.

Once on the Deville névé continue easily in a north direction. A steep snow spur descending from Mount Wheeler runs out into the icefield and must be downclimbed. Continue north, crossing flat icefields to the top of the cliffs above Glacier Circle (see photos on page 261). These cliffs are located immediately west of Mount Topham and are about 100 vertical metres (GR 741672). The cliffs are not too steep to begin with and the first rappel is not a problem. The second rappel, however, is steep and drops you into the top of a snow gully which can be descended easily on foot. There should be plenty of old pitons and slings, but it is best to carry a few just in case. Tend to keep right as you descend and do not get drawn over to the left (west).

From the bottom of the snow gully it is necessary to continue north across a potentially dangerous slope to gain the crest of a moraine. Continue north and west for a short distance across the flats, then climb up and over the shoulder of Mount Fox and down into Glacier Circle. The hut can be tricky to locate and it might be necessary to ski around for a while until you stumble upon it (GR 726689).

Top: Crossing the Spillimacheen Icefield below Twin Towers. Photo Chic Scott
Bottom: Crossing the head of Grand Glacier. The route to Grand Glacier crosses the lefthand
shoulder of the lefthand peak just below the summit of Mount Sugarloaf. Photo Chic Scott

The most reasonable way to climb out of Glacier Circle is to work your way west to reach a small glacier underneath The Witch's Tower. Ascend the glacier, then turn north and continue climbing under The Witch's Tower until it is possible to turn northeast and ski out onto the Illecillewaet névé. Continue climbing gently as you travel north onto the névé. Cross the névé in a northeast direction towards Lookout Mountain and the Illecillewaet Glacier. Descend into the Illecillewaet Valley, staying on the left side near the slopes of Glacier Crest, then follow the trail along the right bank of the river to reach the Wheeler Hut (see page 152).

Have a cup of tea and take off your pack.

Photo taken In 1973 shows skiers ascending the steep snow spur of Mount Wheeler on the Deville névé. Photo Chic Scott

*Looking across to the Deville névé from the Illecillewaet névé. Photo Stan Wagon
Top and left: Arrows marks the descent route through the cliffs to Glacier Circle.*

Photo Chic Scott

Planning Notes

The route does not really parallel a highway so when you are in the middle of the trip you are about 50 km from civilization. There are no easy ways out and you must be prepared to look after yourself.

The traverse normally takes about two weeks and is usually done with a food cache midway at the McMurdo Creek Cabin. This can be placed by helicopter from Golden or by skidoo up the Spillimacheen River. Be sure to secure your cache well as there is lots activity at this hut and it may be vandalized.

The trip can be skied in either direction but if you end your trip at the

Bugaboos you may have a problem getting out to the highway. In addition, it is easier to rappel the Deville cliffs than to climb them. To reach the Bugaboos you must make arrangements with Canadian Mountain Holidays in Banff. Phone (403) 762-7100. You must fly on their changeover day which is Saturday.

The route is quite complex and presents a great deal of potentially dangerous terrain. In periods of high avalanche hazard this traverse can prove quite difficult.

There are four huts on the route which are a very pleasant change from camping each night. These are the Conrad Kain Hut, the Malloy Glacier Igloo, the McMurdo Hut and the Glacier Circle Hut.

This traverse is best done in late April but in heavy snow years is possible into mid-May.

Note: The photos in this section were taken in 1973 when the route was skied in reverse direction.

Maps
1:50,000
82 K/10 Howser Creek
82 K/15 Bugaboo Creek
82 K/14 Westfall River
82 N/3 Mount Wheeler

1:250,000
82K Lardeau
82N Golden

Further Reference
French, R.: "Skiers Travel 110 Miles Across Mountain Ranges", Summit, Vol. 5, Jan. 1959, pp. 6-11.
French, R.: "Bugaboo Ski-Mountaineering", Canadian Alpine Journal, 1960, P.76.
Scott, C.: "The Great Canadian High Level Ski Tours", Canadian Alpine Journal, 1978, pp. 2-4.
Scott, C.: "Odyssey in the Canadian Icefields", Nordic World, Volume 7, No 6, February, 1979, p 36.
Scott, C.: "High Level Ski Tours", Polar Circus, Volume 1, 1986, p 15.
Wagon, S. "The Haute Route", Canadian Alpine Journal, 1991, pp. 52-54.

The Vowell/Malloy Igloo

This hut is one of the two original fibreglass structures which were previously erected at Boulder Camp, in the Bugaboos. They were designed by architect Philip Delesalle and erected at Boulder Camp in 1965. When the Conrad Kain hut was built in 1972 the igloos were moved. The first location near the Malloy Glacier was unsatisfactory and the igloo was moved again to its present location in 1976.
Map 82 K/15 Bugaboo Creek
Location GR 104262 at 2680 m
Capacity 4-5
Facilities none, bare-bones shelter

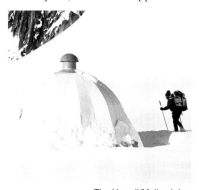

The Vowell/Malloy Igloo.
Photo Stan Wagon

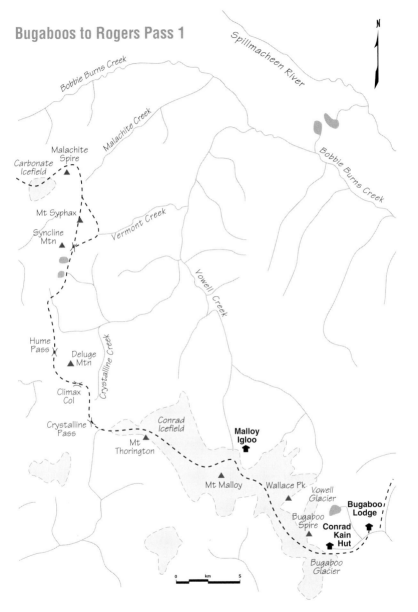

Bugaboos to Rogers Pass 1

N

Spillmacheen River

Bobbie Burns Creek

Malachite Creek

Bobbie Burns Creek

Carbonate Icefield

Malachite Spire

Mt Syphax

Syncline Mtn

Vermont Creek

Vowell Creek

Hume Pass

Deluge Mtn

Crystalline Creek

Climax Col

Crystalline Pass

Conrad Icefield

Mt Thorington

Malloy Igloo

Mt Malloy

Wallace Pk

Vowell Glacier

Bugaboo Lodge

Bugaboo Spire

Conrad Kain Hut

Bugaboo Glacier

0 km 5

The Grand Traverses 263

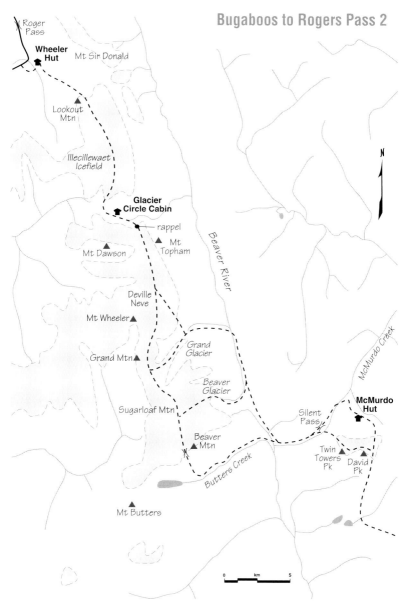

Roger Pass

Wheeler Hut

Mt Sir Donald

Lookout Mtn

Illecillewaet Icefield

Glacier Circle Cabin

rappel

Mt Topham

Mt Dawson

Beaver River

Deville Neve

Mt Wheeler

Grand Glacier

Grand Mtn

Beaver Glacier

McMurdo Creek

Sugarloaf Mtn

Silent Pass

McMurdo Hut

Beaver Mtn

Twin Towers Pk

David Pk

Butters Creek

N

Mt Butters

0   km   5

THE SOUTHERN PURCELLS TRAVERSE

This traverse has only been done in its entirety once. It is an excellent wilderness ski adventure that takes you through beautiful unspoiled country. There are no cabins or huts on the route and only a handful of logging roads to remind you of civilization.

The route begins at Bugaboo Lodge. From there it works its way down the Southern Purcell Mountains to St. Mary's Alpine Provincial Park where it meets the road again, not far from Kimberley.

In spring 1982 two parties attempted the traverse. Len Potter, Chris Kubinski, Errol Smith and Chic Scott headed up Dewar Creek at the south end of the traverse, while at the same time Bob Saunders and Steve Smith began the traverse from Bugaboo Lodge at the north end. The two parties narrowly missed meeting each other near Mount Findlay.

The Saunders/Smith party completed the route in 13 days. They did the traverse without a cache and started the trip with 35 kg packs containing food for 21 days. The other group successfully skied half the route as far as Toby Creek in eight days, then skied out to civilization via Panorama Ski Resort.

Length of the traverse 150 km
Vertical height gain 11,000 m
Approximate time 2-3 weeks

From Bugaboo Lodge, ski back down the road a short distance then turn right and follow the road up the main branch of Bugaboo Creek. The first objective is Phacelia Pass (GR 228134) which is reached by a steep climb from Bugaboo Creek. This climb offers avalanche potential and should be treated with caution. The descent on the south side of Phacelia Pass is straightforward and after reaching the valley bottom the route turns southwest down Howser Creek for about 5 km.

At GR 198052 turn south and ascend an unnamed creek. After 4 km angle up left and ascend through open forest to reach open slopes which lie on the west flank of the ridge crest dividing the Stockdale and Howser drainages (GR 230994). The route then turns south again and out onto the head of the Stockdale Glacier. Ski through a pass immediately southeast of Birthday Peak (GR 217924) and descend easily onto the Starbird Glacier. At the point where this glacier turns to descend into Horsethief Creek (GR 242872) begin climbing beneath Mount Monica onto the west shoulder of Glacier Dome. Cross the shoulder (GR 250858), then descend into the Jumbo Creek drainage. Soon logging roads are encountered and are followed to a bridge over Jumbo Creek (GR 304778). You should have a cache placed here and spend a luxurious night around the camp fire eating and drinking various goodies.

From the Jumbo Creek bridge ascend a small unnamed creek south up to a col between Blockhead Mountain and Redtop Mountain (GR 299729). Descend steeply for about 700 vertical metres to the creek below. Then at about 1820 m elevation begin a high traverse, contouring above the valley floor for 6 km to reach Earl Grey Pass. Although this looks difficult, the travelling is quite reasonable. From Earl Grey Pass descend steeply to the east to reach open flats below.

Ascend the Toby Glacier to a pass just west of Mount Katherine (GR 345614), then descend steeply in a southwest direction to the creek (GR 331591). From here the descent down the creek for about 4 km to the junction with Carney Creek is threatened by many avalanche paths. It is best to do this section of the trip early in the morning and as quickly as possible. Turn left (GR 337559) and ascend Carney Creek for about 4 km, then take the right hand branch (at GR 378541) and climb to a pass 1 km north of Trikootenay Peak (GR 395527). Traverse around the east flank of this peak to another pass (GR 395514).

From this pass remain high and traverse above treeline across the eastern flank of Mount Findlay. High on Mount Findlay (at about GR 365476) is a distinct notch in the ridge that you pass through. From this notch descend steeply on foot for about 150 vertical metres to reach easier ground, then ski to a frozen lake below. Staying high above the head of Granite Creek, you contour around above treeline until below Mount Lees. At about GR 376446 descend about 150 vertical metres to an elevation of 1970 m, then curve around the lower north ridge of Mount Clutterbuck into upper Granite Creek.

Ascend Granite Creek for about 2 km to a small lake (GR 400439) below a steep slope. Climb on foot to the pass (GR 404437). The descent down the south side of this pass to reach the glacier is very steep and technical, requiring rope and belays (see photo). The crossing of this pass is the crux of the whole traverse. It was noted in 1982 that the steep slope further west which climbs to another col (GR 394433) should be investigated if snow stability is good. It could provide an easier alternative.

The south side of pass GR 404437 (the crux). Photo Chic Scott

Top: Mount Toby from the Toby Icefield.
Bottom: Looking towards Mount Finlay from the north. Both photos Bob Saunders

From here ascend the glacier south of Mount Clutterbuck to a pass west of Duchess Peak (GR 386411). Descend steep open slopes for about 300 vertical metres until at 2425 m when you begin contouring around the drainage. Climb to a ridge on the northeast side of Mount Klahowya. Then traverse south across a small snowfield to reach another col (GR 405372) from which you descend south into the drainage below.

At GR 437348 begin climbing towards Mount St. Mary's. The drainage itself is very narrow and it is best to follow a draw about 300 m east of the creek. Ascend to a lake (GR 429329), then continue climbing to reach a pass on the southwest ridge of Mount St. Mary's. A short steep descent down the south side of the pass leads to Bleak Lake.

From here the route traverses St. Mary's Alpine Provincial Park in a southerly direction for about 15-20 km to reach a pass about 1 km east of Mount Manson. The route finding is intricate and the route meanders up and down and around many small hills and peaks. From Bleak Lake descend to Nowita Lake and continue down to Lyallii Lake. Work your way south over a wooded ridge to Keer Lake and on to Totem Lake. Descend Price Creek and round the corner to reach Huggard Lake. Ascend Spade Creek, then cross another ridge to reach Bird Lakes. Continue south under the slopes of Mount Manson to the pass (GR 468181). This pass may be difficult to cross due to a large cornice.

Descend the drainage on the south side of the pass for several kilometres until logging roads are reached. These roads descend, zig-zagging back and forth, to reach a major logging road on the east flank of the valley above Dewar Creek. Continue south down this road for about 6 km to reach the St. Mary River Road and your waiting vehicle (GR 448081).

Planning Notes

The trip is best done with a cache half way along the route. Probably the best place for a cache is along Jumbo Creek where the road crosses a bridge over the creek not far from Jumbo Pass (GR 304778). This point can be reached by driving up Toby Creek beyond the Panorama Ski Resort then by skiing up logging roads.

It is best to begin the trip from the northern end by flying in to Bugaboo Lodge. You must do this on a Saturday when the heli-skiers change over. Arrangements can be made by phoning Canadian Mountain Holidays (403-762-7100). Leave a car where Dewar Creek reaches the road along the St. Mary River about 35-40 km from Kimberley (GR 448081).

Maps
1:50,000
82 F/9 St. Mary Lake
82 F/16 Dewar Creek
82 K/1 Findlay Creek
82 K/2 Lardeau
82 K/7 Duncan Lake
82 K/10 Howser Creek
82 K/15 Bugaboo Creek

1:250,000
82F Nelson
82K Lardeau

For Further Reference
Scott, C.: "High Level Ski Tours", Polar Circus, Volume 1, 1986, p 15.

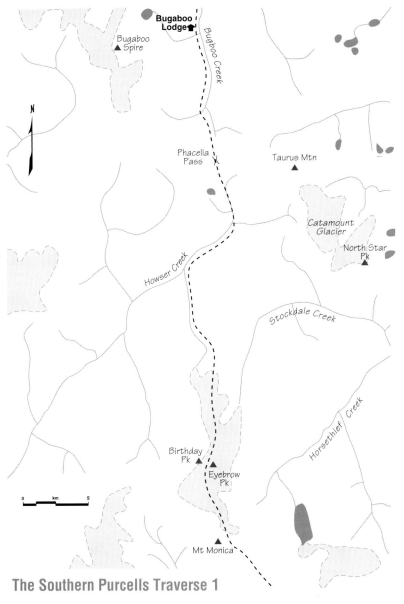

Bugaboo
Lodge

Bugaboo
▲ Spire

Bugaboo Creek

N

Phacelia
Pass

Taurus Mtn ▲

Catamount
Glacier

Howser Creek

North Star
Pk ▲

Stockdale Creek

Horsethief Creek

Birthday
Pk ▲

▲
Eyebrow
Pk

0   km   5

▲ Mt Monica

The Southern Purcells Traverse 1

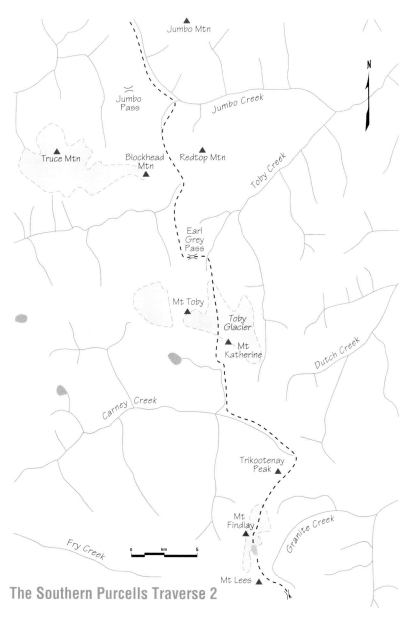

The Southern Purcells Traverse 2

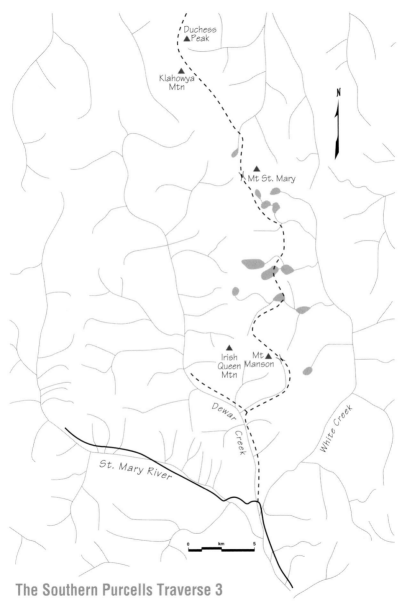

Duchess
▲ Peak

Klahowya
Mtn

N

Mt St. Mary

Irish
Queen
Mtn
Mt
Manson

Dewar
Creek

White Creek

St. Mary River

0   km   5

The Southern Purcells Traverse 3

THE VALHALLA TRAVERSE

This is a great ski adventure and offers complicated routefinding over intricate terrain. The scenery is outstanding, the traverse is very serious and you are forced to continually make decisions about snow stability. Escape would be difficult in the event of bad weather or accident. To the east the valleys lead to the uninhabited west bank of Slocan Lake and to the west it would be a very long trudge along logging roads to reach civilization. In other words, this traverse is not to be taken lightly and should be attempted by experienced skiers only.

Length of the traverse 55 km to Wragge Lake, 60 km to Shannon Creek (it is then a further 10 km to Highway #6 along logging roads)
Vertical height gain 4575 m to Wragge Creek, 4965 m to Shannon Creek
Approximate time 7-8 days

Historically there have been two approaches to begin this tour. Some parties have followed logging roads up Hoder Creek to reach the high country at Drinnon Pass. Unfortunately, this approach misses some of the most beautiful terrain on the traverse. A party in the mid 1980's flew in by helicopter to Mulvey Basin and began their traverse from there. This is the recommended way to begin.

From the old hut site (GR 549136) in Mulvey Basin the route ascends past Mulvey Lakes to Upper Mulvey Lake, then turns north and climbs steeply to a small col on the northeast ridge of Asgard Peak (GR 534148). From the col descend steeply down the other side to about 2300 m, then contour west and cross a shoulder (GR 525157) into the next basin.

Descend to the west about 180 vertical metres to a creek which is ascended in a southerly direction to the upper of two unnamed lakes below Mount Prestley. From here climb for about 210 vertical metres to another col (GR 508148).

From this col descend northwest for about 150 vertical metres to a small unnamed lake, then angle down, still heading northwest, to the northern tip of Valhalla Lake. Climb from Valhalla Lake to the southwest for about 60 vertical metres to circumvent a large field of giant boulders, then descend for about 150 vertical metres to the bowl northwest of Drinnon Peak (near a small sink lake marked on the map at GR 494157). Continue heading north, contouring at the 2000 m level to the shoulder overlooking Gwillim Creek (GR 490165). From here, climb back up southwest, following a draw to reach a pass just north of Drinnon Peak (GR 486156). Descend to the west for about 240 vertical metres before contouring to the right (north) into Drinnon Pass (GR 477164).

Descend north for about 0.5 km to a small unnamed lake, then turn west-northwest and follow gentle terrain which gradually curves north and descends into Gwillim Lakes. Ascend the headwall north of Gwillim Lakes to the upper lakes (steep), then ascend to the north under the southwest flank of Lucifer Peak to Lucifer Col (GR 470194). A moderate descent down the north side for 450 vertical metres takes you to Rocky Lakes from where easy terrain

Opposite; Mount Gimli from above Mulvey Basin. Photo Dave Smith

continues north to Hird Lakes. Climb from Hird Lakes up to Urd Col just west of Urd Peak (GR 481236). Descend the other side for about 450 vertical metres, contouring right over a shoulder to a small unnamed lake (GR 484249). In the event of an emergency, escape to logging roads might be feasible down Ice Creek to Snow Creek.

The next section of the trip is a tree bash for a short way, but it is safe from avalanches. From the small lake descend the right flank of the creek to the valley, then follow along the right flank of Ice Creek for a little more than 2 km. Turn right and climb through steep forests into a high basin, then make your way up to a pass (GR 492278). Descend only a short distance down the east side of the pass before heading northeast along a bench. Continue traversing about 120 vertical metres above Avis Lakes, then angle up and climb to a col (GR 508296). From here you can traverse along the broad crest of Snow Ridge for a little over 2 km, heading east, before descending to Snow Pass (GR 534293).

The entire section between Hird Lakes and Snow Pass has been done in different ways. This variation tackles some steep and risky slopes. From Hird Lakes you can climb east up onto the south shoulder of Urd Peak, then traverse around on very steep terrain into a col on the west side of Urd Peak (GR 488237). This ascent is potentially very hazardous and you can be carried over cliffs in the event of a slide. The angle of the terrain is about 35-40°. However, if you do reach this col you have a great 550 vertical metre descent to Upper Demers Lake.

From Upper Demers Lake the variation continues climbing north up reasonable slopes to a col overlooking Upper Beatrice Creek. The descent to the north is, however, very steep. It begins by descending an extremely steep chute which takes you into a bowl, then angles over left to descend another steep chute at the edge of the trees. Upper Beatrice Creek is followed easily for 2 km then the route turns east for a short distance down Beatrice Creek. Begin angling up left through the forest at about GR 523280 and work your way over a shoulder and into Snow Pass (GR 534293) where the two routes join.

Descend the drainage north from Snow Pass for about 2 km, then at about 1850 m start angling up right, gradually ascending through the trees for about 1 km. Turn east and climb to a pass (GR 549322) above Nemo Lakes.

Descend about 120 vertical metres to the Lower Nemo Lake. Now climb for about 60 vertical metres to the north and cross a crest (GR 562326) into the next drainage. (At this point escape to the north over a pass into Caribou Creek would take you to logging roads which lead to Shannon Creek and out to Hills, in the event of emergency).

From here a long and serious climb takes you to the summit of Mount Meers. It is best to camp overnight before attempting this ascent, then do

Ascending steep southwest facing slopes en route to Mount Meers. Much of the terrain on this traverse presents avalanche risk.
Photo Dave Smith

the climb early in the morning when the south facing slopes are frozen (see photo above). Begin by traversing east across steep slopes on the south flank of two unnamed peaks, then climb steeply for about 300 vertical metres to gain the crest (GR 673338). Turn east again and climb gentle slopes to a pass (GR 583341) where you turn right and climb southeast to the summit of Mount Meers.

From here an excellent descent of about 575 vertical metres takes you down a shoulder to an unnamed lake

(GR 597338). Turn north here and descend the drainage to Wee Sandy Lake.

Continue north from Wee Sandy Lake for about 1 km to an unnamed lake (GR 596385). Continue climbing steeply to the north above the lake to North Boundary Col (GR 588397). Descend about 180 vertical metres to the north, then contour into Wragge Pass (GR 592410).

If you have had enough at this point you can descend from Wragge Pass to the east, past two unnamed lakes and down to Wragge Lake (GR 606420). Be careful here and do not descend directly to Wragge Lake but traverse to the east to GR 610415 before heading down. Descend Wragge Creek to logging roads. The Wragge Creek logging road joins up with the Shannon Creek logging road and leads to Highway #6 at Hills.

If you want to push the route a little farther north it is said to be possible to continue north from Wragge Pass. You cross the shoulder of an unnamed peak and descend to an unnamed lake (GR 589427). From here ascend a pass to the west of Mount Vingolf (GR 587435). Descend the drainage to the north to Shannon Lake, then continue down Huss Creek to reach logging roads in Shannon Creek. These roads can then be followed for about 10 km to Highway #6 at Hills.

Planning Notes

Have a good talk with the folks at the Nelson Regional Forestry Office, (250) 354-6200, about the state of logging roads in the area before heading out. In the event of emergency or prolonged bad weather you may want to abort the trip and follow these logging roads back to civilization. At the end of the traverse you will want to know the precise location of the logging roads in Wragge Creek and Shannon Creek.

If you abort the trip to the east (for example down Wee Sandy Creek) you will end up on the west shore of Slocan Lake looking across at civilization on the other side. In that situation all you can do is light three large fires and hope that someone comes across the lake to pick you up.

It may or may not be possible to fly by helicopter into Mulvey Basin to begin the trip. You should contact the West Kootenay District Office of BC Provincial Parks, (250) 825-3500, to arrange for permission to land in Valhalla Park. Do not attempt to ski up Mulvey Creek to begin the trip. The headwall at the end of the valley offers a steep and very dangerous avalanche slope which should not be attempted.

Maps
1:50,000
82 F/13 Burton
82 K/4 Nakusp

1:250,000
82F Nelson

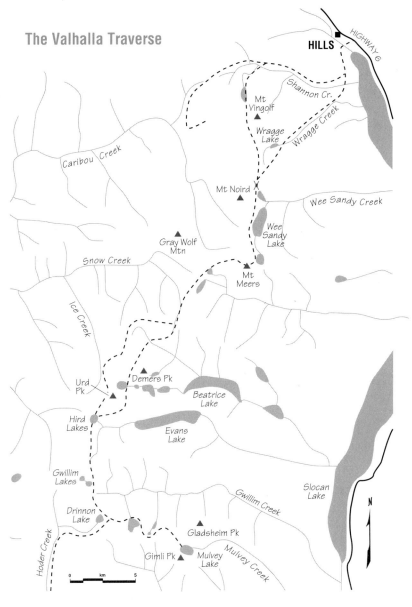

The Valhalla Traverse

HILLS

HIGHWAY 6

Mt Vingolf

Shannon Cr.

Wragge Lake

Wragge Creek

Caribou Creek

Mt Noird

Wee Sandy Creek

Wee Sandy Lake

Gray Wolf Mtn

Snow Creek

Mt Meers

Ice Creek

Demers Pk

Urd Pk

Beatrice Lake

Hird Lakes

Evans Lake

Gwillim Lakes

Gwillim Creek

Slocan Lake

Drinnon Lake

Gladsheim Pk

Hoder Creek

Gimli Pk

Mulvey Lake

Mulvey Creek

km 0 — 5

N

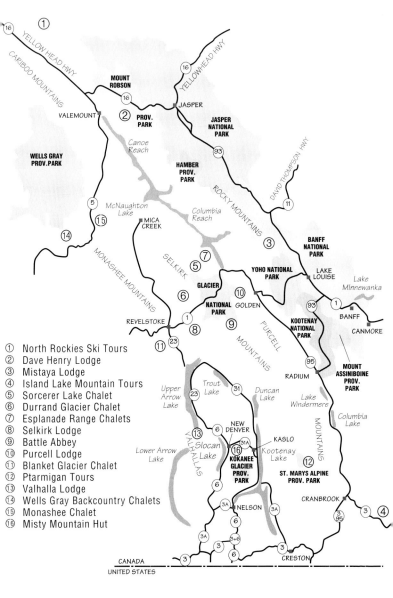

① North Rockies Ski Tours
② Dave Henry Lodge
③ Mistaya Lodge
④ Island Lake Mountain Tours
⑤ Sorcerer Lake Chalet
⑥ Durrand Glacier Chalet
⑦ Esplanade Range Chalets
⑧ Selkirk Lodge
⑨ Battle Abbey
⑩ Purcell Lodge
⑪ Blanket Glacier Chalet
⑫ Ptarmigan Tours
⑬ Valhalla Lodge
⑭ Wells Gray Backcountry Chalets
⑮ Monashee Chalet
⑯ Misty Mountain Hut

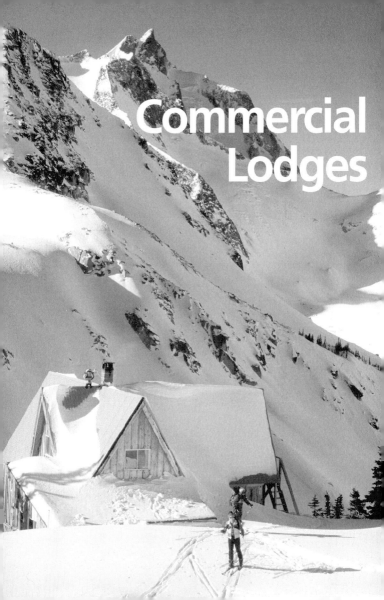

Commercial
Lodges

Mistaya Lodge

Location The lodge is located northeast of Golden near the border of Banff National Park. The hut sits on the edge of a small lake at an elevation of 2060 m in the upper Wildcat Creek Basin (GR 254274).

Map 82 N/10 Blaeberry

Access A twenty minute flight by helicopter from Golden. You can also reach Mistaya Lodge by skiing across the Wapta Icefields. From the Bow or Peyto Huts ski to Baker Col, then descend to the hut.

Facilities The luxurious lodge offers rooms for 12 guests (three 3-4 person rooms and two with double beds). Hearty meals are prepared by cooks and served family style. There is a sauna cum bathhouse which is a treat at the end of the day and all trips are led by certified guides. The lodge has hot and cold running water, private washroom, solar electricity and small hydro plant for electric lights and a radio for emergency response.

Hosts Ron Blaue and Jane Girvan

Address Mistaya Lodge and Alpine Tours, Box 809, Golden, BC, V0A 1H0, Phone/Fax (250) 344-6689, e-mail: mistayalodge@redshift.bc.ca, website: www.mistayalodge.com

Cost Varies from $735/person (3 nights) to $1,495/person (7 nights) during high season. Includes meals, linen, avalanche transceivers, guiding and helicopter flight to the lodge.

Skiing The upper basin of Wildcat Creek offers excellent skiing on glaciated and open treed terrain. There is abundant snow with the area receiving roughly twice the snowfall that Bow Summit does! The runs are generally about 700 vertical metres. You can also access parts of the Wapta

Icefields from this lodge. There is good tree skiing for those white out days and for the peak baggers it is possible to ascend six peaks in the area. Excellent spring skiing in April and early May.

Dave Henry Lodge

Location In the Selwyn Range of the Rocky Mountains, approximately 20 km east of Valemount, BC, near Mount Robson Provincial Park. The lodge is located at an elevation of 1829 m at the head of Dave Henry Creek (GR 686588).

Maps
83D/15 Lucerne
83D/14 Valemount

Access By helicopter from Valemount. You can ski out (27 km), the average time is five hours.

Facilities Two-storey log building with upstairs accommodation for ten people. The lodge has propane lighting, a full sized kitchen stove for cooking, a fully-equipped kitchen and a wood stove to heat the building. Foam mattresses are provided, but guests must bring their own sleeping bags. There is a wood heated sauna and a radio for emergency communication.

Hosts Liz Norwell and Brian McKirdy
Address Headwaters Outfitting Ltd., Box 818, Valemount, BC, V0E 2Z0, Phone (250) 566-4718, website: www.davehenry.com.

Cost $38/person/night (self sufficient), $78/person/night (catered), Helicopter access one way is $133/person.

Skiing The area is perfectly suited to Telemark skiing and is also popular with the Alpine touring crowd. There is a wide mixture of terrain—alpine basins, open meadows and good tree skiing in subalpine forests. There are gentle slopes beside the lodge and more challenging terrain for the expert farther afield which can be accessed on day trips. The outstanding scenery of Mount Robson Park surrounds the area. This is a place that skiers of all ages and abilities can enjoy.

Photo Alf Skrastins

Swift Creek Cabins

Location In the Selwyn Range of the Rocky Mountains, approximately 15 km northeast of Valemount near the headwaters of Swift Creek (GR 608638).

Map 83D/14 Valemount

Access By helicopter from Valemount. You can also ski over from Dave Henry Lodge, a 15 km tour that takes you through subalpine meadows, mature timber and high alpine terrain.

Facilities Two frame cabins—one for cooking and dining and one for sleeping. Both cabins are wood-heated. The cooking cabin has propane lights and a small, four-burner propane stove with oven. The kitchen is fully-equipped. Foam mattresses for sleeping. Comfortable for up to eight people. Radio for emergency communication.

Hosts Liz Norwell and Brian McKirdy

Address Headwaters Outfitting Ltd., Box 818, Valemount, BC V0E 2Z0, Phone (250) 566-4718.

Cost $38/person/night (self-sufficient). Helicopter access one way is $100/person.

Skiing Mostly advanced terrain. Alpine runs of up to 650 vertical metres. Lots of 30° plus slopes on all aspects. Some tree skiing but most skiing below timberline is on avalanche paths. It offers exceptional high-elevation touring. Groups should be experienced or hire a guide.

Opposite top: Skiing at Dave Henry Lodge
Opposite bottom: Skiing at Dave Henry Lodge. Photo Alf Skrastins

Swift Creek Cabins. Photo Alf Skrastins

North Rockies Ski Tours

Location In the Dezaiko Range of the Rocky Mountains, 100 km northeast of Prince George.

Maps 93I Monkman Pass (1:250,000), 93 I/3 Gleason Creek (1:50,000)

Access By road from Prince George to the staging area, then by helicopter to the lodge. Road and helicopter transportation is provided and included in the price.

Facilities Two-storey lodge located at timberline (1500 m). Dormitory sleeping arrangements with mats and sleeping bags provided. Room for up to eight guests. Wood heating and cook stove as well as propane stove. Emergency radio, sauna and outdoor toilet.

Hosts Craig Evanoff and Bonnie Hooge

Address Box 2791, Prince George, BC, V2N 4T6, Phone/Fax (250) 962-5272, e-mail: cevanoff@mag-net.com.

Cost $750 (5 days), $900 (7 days). No GST. All inclusive and fully catered.

Skiing Guided daily excursions from the lodge for Telemark and touring. Varied terrain from high alpine bowls and open slopes to treed glades, all in close proximity to the lodge. Suitable for any age or any ability. (Note that a variety of wildlife inhabits the area and it is common to see mountain goat, caribou, wolf and wolverine).

Island Lake Mountain Tours

Location In the southern Rockies, in the Lizard Range 8 km west of Fernie, BC (GR 321855).

Maps 82G/11 Fernie
82G/6 Elko

Access By snowcat from Mount Fernie Provincial Park (20 minutes).

Facilities A log lodge that sleeps 24 in six rooms, bunk style. Licensed lounge, showers, central heating.

Host Bob Langfield

Address Dale Bowman, Box 1229, Fernie, BC, V0B 1M0, Phone (250) 423-3700.

Cost Three and four day packages start at $1280 (fully catered and guided).

Skiing Although ski touring has been offered in the past, this area is now exclusively for cat skiing. The runs are about 650 vertical metres mainly on slide paths. Good tree skiing. The area gets a lot of snow, but it can rain.

Photos by Alf Skrastins

Sorcerer Lake Lodge

Location 25 km north of the Rogers Pass beneath the north flank of Nordic Mountain. The hut is on the edge of a small lake at an elevation of 2050 m. (GR 513997).

Maps 82 N/5 Glacier

Access By helicopter from Heather Mountain Lodge 55 km west of Golden.

Facilities Four bedrooms that sleep 16 guests, plus a loft. Fully equipped kitchen with propane cookstove. Electric lights. Wood stove for heat. Sauna.

Hosts Tannis Dakin

Address PO Box 161, Golden, BC, V0A 1H0, Phone (250) 344-2804, Fax (250) 344-2805, e-mail: sorcerer@rockies.net, web site: www.sorcererlodge.com.

Cost For groups: $3200 to rent the cabin for one week (Saturday to Saturday) plus $220 per person for the helicopter. Custodian provided. To join a fully catered and guided week the rate is $1175 per person (helicopter, accommodation, meals and guide provided).

Skiing Sorcerer Lake can offer excellent skiing in truly alpine terrain. Some of the more popular runs are:

• The descent from White Russian Col (GR 524974) both to the north back towards the hut and to the west towards Alder Creek.

• The descent from the West Peak of Nordic Mountain (GR 498965) back NE towards the hut.

• The south slopes of a small peak (GR 535995) into Alder Creek.

Photo Alf Skrastins

• The descent northeast down the Perfect Glacier starting about GR 527978.

• There is also some tree skiing in the immediately vicinity of the lodge.

Durrand Glacier Chalet (Selkirk Mountain Experience)

Location One main lodge and one high alpine chalet are located 45 km and 53 km northeast of Revelstoke in the northern Selkirk Mountains. The main lodge, Durrand Glacier Chalet, is located on a knoll at 1950 m, 45 minutes from the Durrand Glacier (GR 317799). The higher alpine chalet, Mount Moloch Hut is located 8 km to the northeast at an elevation of 2200 m. It sits on a bedrock knoll in the middle of the glaciated amphitheatre of the Dismal Glacier (GR 365846).

Maps 82 N/5 Glacier [mainly this map]
82 N/4 Illecillewaet
82 M/8 Downie Creek
82 M/1 Revelstoke

Access Helicopter from Revelstoke.

Facilities The Durrand Glacier Chalet is a pine and cedar Swiss-style alpine chalet. It offers deluxe accommodation for up to 18 guests in two-person

Durrand Glacier Chalet

bedrooms. A highly qualified cook and pastry chef prepares fine meals which are served family style. Showers and sauna are available, as well as indoor plumbing. The Mount Moloch Hut is a smaller and more rustic Swiss Chalet, but can accommodate a group of 11 guests.

Mount Moloch Hut. Photo Peter Thompson

Hosts Ruedi and Nicoline Beglinger
Address Selkirk Mountain Experience
Ltd., PO Box 2998, Revelstoke, BC,
V0E 2S0, Phone (250) 837-2381,
Fax (250) 837-4685,
e-mail: selkirk@junction.net
Cost: Selkirk Mountain Experience
offers three packages through the winter.
• Around Christmas and New Year you
can book three or six day powder
holidays for $1080.

• For the rest of the winter seven
day packages are available. If you wish
to   participate in one of the hut-to-
hut seven day ski weeks, or simply enjoy
a fun filled powder week based at
the Durrand Glacier Chalet, from
January to early May the cost is $1185
(low season) and $1250 (high season).
• Several week long avalanche safety
and ski mountaineering leader-
ship courses are offered in January
for $1185.
All prices include:
• helicopter to and from the Durrand
  Glacier Chalet
• bus service from Revelstoke to the
  heliport
• lodging (full bedding) and all meals
• guiding and instruction by UIAGM and
  ACMG guides
• use of avalanche safety beacons.
Skiing There are about 40 major ski
routes on the 25 different peaks and
glaciers surrounding the two chalets.
Near the Durrand Glacier Chalet, the
north glacier of Tumbledown Mountain
offers 800 vertical metres of excellent
skiing. Many other fine ski tours are
accessible from this lodge. In the event
of poor visibility there is excellent tree
skiing near the lodge and in Excalibur
Bowl, offering runs from 600-1200
vertical metres. From the Mount Moloch
Hut you can tour on the Graham and
Zwilling's Glaciers, making ascents of

Mount Graham and Zwilling's east and
west. The two lodges can be linked via
the Philharmonic and Juliana Glaciers,
Mount Ruth and either the Concordia
Icefall or Ruth Glacier. This area offers
70 km^2 of mainly glacier skiing and high
peaks. It is for those in search of a
challenging ski mountaineering
experience and for those who like steep
powder slopes in the subalpine and
lower alpine.
Note For all programs with Selkirk
Mountain Experience you must be a
stable intermediate downhill skier on
Telemark skis or alpine randonee
equipment. The guests ski in two
medium sized groups, one slower and
one faster.
For Further Reference:
Thompson, P.: *Sea of Summits. Ski
touring in the Selkirks*, Explore, Oct/
Nov, 1992.   *All photos by Ruedi Beglinger
(Selkirk Mountain Experience)*

Esplanade Range Chalets (Golden Alpine Holidays)

Location There are three huts in the Esplanade Range of the Selkirk Mountains. They are all located at about 2100 m near timberline. Sunrise Chalet at the head of Wisted Creek on the edge of a small lake (GR 109619), Meadow Chalet at the head of Carrol Creek (GR 133596), and Vista Chalet at the head of Schlicting Creek (GR 155589).

Map 82 N/12 Mount Sir Sandford

Access By helicopter from staging area west of Golden.

Facilities All three chalets are identical and offer six double occupancy bedrooms. Wood stoves heat the chalets while propane is used for lighting and cooking. Sauna. Chalets are outfitted with cooking equipment and utensils. Linen is provided.

Host Alison Dakin

Photo Pat Morrow

Address Golden Alpine Holidays, Box 1050, Golden, BC, V0A 1H0, Phone (250) 344-7273, e-mail: goalpine@rockies.net.

Cost A fully catered seven-day package costs $1200. This includes the helicopter flight to and from the chalet, all meals, guiding and accommodation. It is normal for groups to book at least six months to a year in advance but small parties of one, two or three individuals can usually squeeze in with a week or two notice.

Skiing The skiing is superb at Golden Alpine Holidays. The runs are located on ridges and peaks above high alpine meadows. By February there is normally a three-metre base of snow. Skiable terrain is extensive at all lodges and it is unlikely that you will run out of untracked powder. GAH is blessed with plenty of tree skiing for those overcast days. The runs are 500-700 vertical metres. No glacier skiing. Groups usually traverse between chalets mid week.

Photo Brett Baunton

Photo Gillean Daffern

Selkirk Lodge

Location Located at the Albert Icefields in the Selkirk Mountains east of Revelstoke, BC, at an elevation of 2200 m (GR 490548).
Map 82 N/4 Illecillewaet
Access By helicopter.
Facilities A two-storey lodge, that accommodates 12 guests in four bedrooms. Wood heating, shower, sauna, Propane fridge and stove, indoor toilet and solar lighting. Daily radio communication with Revelstoke.
Host Grania Devine
Address Selkirk Lodge, Box 1409, Golden, BC, V0A 1H0, Phone (250) 344-5016 or 1-800-663-7080, Fax (250) 344-7102
Cost $1150 per week. Fully catered and guided (includes ground transportation from Revelstoke, helicopter flight in and out and the use of avalanche transceivers).

Photo M. Morris

Skiing This area offers intermediate and advanced terrain with a mix of tree skiing, open bowls and high glacier skiing. The snowpack is deep with an average of 4 m settled snow at the lodge. There is a long season at Selkirk Lodge—from December to May. ACMG/UIAGM certified guides.

Photo Kevin Wiley

Purcell Lodge

Location The Purcell Lodge is located at 2180 m near timberline at the head of the Spillimacheen River (GR 782788). This location is in the Bald Mountains in the northern Purcells southwest of Golden and directly east of Mount Sir Donald on the edge of Glacier Park.

Map 82 N/3 Mount Wheeler

Access By helicopter from the Golden airport.

Facilities This is truly a deluxe lodge, and, in fact, is almost a hotel high in the mountains. There is hot and cold running water, showers, flush toilets and electricity as well as forced-air heating. The meals are prepared by European chefs. There are beds for 24 guests in ten private rooms, complete with balcony. There is a fireplace, licensed dining room, conference facilities and sauna.

Hosts Paul Leeson and Russ Younger

Address Places Less Travelled Ltd., PO Box 1829, Golden, BC, V0A 1H0, Phone (250) 344-2639, Fax (250) 344-5520, e-mail: places@rockies.net, web site: www.purcell.com.

Cost Three, four and seven night packages are available. There are high season rates and low season rates. Costs will also vary depending on the type of room selected. Rates range from $1195-$1475 per week (double occupancy). Accommodation, meals, helicopter access and guiding are included.

Skiing Purcell Lodge offers a real variety of skiing. Nearby are endless rolling meadows offering excellent light touring. For the Telemark fans there are descents of up to 700 vertical metres and in the event of poor visibility there is tree skiing below the lodge.

Photo ABC Wilderness Adventures

Battle Abbey

Location Battle Abbey is spectacularly located near the headwaters of Butters Creek in the Battle Range of the Selkirk Mountains at an elevation of 2,195 m (GR 761476).

Map 82 K/14 Westfall River

Access By helicopter from the Bobbie Burns Heliport, 1 km west of Parsons, BC. The helicopter flies on Saturday at 3:30 PM.

Facilities The hut consists of a kitchen/dining room, living room, small bar (bring your own booze!), and four sleeping lofts. Electricity is supplied via a wind generator and solar panels. Solar heat is also used for hot water. There is hot and cold running water and two indoor toilets which can be used at night. The hut can comfortably accommodate 16 people. There is radio phone communication with the outside world.

Host There is a cook and two guides in attendance.

Address Canadian Mountain Holidays, PO Box 1660, Banff, Alberta, T0L 0C0, Phone 1-800-661-0252, (403) 762-7100, Fax (403) 762-5879

Cost $1458 per week. This includes return transportation between Calgary and Battle Abbey, all meals, accommodation (dormitory style), guide service (ACMG/UIAGM) and the use of avalanche transceivers. The lodge only operates for the general public five weeks per year, from early March to mid-April.

Skiing The skiing is mostly above treeline. The terrain is complex, a mixture of mellow and steep slopes. Runs are generally 300-500 vertical metres. All parties are guided.

Photo Alf Skrastins

Top: On the Typee Glacier.
Photo Roger Laurilla
Bottom: Photo Vance Hanna

Commercial Lodges 295

Ptarmigan Tours

Location In the Southern Purcells, in the mountains east of White Creek near Kimberley, B.C. (Boulder Cabin GR 543103, Ptarmigan Cabin GR 543150).
Maps 82F/16 Dewar Creek
82F/9 St Mary Lake
Access Helicopter in and out from Kimberley.
Facilities There are two locations, Boulder and Ptarmigan. Boulder has two buildings that sleep 10 people, propane kitchen, wood heating stove, outdoor toilets and a hot tub. Ptarmigan offers similar accommodation but has a sauna rather than a hot tub. Bedding is provided (sleeping bags and sheet liners).
Hosts Margie Jamieson
Address Box 11, Kimberley, BC, V1A 2Y5, Phone/Fax (250) 422-3270, e-mail: ptarmigan@cyberlink.bc.ca, web site: www.cyberlink.bc.ca/-ptarmigan.
Cost The rate for an eight day package is $1095. The week includes skiing at both Boulder Cabin and Ptarmigan Cabin with a traverse day mid-week. All weeks are fully catered and guided and the price includes the helicopter flight in and out.
Skiing Excellent Telemark skiing for the more advanced skier and great touring. The runs are in high alpine bowls and are up to 600 vertical metres. There is also lots of good tree skiing. No glaciers.

Top: Boulder Cabin. Photo Art Twomey
Bottom: Photo Art Twomey

Opposite: Skiing at Blanket Glacier.
Photo Alf Skrastins

Blanket Glacier Chalet

Location South of Revelstoke in the Monashee Mountains (GR 122277).
Map 82 L/16 Revelstoke
Access The hut is a short helicopter flight from Revelstoke.
Facilities The chalet is a three-level A-frame building with sleeping space for up to 16 on two sleeping levels. It is equipped with all cooking and eating utensils, propane cooking stove and wood heating. There is no indoor plumbing, but a propane lighting system lights the way. There is a separate sauna building with a large change room and a shower.
Hosts Al and Marion Schaffer
Address Nordic Ski Institute, Box 8150, Canmore, Alberta, T1W 2T9, Phone (403) 678-4102,
e-mail: aschaffe@Banff.net.
Cost You can rent the whole chalet for the exclusive use of your group (maximum of 16 spaces) for a cost of $500 per person per week (includes helicopter access flight). You can also

Photo Al Schaffer

sign up for one of the instructional telemark weeks at the chalet with Al or Marion. They are $700 per person per week and include the helicopter lift in and out of the chalet as well as telemark instruction.
Skiing The Blanket Glacier area receives an average winter snowfall of 8 m and is unsurpassed with its limitless ski terrain. There are a multitude of open or treed runs near the chalet and glaciated ski runs on the glacier itself. The descent from Blanket Peak offers a run of over 1000 vertical metres.

Valhalla Lodge

Location In the Valhalla Range, northwest of Nelson at an elevation of 2,130 m.

Map 82 F/13 Burton

Access By helicopter (10 minute flight from Burton).

Facilities Post and beam, two-storey building. Propane lights and stove. Wood heating. Sauna. Accommodation for 10 in 3 double and 1 quad bedrooms, sheets, pillow cases and blankets provided.

Hosts Jeff Gfroerer and Leo Jansma

Address Kootenay Mountain Huts Inc., Box 1167, Kaslo, BC, V0G 1M0, Phone (250) 353-7179, Fax (250) 353-2317, web site: www.netidea.com/kmh.

Cost "$1200/person/week fully guided and catered. Lodge rental only is $680/person/week. All prices include helicopter access.

Skiing There are ten large alpine bowls within comfortable touring distance which offer excellent skiing. The runs are 300-600 vertical metres. There is lots of excellent tree skiing near the lodge.

Opposite:Top: Trophy Chalet
Opposite Bottom: Skiing at Fight Meadows

Photo Valhalla Lodge

Wells Gray Park Backcountry Chalets

Location These chalets are located in the southern part of Wells Gray Provincial Park north of Clearwater. (Note that Clearwater is only 5.5 hours by car from Vancouver.) They are in the Trophy Range at the south end of the Cariboo Mountains. (Trophy Mountain Chalet GR 049386, Fight Meadow Chalet GR 001560, Table Mountain Cabin GR 046452).

Map 82 M/13 West Raft River

Access Helicopter, snow cat or ski in.

Facilities There are three buildings: Trophy Mountain Chalet, Discovery Chalet and Fight Meadow Chalet. The Trophy and Fight Chalets are identical: they both sleep 10-12 and are provided with mattresses, bedding and a propane-equipped kitchen. There are propane lights and a sauna as well. The Discovery Chalet is new as of 1995, sleeps 8-10, has mattresses, bedding and a propane-equipped kitchen.

Host Ian Eakins and Tay Briggs

Address Box 188, Clearwater, BC, V0E 1N0, Phone (250) 587-6444, Fax (250) 4587-6446, toll free number: 1-888-754-

8735, e-mail: skitrek@wellsgray.net.

Cost Fully catered and guided trips are $110/person/day (5 and 7 days duration). For those prepared to guide themselves and provide their own food the rate is $33/person/day.

Skiing There is a reliable 3 metre base in this area. The Trophy Mountain Chalet is located at timberline and is surrounded by steep and deep Telemark terrain. The Fight Meadow Chalet is surrounded by rolling meadows which are more suitable for cross country touring and less experienced skiers. However, good Telemark terrain can be found not far away, as well. Discovery Chalet offers excellent intermediate telemark terrain just out the back door on Table Mountain.

Monashee Chalet

Location In the Monashee Mountains, 20 km southeast of Blue River above Finn Creek at an elevation of 1820 m (GR 467614).

Maps 82 M/14 Messiter
83 D/3 Blue River

Access By snowcat (45 minutes). Ski out (two hours).

Facilities A-frame building divided into seven rooms. Lots of windows! Propane for cooking and wood heating stove. Electric lights.

Host Adolf Teufele

Address Interior Alpine Recreation Ltd., 1408 - 8 Ave., New Westminster, BC, V3M 2S4, Phone (604) 522-1239.

Cost : Self guided and catered: $38/person/day (up to eight people) or $35/person/day (more than eight people). Low season rate: $30/person/day (minimum of three nights).

Skiing Tree line skiing and touring suited for the intermediate and novice skier. Lots of short runs and good tree skiing. The ski-out is a lot of fun. It is almost all downhill and you can sneak off the cat track and get some turns.

Photo Alf Skrastins

Flint Lakes Cabin

Location In the Kokanee Range 20 km north of the Kokanee Glacier and west of Kaslo BC at an elevation of 2000 m.

Maps 82 F/14 Slocan
82 K/3 Rosebery

Access By helicopter. Three hour ski out.

Facilities Conventional frame cabin which accommodates six guests dormitory style. Wood heating, propane cooking, hot showers and separate dining room.

Host Jeff Gfroerer

Address Kootenay Mountain Huts Inc., Box 1167, Kaslo BC, V0G 1M0, Phone/Fax (250) 353-7179.

Cost "$1100/person/week fully guided and catered. Lodge rental only is $650/person/week. All prices include helicopter access.

Skiing Large open bowls with terrain for intermediate to expert skiers. Excellent tree skiing with runs up to 500 vertical metres.

Opposite: Skiing at the Durrand Glacier Chalet. Photo Ruedi Beglinger (Selkirk Mountain Experience)

Last Run

INDEX

Chic Scott

The author discovered ski mountaineering in 1962 and took to it with a passion. Only five years later, at the age of 21, he successfully completed the Great Divide Traverse across the icefields of the Continental Divide between Jasper and Lake Louise—the first ever crossing. Since then he has completed another nine major ski traverses.

Photo Doug McConnery

Chic's career as a mountaineer is extensive and includes expeditions to the St. Elias Mountains of northern Canada, many ascents in the European Alps, expeditions to the Nepal Himalaya and new rock and alpine routes in the Canadian Rockies.

For many years Chic has worked as a mountain guide. During the 1960's and 1970's he was employed by Dougal Haston at the International School of Mountaineering in Leysin, Switzerland. In recent years he organized and guided many camps, courses and expeditions for the Alpine Club of Canada.

Chic is author of *Ski Trails in the Canadian Rockies* and since 1995 has been researching and writing *Pushing the Limits - the story of Canadian Mountaineering,* which should appear in the spring of 2000.

IN AN EMERGENCY

RCMP Offices

Canmore	(403) 678-5516
Banff	(403) 762-2226
Lake Louise	(403) 522-3811
Jasper	(780) 852-4421
Golden	(250) 344-2221
Revelstoke	(250) 837-5255
Valemount	(250) 566-4466
Nelson	(250) 352-2156

Park Ranger or Warden Offices

Banff emergency (Banff Park)	(403) 762-4506
Banff regular (Banff Park)	(403) 762-1470
Field (Yoho Park)	(250) 343-6324
Sunwapta (Jasper Park)	(780) 852-5383
Jasper (Jasper Park)	(780) 852-6155
Rogers Pass (Glacier Park)	(250) 814-5202
Bugaboo Provincial Park	(250) 422-4200
Kokanee Provincial Park	(250) 825-3500
Valhalla Provincial Park	(250) 825-3500

AVALANCHE HAZARD AND SNOW STABILITY

Public Avalanche Information Bulletin
(Canadian Avalanche Association)

1-800-667-1105
web site: www.avalanche.ca

Toll free number not accessible from the USA
If calling from the USA call either the Vancouver or Calgary numbers

If calling from the Vancouver area call (604) 290-9333
If calling from the Calgary area call (403) 243-7253 (code 7669)

Banff/Yoho/Kootenay National Parks Avalanche Information (403) 762-1460
(recording)